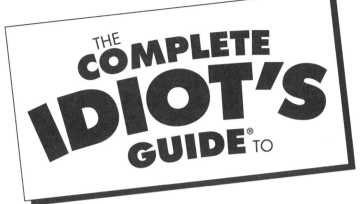

THE COMPLETE IDIOT'S GUIDE® TO

Macromedia®
Dreamweaver® MX

by David Karlins

ALPHA

A Pearson Education Company

To everyone for whom the chimes of freedom are flashing.

For marketing and publicity, please call: 317-581-3722

The publisher offers discounts on this book when ordered in quantity for bulk purchases and special sales.

For sales within the United States, please contact: Corporate and Government Sales, 1-800-382-3419 or corpsales@pearsontechgroup.com

Outside the United States, please contact: International Sales, 317-581-3793 or international@pearsontechgroup.com

Publisher: *Marie Butler-Knight*
Product Manager: *Phil Kitchel*
Managing Editor: *Jennifer Chisholm*
Acquisitions Editor: *Eric Heagy*
Development Editor: *Clint McCarty*
Production Editor: *Katherin Bidwell*
Illustrator: *Chris Eliopoulos*
Cover/Book Designer: *Trina Wurst*
Indexer: *Tonya Heard*
Layout/Proofreading: *Angela Calvert, Megan Douglass, John Etchison, Becky Harmon, Mary Hunt, Vicki Keller*

Contents at a Glance

Appendixes

Contents

Foreword

Once upon a time, there was a web with only HTML <Carrot, slash, break, crash/> …
View source, beg borrow and steal. Coding is for warriors. I need help.

Enter Dreamweaver, David Karlins, and *The Complete Idiot's Guide to Macromedia
Dreamweaver MX*.

As well-seasoned as Dreamweaver has become at every level of web design, MX launches
it to new heights. Indispensable, essential, requisite. This is both David Karlins and his
new book.

And whoever thought editing web pages could be fun? David's sense of humor and style
have become well-honed, teaching both live and online courses for San Francisco State
University's Multimedia Studies Program. He respects his tools and his audience and has
his own characteristic knack for breaking down intimidating programs into digestible
chunks. Each chapter sets up the objectives of content to be conveyed and then serves it
up to be consumed with ease and delight.

David's hands-on experience in the web design world, and his experience working with
students lends itself to insights that help you construct your own intuitive process. By the
end of this book, who knows, maybe you'll even develop a new sense of humor.

As one of his students said as he evaluated David's live Dreamweaver class, "I feel empowered and ready to rule the World Wide Web." And so will you.

—Cathy Flight
Program Director
Multimedia Studies Program
San Francisco State University
http://msp.sfsu.edu

Introduction

Introducing Dreamweaver calls to mind the ancient fable of the blind men describing an elephant. To one who grabbed the tail, the elephant was like a snake. To another who grabbed the trunk, it was like a hose. And so on. The point being that Dreamweaver does *many* things.

Many people are familiar with Dreamweaver as a page design tool. You format text and images just like you were working with a word processor or page layout program, and Dreamweaver generates all the HTML (HyperText Markup Language) code you need to make your vision come to life on the web.

True, Dreamweaver is an unparalleled page design tool, but that's only the beginning of the story. You can also use Dreamweaver to create pictures that fly around on your page, menus that visitors use to navigate your site, and to present media such as videos and songs.

I think you'll find this book covers a rather astonishing amount for a so-called *Complete Idiot's Guide*. That's because I'll skip much of the technical jargon and focus on showing you how to use all the cool features in Dreamweaver. Then, for the technically non-challenged, I'll point you toward tools for more complex web design. I guarantee you'll be surprised at how much you'll be able to do with your site by just using this book.

Extras

To help you understand the online jungle, this book also gives you extra secrets, inside tips, and bits of information that will help you get the most out of your money. You'll find them in these boxes:

By the Way

These sections throughout the book point out things that are noteworthy, stuff to be leery of, tips, tricks, and stuff to avoid—basically, they are full of information that adds to your understanding of Dreamweaver or gives insightful background.

Caution

These are warnings of things to avoid, be sure about, or be careful of as you create your Dreamweaver site. Treat them like stop signs as you fly through this book—pause and read them before plunging ahead.

> **Inside Info**
>
> These boxes highlight terms, methods, or behind-the-scenes stuff that you don't necessarily need to know, but that definitely help you make more sense out of how Dreamweaver does that thing it does.

> **Definition**
>
> These boxes are used to identify new or particularly important terms and provide detailed descriptions of those terms so that you fully understand as you proceed.

How to Use This Book

I've organized this book into six parts. Each part explores a realm of web design with Dreamweaver, like page design, forms, table design, and so on.

Part 1, "Organizing a Dreamweaver Site," is an essential starting place. Even if you end up jumping around the rest of the book, make sure you check in here first. I think you'll find the overview of how Dreamweaver fits into the world of web design eye-opening. And you'll definitely want to understand how sites and files fit together to make up a website. Plus, I'll introduce new additions to Dreamweaver MX. Finally, I'll demystify and walk you through the sometimes murky waters of connecting your local site to a remote server so the whole world can enjoy it.

In **Part 2, "Adding Pictures and Text,"** I'll show you how to design web pages, how to add text and pictures, and how to format your pages. You bring the text and pictures, and I'll cover the rest here. Don't have text or pictures? I'll share some suggestions for that as well. Plus, I'll explain how to define a well-organized set of links that connect your pages to each other, and to the rest of the World Wide Web.

In **Part 3, "Tables, Layers, and Frames,"** I'll explain how to use the three main tools for organizing page content. I'll show you how to design pages using tables to place pictures and text. I'll show you how to design with 3-D, overlapping layers. This part also shows you how to define and attach external style sheets, a powerful site-wide formatting feature of Dreamweaver. And, you'll learn to create framed pages that, in the immortal words of Vincent Flanders, don't "suck."

Part 4, "Managing Your Assets," introduces you to some underrated but productive tools for speeding up your work in Dreamweaver MX. You'll learn to take advantage of Dreamweaver Assets to make repetitive tasks easier. And I'll show you how to use special assets called Library Items to create revisable embedded objects throughout your site.

In **Part 5, "Good Form (Input Forms),"** you'll examine forms and online databases. You'll learn to create jump menus that run off of Dreamweaver-generated JavaScript. You'll design input forms and learn to display data from an online database using powerful new application tools in MX.

In **Part 6, "Putting On a Show (Multimedia),"** you'll incorporate media in your site. You'll learn to add Flash movies and even to create (simple) Flash animation buttons right in Dreamweaver. You'll add sound to your site and embed movies in pages. Plus, you'll find out how to use behaviors to add animation and interactivity right in Dreamweaver.

Finally, in **Part 7, "Site Management and Maintenance,"** you'll learn how to use some hard-working Dreamweaver tools to do much of the dreary grunt work of proofreading and testing your site. Bad links make bad sites, so use Dreamweaver to test your links. I'll turn you on to tools you can find outside Dreamweaver to add extra goodies like calendars, counters, and search boxes to your site.

Acknowledgments

Thanks to the team that put this book together, especially Eric Heagy at Alpha Books, and my agent Lisa Swayne.

The editors, layout folks, and designers who put this book together all made big contributions to the book you have in front of you.

Special thanks are due to my associate Thais Nye who contributed much to the nice mix of Mac and PC screenshots that illustrate this book. Visit her at www.hiretowrite.com.

Special Thanks to the Technical Reviewer

The Complete Idiot's Guide to Macromedia Dreamweaver MX was reviewed by an expert who double-checked the accuracy of what you'll learn here, to help us ensure that this book gives you everything you need to know about Macromedia Dreamweaver MX. Special thanks are extended to Bill Bruns.

Trademarks

All terms mentioned in this book that are known to be or are suspected of being trademarks or service marks have been appropriately capitalized. Alpha Books and Pearson Education, Inc., cannot attest to the accuracy of this information. Use of a term in this book should not be regarded as affecting the validity of any trademark or service mark.

Part 1

Organizing a Dreamweaver Site

Before you don your artist beret and start designing beautiful web pages, you need to put on your overalls and do the dirty work of setting up your website.

In these first chapters, you'll learn how to gather the text, images, and other files you need to launch your site, and I'll show you how to publish these files to a remote web server so the whole world can see your stuff.

Chapter 1

Dreamweaver— the "Do It All" Package

In This Chapter

- ◆ Dreamweaver in the world of web design
- ◆ Surveying the Dreamweaver interface
- ◆ Customizing Dreamweaver
- ◆ What's new in Dreamweaver MX

Dreamweaver is kind of the Swiss army knife of web design—you'll find a tool for almost anything you need for your website.

You want page design? You got it. But Dreamweaver also generates JavaScript for objects that react to visitors or bounce around the page. Dreamweaver generates something called CSS—or Cascading Style Sheets—to apply formatting to your entire web page. Dreamweaver manages your files for you. Heck, Dreamweaver even creates little "glow-when-you-roll-over-'em" Flash buttons.

All these features can be a little overwhelming. No problem. I've taught hundreds of students to use Dreamweaver in my live and online web design classes. They start throwing spitballs at me if they get confused so I've learned to break Dreamweaver down into digestible chunks for them. I'll take that same approach in this book.

The Wide World of Dreamweaver

Let's start by breaking down just what Dreamweaver does. There are two main things that you do with Dreamweaver. You organize and manage a *website*, and you create and format web *pages*.

Dreamweaver's *site* management tools allow you to organize the files in your website, and then later transfer those files from your computer to a remote (far away) web server in a way that ensures that the files will all work together well. These site management tools are generally found in Dreamweaver's Site window.

Dreamweaver's *page* tools allow you to add, edit, and format content on your web page. Page design and formatting is done by opening (or creating) a page in the Document window. Most of this book, and some of this chapter, will be spent digging around in the Document window and learning to use the page design tools found there.

What Are Websites Made Of?

Dreamweaver is often thought of as a page design tool. But it's so much more. Like an orchestra conductor, Dreamweaver organizes and manages all kinds of website objects.

When you visit a website, you see a web page. But, underneath the surface of that page, you're actually looking at many different objects.

The page itself, with text, links to other pages, and text formatting, is an *HTML* file.

Definition

HTML stands for HyperText Markup Language and is the way web browsers (like Internet Explorer or Netscape Navigator) look at and display text and images on your page.

A page will also often include pictures. These are actually separate image files, which just appear as part of the page.

A web page might also include media, like sound or video. That media might be a QuickTime movie, a Windows Media movie, an MP3 sound file, a Real-Media video, or a Flash movie. Again, these objects might appear to be part of a web page, but actually they're separate files—even though they might be embedded (placed) on a web page.

There's more! Web pages might include objects that react to actions of a visitor—like a drop-down menu that allows visitors to jump from one page to another. Or an object that flies around on the page. Or activities like new browser windows that open. Dreamweaver creates interactive and animated page objects by generating Javascript code.

Finally, a website might contain a data entry form, and connect that data to an online database. This requires that forms in a web page connect with programs at a remote server that manage this data.

What Does Dreamweaver Do?

"All right," you say, "So websites are made up of all kinds of stuff. How much of that does Dreamweaver do?"

The short answer is, a lot!

Much of the popularity of Dreamweaver stems from the fact that it handles so much more than page design. I often find history boring, but it's worth a one-paragraph trip down memory lane to understand what Dreamweaver does.

Earlier generations of web design tools let folks who didn't know HTML design web pages. Instead of needing to memorize a coding language, we could just use word-processor type formatting tools to layout web pages. The new generation of web design tools, with Dreamweaver in the front of the pack, allow us not just to design *text* and *images*, but to add just about any other website object to our pages.

The early chapters in this book will show you how to create a website, and how to create and format web pages with text and graphics. But after that, I'll show you how to add a wide range of features to your site. And, along the way, I'll probably turn you on to some things you didn't know you could do with Dreamweaver.

Table 1.1 will help give you a sense of what you can (and cannot) do in Dreamweaver.

Caution

The one thing Dreamweaver does not do is let you create artwork. For that, you need a graphic design program like Fireworks, Photoshop, Illustrator, or one of the many image-editing programs available.

Table 1.1   Dreamweaver Abilities

Site Element	Done in Dreamweaver?
HTML page formatting	Yes
Image editing	No
Image attributes (like rollover text)	Yes
Create Flash objects	Somewhat
Create animation with Dynamic HTML (DHTML)	Yes
Create interactivity with JavaScript	Yes
Create external style sheets	Yes
Manage file transfer (FTP)	Yes
Design forms and connect them to online databases	Yes

The Dreamweaver Interface

Dreamweaver MX is loaded with features. Almost *too* loaded until you clear away some of the chaotic interface.

In general, I'll identify important elements of the interface as we need them, rather than force you to memorize them in advance and flunking you if you forget one!

But it will be helpful to identify some of the main elements of the Dreamweaver interface right away.

Mac and PC—Can We All Get Along?

I always thought that one of the nice things about Dreamweaver was that it looked pretty much the same no matter what operating system you ran it under.

That's changed a bit. I guess the logic is that the folks at Macromedia wanted to take advantage of features in the new versions of the operating systems for Macs and PCs (Mac OS X and Windows XP, respectively). In fact, with all the X's everyone's using, they even added an "X" to Dreamweaver—Dreamweaver MX.

So, you'll find that some menu commands are a bit different, depending on the operating system. And some features look different—for instance, Windows users will see little tabs on the bottom of their page that allow them to jump between open pages, while Mac users don't have that option.

Deep down inside, however, we're all the same, and so are the different versions of Dreamweaver. We (myself and my staff, plus the editors) tested this book on Macs and PCs. We set out to create a number of screenshots scientifically mixed to exactly match the ratio of Mac and PC users that our extensive reader research told us to expect.

The point is, both versions are almost the same, and where there is a difference, I'll note it for you.

A Quick Look Around

Exactly which elements of Dreamweaver appear when you start the program depends on which elements of Dreamweaver you had open in your last session. But just to demystify the chaos, the main elements you'll see when you launch MX are identified in Figure 1.1.

The document window is the largest area of the Dreamweaver interface. This is the large page on the left side of the screen where you design page content.

Insert panel   Document window   Docked panels

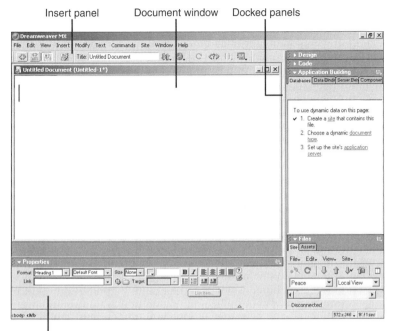

Properties panel

Figure 1.1

The document window and floating panels greet you when you start Dream-weaver MX. This is how Dreamweaver looks in Windows XP—your system might look a little different.

Panels float about outside or inside the document window. They provide access to Dreamweaver's tools, and you turn them on or off by selecting or deselecting them from the Window menu. The Insert panel has shortcut icons that allow you to insert objects. All these objects can also be inserted using the menu.

The most important panel is the Properties panel. By default, it docks on the bottom of the screen. The Properties panel changes depending on what object you've selected. For instance, different properties are available for pictures than are available for text.

Finally, the right side of the screen displays a series of docked panel groups. These panel groups can be undocked from their perch on the right side of the document window and dragged around the screen.

You can close a docked panel by choosing Close Panel Group from the drop-down Panel menu on the right side of the Panel title bar, as shown in Figure 1.2.

Figure 1.2

Ditching a panel.

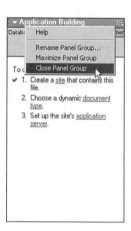

Before moving on, Figure 1.3 shows the main elements of the Dreamweaver layout on a Macintosh.

Figure 1.3

The Mac version of the Dreamweaver Document window.

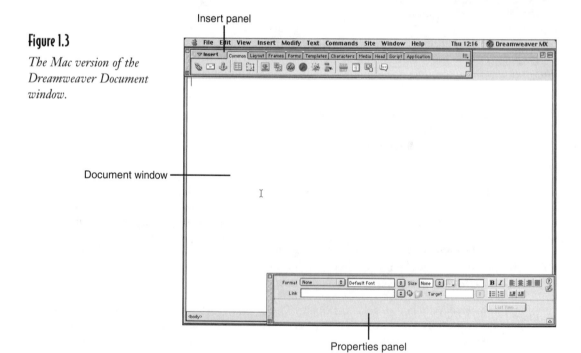

Customizing Dreamweaver

Dreamweaver is an extremely accommodating program. You can customize how it acts and how it looks.

Mostly, I'll identify ways you can customize Dreamweaver as I show you how to use different features. But I want to quickly introduce you to the options for changing your Dreamweaver interface.

Many of the menu options in Dreamweaver have keyboard shortcuts. For instance, the File, New menu option can be performed by pressing Command (on a Mac) or Ctrl (on a PC) plus "N." In this book, I'll refer to that command as **Command/Ctrl+N** where I use keyboard shortcuts.

You can see, or change, all the keyboard shortcuts by choosing **Edit, Keyboard Shortcuts** on a PC, or **Dreamweaver MX, Keyboard Shortcuts** in Mac OS X.

Other customizable elements of Dreamweaver can be changed by choosing **Dreamweaver MX, Preferences** (in Mac OS X) or **Edit, Preferences.** I'll note many ways you can adapt Dreamweaver to your needs in the course of this book.

What's New?

Writing lots of computer books as I do, I sometimes become jaded in looking at new versions of software. OK, they added a new doohinky. So what?

Not so with Dreamweaver MX. This is a major development. The interface has been radically redone—something I'm not totally wild about. But more importantly, the folks at Macromedia actually combined two products into one.

MX is actually a combination of what Dreamweaver was, plus Macromedia's UltraDev—a program used to connect web pages with online databases. UltraDev was a major product in its own right, so you really get two products in one when you buy Dreamweaver MX.

That said, the (formerly) UltraDev features of Dreamweaver MX are, overall, quite a bit beyond the scope of a *Complete Idiot's Guide*, and also beyond the needs and skills of most web designers—amateur or professional. Still, adding UltraDev's database features to Dreamweaver provides a tool for the database-inclined to define their own online data applications. I'll introduce you to these features in Chapter 15.

A Makeover Look

The main change in the look of Dreamweaver is that MX fills much of the workspace with grouped, docked panels (in the Macintosh version, the panels are not docked). These panels are *grouped* because they have tabs that combine many panels into one (and you choose one by clicking on the tab at the top of the panel group). They're *docked* because Otis Redding's immortal "Sittin' on the Dock of the Bay" remains one of the most moving songs you can listen to. No, actually, in this case, docked means locked in place on the right side of the Dreamweaver workspace.

Why are panels grouped and docked? Perhaps the idea is that if we're all going to have 21-inch, 1600-pixel-wide monitors, we need something to fill up that space.

Maybe, but when I'm designing a page, I prefer to have a nice clear space to look at. Therefore, my first act in cranking up MX is to close all the open panels until I need them.

You can do that by selecting **Close Panel Group** from the Panel menu in the top right of each panel.

As I mentioned earlier, tabs at the bottom of the page allow you to switch between open windows (pages). This feature is only available in Windows, and is illustrated in Figure 1.4.

Figure 1.4

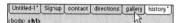

Page tabs allow you to switch between open pages in the Windows version of Dreamweaver MX.

Page Templates

A valuable addition to MX is a nice set of templates that help you save time designing pages. Besides saving time and work, Dreamweaver's nicely designed page templates will tweak your creative juices by providing models to steal ideas from (oops, I mean *get inspiration from*).

To create a page from a template, choose **File, New.** The New Document dialog box displays a list of categories on the left, and then a whole selection of page layouts on the right.

In Figure 1.5, I'm looking at a page design for a Text Journal Entry.

Figure 1.5

Previewing a page template.

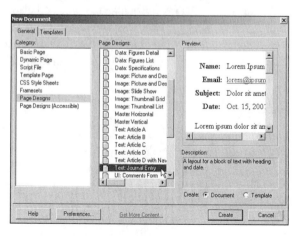

After you pick a template in the New Document dialog box, click **Create** to generate a page. You can edit that page using all the techniques and tricks I cover in this book.

Advanced Features

Some of the new features in Dreamweaver MX are aimed at folks who want to code their own HTML. Good for them and more power to them. I'll note those tools only in the context if showing you how the code generated by Dreamweaver appears. And, once in a blue moon (or once every few chapters), I'll invoke some of these tools to touch up HTML where that's needed.

By the Way

There are some other cool little design tools introduced in MX. One of my favorites is a set of predesigned color schemes developed by web color gurus Lynda Weinmann and Bruce Heavlin.

The single most powerful new tool in Dreamweaver MX is the ability to connect to an online database. Doing this requires more than a little knowledge of how to create and manage a database, as well as more understanding of *server* configuration than I expect will be the norm for readers of this book.

Definition

A **server** is a large computer that stores a website and makes it accessible to others— either over the Internet or via an in-house intranet.

Nevertheless, we'll venture into database territory briefly in Chapter 15 and explore these new features.

The Least You Need to Know

 ◆ Websites contain many files and many types of files. In addition to HTML web page files, they include image files, media files, script files, as well as other files that you'll learn about later in this book.

 ◆ Before you start your Dreamweaver site, collect all the files you already have in a folder.

 ◆ Even if you don't have any files prepared in advance, it's necessary to create a folder on your local computer before you define a site in Dreamweaver.

Chapter 2

Preparing Your Site

In This Chapter

- ◆ Preparing the files you need for a Dreamweaver site
- ◆ Learning where web files come from
- ◆ Creating a Dreamweaver site
- ◆ Opening web pages in Dreamweaver

Think of yourself as an orchestra conductor …. Okay, the lead singer of an alternative rock band, the producer of a hip-hop album … you get the basic idea. You're the one who is taking many different elements and organizing them into a single website.

As I emphasized in Chapter 1, Dreamweaver is both a tool for creating website content, and a way to organize and present content created in other programs.

Web pages are actually, in most cases, composed of many files and often, many kinds of files. Images, for example, are all separate files that are embedded in your web page. Same with plug-in sound files and embedded Flash movies.

In order for all these files to work together, you need to have them properly organized in your website. If your embedded images don't show up in your page, if your frames display with "page not found" messages, and your generated JavaScript is lost in a wrong website folder, your site is a big nothing, as we used to say back home.

So, before you dive into Dreamweaver to put your website together, you'll want to collect and organize much of the content of your website in advance.

The best news is that once you've collected your site content into folders, you're 90 percent of the way to organizing a Dreamweaver site, and turning all the dreary details of managing your files over to Dreamweaver.

Planning Your Site—the Concept

The more you can envision your site in advance, the more smoothly you can implement your site. This is all the more important when you are designing a site for a client, and you need to be sure that you and your client are on the same page as far as what the site will contain and look like.

There are two ways to approach site content: You can start with "What You Got," or you can start with "What You Want." The what-you-got approach begins with making a list of the content you already have that needs to be organized into a website. That content might include text files, images, media files, and so on. The what-you-want approach starts by stepping back and envisioning your site as if you were a visitor. Even after designing hundreds of websites, I almost always end up working out a basic layout for a new site on a piece of scratch paper or the back of a napkin (hopefully over a nice lunch at the client's expense!).

The basic layout you design for a site should start with a home page—the place where visitors will arrive when they come to your site. From there, you'll want to lay out navigation options that a visitor can follow. Figure 2.1 shows the kind of schematic I find helpful in charting out a plan for a website.

Figure 2.1

This simple sketch provides a road map to create a site.

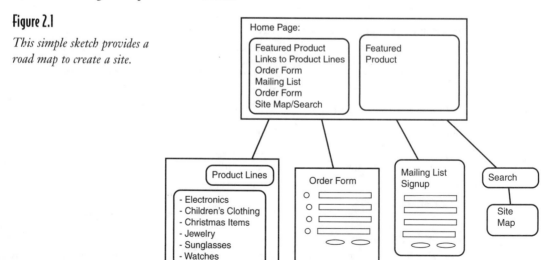

Once you have a basic list of site content, and a vision of how your site should "flow," you can translate your vision and content into a real live site. The home page for the site in Figure 2.2 reflects the site flowchart I designed in Figure 2.1.

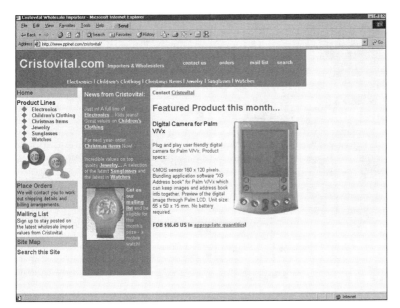

Figure 2.2

The site comes to life—incorporating the rough sketch in Figure 2.1 plus the content provided by a client.

The Recipe Cookbook—What Goes Into a Site

Most of this book will explore website content that you create right in Dreamweaver—formatted text, page design tools like tables and frames, input forms, and even things like Flash animation that can be generated right in Dreamweaver.

But there are many elements of a website you *can't* create in Dreamweaver. After all, if Macromedia put all the tools necessary to create *all* website content in Dreamweaver, who would bother to buy products like Flash for animation, Illustrator for drawings, Photoshop for photos, Premiere for movies, and so on. Seriously, Dreamweaver is a powerful tool for web design, and you *can* create many web objects with it. But you will also want to integrate graphics, media, text, and scripting from other sources.

A site I created for a music production studio, for example, includes video, different types of sound files, and imported graphic art, some of which is shown in Figure 2.3.

Imported art work

Figure 2.3

This web page incorporates imported MP3 and Real Media audio files and graphic art.

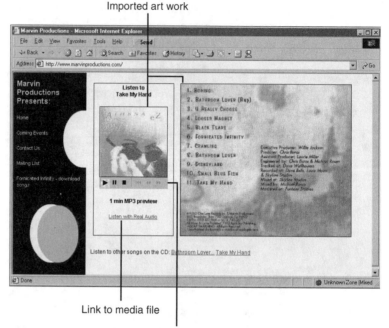

Link to media file

Media file embedded in plug-in

In the following sections, I'll give you an overview of where different kinds of files come from.

Sources and Types of Image Files

As you prepare to launch your web design project in Dreamweaver, one of your first and most important tasks is to accumulate image files in usable graphic file formats.

Web graphics can come from anywhere—scanned images, digital photos, hand-drawn artwork, computer generated graphics, and more.

But before graphics can be displayed in a website, they must be converted to or saved as a web-compatible image file format. The vast majority of web graphics are saved in one of the two image file formats that are interpreted by every browser—GIF and JPEG. I'll discuss how and when to use each of these file types in Chapter 5. But if you are collecting images for a website, you will want to insist they be provided to you in one of these formats.

Graphics programs like Adobe Photoshop, CorelDRAW/Paint, Adobe Illustrator, Macromedia Freehand, and others all can export images to either GIF or JPEG format.

New developments in web browsers, combined with the widespread installation of plug-ins, have opened the door to the display of images in additional formats including Flash (SWF) graphics, Adobe's SVG (Scalable Vector Graphics) images, and also PDF files that display both text and graphics. These additional formats allow web designers additional freedom in presenting better looking and animated graphics. I'll explore using Flash files in Chapter 16.

The following table shows many of the more popular file types that can be used in a website, and where they come from. Web content software producers—please don't sue me if your latest and greatest (but not yet adopted) web file format isn't included. I appreciate what you're doing with your cutting edge, envelope busting new web format. But the following list includes file types that comprise over 90 percent of web page content.

Definition

Plug-ins are programs which allow web browsers to display text, graphics, and media that are not interpreted by the browser itself. Some of the most popular plug-ins are the Flash Viewer (that displays SWF files) and the Adobe Acrobat Reader (that displays PDF files).

Table 2.1   File Types Used in Dreamweaver Sites

File Type	Used For	Created By
HTML	Designing web pages	HTML pages are created right in Dreamweaver, or hand-coding HTML in text processing program
GIF	Presenting graphics on the web	Adobe Photoshop or other graphic design programs
JPEG	Presenting photos and other color-sensitive graphics on the web	Adobe Photoshop or other graphic design programs
PNG	An alternate graphic format similar to GIF	Adobe Photoshop or other graphic design programs
SWF	Presenting embedded animated or vector images in websites using the Flash Viewer plug-in	Macromedia Flash, Adobe Illustrator, CorelDRAW, Macromedia Freehand, or other vector-based (non-bitmap) graphics programs
MPEG, RM, WMF, QT, MP3, AU, WAV	Various media file formats, each with its own proprietary plug-in used to present sound and video in web pages.	Adobe Premiere, Ulead Media Station Pro, Real Producer, Quick-Time, CoolEdit, and a long list of media creating programs
CSS	Cascading Style Sheet files store global formatting for a website	Created in Dreamweaver or hand-coded using CSS code

In addition, Dreamweaver creates its own proprietary file types, like LIB files to store library items—global site elements that I'll explain in Chapter 12.

Using Media Files

Sound and video files can be integrated in your website in two ways. They can be integrated seamlessly in your site using Dreamweaver's plug-in features, or you can simply provide links to media files at your site, in which case the files will open in an independent browser window, provided your visitors have the appropriate media player installed on their system.

I'll give you more advice on what kinds of media files work best, how to integrate them into your site, and what to watch out for in Chapter 17 and Chapter 18.

Don't Take No Hardcopy—Importing Text

Text remains the basic content tool for websites. I don't know about you, but with all the carpal tunnel going around these days, the less typing I have to do, the better! So I try to get text files in a format where I can quickly and easily import them into Dreamweaver web pages.

Dreamweaver has special tools for importing Microsoft Word files. I'll discuss these briefly in Chapter 4. But if text files don't import smoothly, you can always copy and paste text into Dreamweaver.

The important point to keep in mind as you prepare to launch your website project is that you need text files in some kind of digital format. And you'll want to collect these files in advance, before you start designing your site.

Including Scripts

You can incorporate *scripts*, programs, or *applets* in your Dreamweaver site. These applets are usually created for websites in programming languages like JavaScript or ActiveX.

Definition

Applets and **scripts** are little programs—composed of a few or a few dozen lines of programming code.

Scripts can add interactivity to your site. For example, you can use a JavaScript to respond to a menu option a visitor selects, by sending the visitor to a selected web page. Or, you can use a script to manage input data entered in an online form.

Often you'll add scripts only later in the site design process, after you have created elements like input forms, graphics, and text that will be included in your scripts.

Even though it's not essential to collect scripts in advance, if you do have scripts you want to use on your site, you can include them in your site organizing plans by saving them in an accessible folder.

Dreamweaver also allows you to create your own JavaScript applets. I'll show you how to do that in Chapter 19 when we explore Dreamweaver Behaviors.

File Naming Faux Pas

Your operating system—Mac or Windows— accommodates all kinds of filenames including those with spaces, upper- and lowercase letters, and multiple periods.

But guess what? The web server, the remote computer to which you will eventually publish your site, is probably much grumpier when it comes to filenames. Many, if not most web servers use some version of the Unix or Linux operating system. Upper- and lowercase filenames tend to confuse Unix servers. Personally, I can't break myself of the habit of naming files with uppercase letters, but at least I know that if I have trouble uploading my site, this might be the problem. If you're not hooked on upper- and lowercase filenames, it's best to avoid them in your site. Further, filenames with spaces sometimes cause upload problems to a server.

None of this poses a problem at this point, when you are defining your local site on your own, file-friendly computer. But particularly filenames with spaces *will pose problems* when you upload your site to a remote server. You'll learn to do that in the next chapter, but I'm warning you now so you can avoid spaces in your filenames as you assemble your site.

By the Way

As you prepare to launch your website, you may well need to get content in various forms from others. Use the notes in this section to provide guidance to people submitting content to your site. For example—tell people providing text that you need it in a file, not hard copy. Tell folks providing you with graphics to submit them in GIF or JPEG format.

Inside Info

One alternative to using spaces in file names is to use the underscore character (_) to separate words in a file name. For example, "Home_Page".

Creating a Dreamweaver Site

As I mentioned in the beginning of this chapter, web pages often include many different files, and part of what you are paying Dreamweaver to do for you is to keep those files organized and plugged in where they are supposed to go.

Dreamweaver will be happy to do that for you. No need for you to remember that the image file you plugged into your home page got renamed and moved to a different file folder. Dreamweaver will handle that for you—as long as you do a little work first to organize your files into a Dreamweaver site.

By the Way

You will need a folder for your Dreamweaver site, even if it's empty right now. As you create files in Dreamweaver, you'll need a place to organize them. So, even if you don't have any files for your site yet, create an empty folder before you start to define your site in Dreamweaver.

The process of creating a Dreamweaver site has three basic parts:

◆ Collect the files you need for our site in a local folder on your computer.

◆ Organize those files into a local website.

◆ Upload your files to a remote site, and test them in as many browsers and browser versions as you can.

I'll discuss the uploading to a remote browser part of the process in the Chapter 3. Here, I'll focus on creating your Dreamweaver site.

Defining a Site

If you have organized all your site files into a folder on your local computer, you're ready to plug them into a Dreamweaver site.

You don't *have* any files yet? OK, that's cool. You don't have to. You can create a Dreamweaver site on the fly, and create content as you go.

Generally speaking, especially as you begin to take on large or professional level projects, you *will* have some image and text files that will go in your site.

If you have a *lot* of files ready for your site, you'll want to organize them into subfolders. Use a logical system to organize your files, so you can find them when you need them.

Inside Info

There are two schools on how to organize files into subfolders. You can organize files by content, or by type. I use both. For example, if I have a lot of media files, I might create folders for video, audio, Flash movies, etc. In that case, I'll have folders organized by file type. Or, if I'm doing an e-commerce site, I might organize files by product type, grouping text, graphics, sound, and other files in the same subfolder, and having separate subfolders for each product line.

With your site files organized into a folder on your local computer, follow these steps to define a Dreamweaver site on your local computer:

1. Launch Macromedia Dreamweaver MX.

2. Ignore (or briefly note and then move on) the massive amount of stuff on your screen. You don't need that yet. Instead, focus on the main menu, and choose **Site, New Site** to open the Site Definition dialog box. In the Site Definition dialog box, click the Advanced tab. Believe it or not, the "Advanced" tab is an easier way to define your site than the options in the "Basic" tab.

3. In the Site name area of the dialog box, type a name your site.

4. Click the Folder icon next to the Local Root Folder area of the dialog box to navigate to the folder with your files (the folder on your computer where you collected the files used in your site). The Refresh Local File List Automatically check box should be selected—this synchronizes the files on our local computer with the display of files in Dreamweaver. Your Site Definition box should now look like Figure 2.4.

By the Way _____

If you don't own Dreamweaver, you can start with the 30-day trial download version—you'll find a link to the download at the macromedia.com website.

Inside Info

Earlier in this chapter I warned you to keep file names simple, and avoid spaces in them. However, the site name is just information stored on your local computer by Dreamweaver, so feel free to use spaces, and any character you wish in this area.

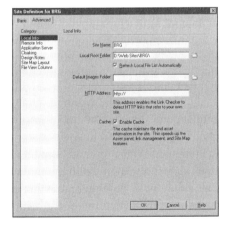

Figure 2.4

Use the Site Definition dialog box to tell Dreamweaver where you'll be storing files.

5. The Default Images Folder area allows you to define a folder on your local computer where images for your site will be stored. This is optional. Use it if you have your image files all organized into a distinct folder. In that case, click on the folder icon and navigate to the folder with your image files.

6. OK the dialog box. You'll be prompted with a little dialog box noting that an initial "site cache" is being created. That just means Dreamweaver will see what's in the folder within which you organized your site files, and will display that information. Click OK and let Dreamweaver open your site.

A Holy Site

Give yourself a pat on the back, a hug, a high-five, or something (perhaps there's a tasty snack in the fridge that would be appropriate?). You've accomplished quite a bit at this point.

By defining a Dreamweaver site, you organized your files into a folder, and synchronized that folder with Dreamweaver's site management features. This is going to make it easy to design web pages, and later on (in Chapter 3), to upload those pages and all the files within them onto a remote server so the whole world can share them.

From now on, it's very important that all the file management you do with files in your site is done in Dreamweaver, and not using your operating system's file management tools.

A File Management Detour

When I teach Dreamweaver, I alternate between teaching Mac folks (on Macs) and Windows users (on PCs). For some left brain/right brain reason, Mac folks find the concept of file management a little more confusing than PCers, who confront file management a bit more overtly in their operating system.

At the same time, since Windows users are sometimes more confident (or brash) about managing files using Windows file management features, they can tend to get into trouble more easily by corrupting the carefully managed file relationships maintained by Dreamweaver. So, *everyone*—take note:

Files on your computer are organized into folders. This is sometimes important when you want to find a file. (Where did I leave that resignation letter I wrote on my computer in a fit of rage last week???) But they're even more important when other files and programs want to find a file. For example, web pages almost always include embedded files—like image files. It's critical that these embedded files be stored where they are supposed to be. Sans Dreamweaver, we'd all be keeping piles of paper, covering ourselves with post-its or going nuts trying to make sure that every file in our site was where it was supposed to be. Otherwise, when a web browser went to look for an image and couldn't find it, one of those annoying x's would show up on the browser where the file was supposed to appear.

The point is, as long as you do *all* file management with Dreamweaver, you don't need to worry very much about any of this. That means, don't rename files in your site, don't move files in your site, and don't delete files in your site, except when using the Dreamweaver Site window, which I'm about to introduce you to.

OK, you've had your lecture, let's move on to the Site window.

Organizing Files in the Site Window

You'll spend most of your time creating web pages in Dreamweaver's Document window—the *WYSIWYG* web page design tool that is the most powerful part of Dreamweaver. But you'll also spend a good chunk of your design time in the Site window. This is where you can see, and organize, *all* the pages and files in your site.

Definition

WYSIWYG stands for "What You See Is What You Get." Dreamweaver's page design tools allow you to format your page much as you would a word processing document. As you do, Dreamweaver generates HTML (HyperText Markup Language) that allows web browsers to interpret the formatting you apply to a page. But in Dreamweaver, the HTML generation goes on *behind the scenes*. Instead, formatting is displayed as visitors will see it in the Dreamweaver document window.

While you use the Document window to define specific page content, the Site window is where you organize *all* the files of your site.

To view the Site window, choose **Site Files** from the Site menu, or press the F8 function key. If the Site window appears docked, on the right side of the Document window, you will want to expand it to a useful size. Do this by clicking the **Expand/Collapse** icon in the collapsed Site panel (it's the icon on the far right in the set of seven icons atop the panel).

The expanded Site window is divided into two parts. The section on the left displays your local site—the version of your website stored on your local computer. Figure 2.5 shows the expanded Site window.

The area on the left side of the Site window can either display a site map—a graphical representation of your site, or it can display the remote version of your website—the version stored on a remote web server. I'll explain how to work with your remote site in the next chapter.

You can create new folders in the Site window by choosing **File**, **New Folder**. To collapse a folder (and hide it's content), click the "-" icon next to the folder name. To expand a folder (and see it's content), click the "+" symbol next to the folder icon.

Figure 2.5

The right side of the expanded Site window shows the files in the local version of your website.

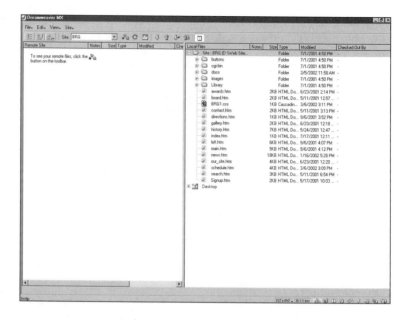

To sort your list of files by name, size, type, modified date, or any other column in the Site window, click on the column heading.

Design notes are comments you can add to a file that don't appear when the file is viewed by a visitor to your site. To add a design note to a file, select the file in the Site window, and choose **File, Design Notes.** You can choose a status for the file in the Status list, and/or enter comments in the Notes area. Assigning a status like draft, final, or needs attention to your files makes it easier to organize your work. If you select the Show When File is Opened checkbox, your design note will display when you open the selected file. The Design Notes dialog box is shown in Figure 2.6.

Figure 2.6

Comments and notes show up in the Site window and can be used as sort categories to prioritize tasks.

You can move files from one folder to another in the Site window by simply dragging them with your mouse. Select a file and press the **Delete** key to delete it.

You can rename a file in the Site window by selecting it, and choosing **File, Rename** from the Site window menu.

> **Caution** _____
>
> It's so important, I'll say it again: When you rename files in your website, you do it in the Dreamweaver Site window, and *not* in your Mac or PC file management programs. When you rename files in the Site window, Dreamweaver automatically checks to see if those files are linked to or embedded in another file, and if so, Dreamweaver *changes* the affected links so that your web pages will still work. *Don't* rename files in your website outside of the Dreamweaver Site window.

If you imported already existing web pages into your site—for instance if you hand-coded some HTML files, you can open those files in the Dreamweaver document window by double-clicking on them in the Site window.

In short, use the Site window as your file manager, to organize, rename, delete, and add comments to all the files in your website.

Creating Web Pages in the Site Menu

Now that you have your files (or at least a blank folder) defined as a Dreamweaver site, you can start to create web pages.

To create a new web page from the Site menu, first click on the folder in which you want to store the file.

With a folder selected, choose **File, New File** to generate a new web page. The new page will appear in the Site window as untitled-1.htm. Figure 2.7 shows a web page being generated in the Dreamweaver Site window.

You'll want to rename the page file to something more descriptive. If the page is going to be your site's *home page*, name it index.htm.

If you create multiple pages without renaming them, Dreamweaver will assign sequential file names starting with untitled-2.htm, untitled-3.htm, and so on.

> **Caution** _____
>
> Most files can be stored in any folder. But some files *must* be stored in the root—or top folder in your site. Most importantly, the home page, which is usually called index.htm, or index.html (but *never* both) must be stored in your *root* folder or visitors to your site will not be able to find it.

Definition _____

A **home page** is the page visitors see when they type your URL (website address) in their browser's address bar. It's not necessary, for example, for a visitor to type www.ppinet.com/index.htm to see my site's home page—they can simply type www.ppinet.com and they'll go to the index.htm page automatically. Every site needs a home page. Alternate names for home pages include index.html, default.htm, or default.html. But since you only want (and can only have) *one* home page, don't use these other options unless your web server host requires that you use them. Almost all servers will recognize index.htm as a home page file name.

Figure 2.7

The safest way to add web pages to your site is to create them in the Dreamweaver Site window.

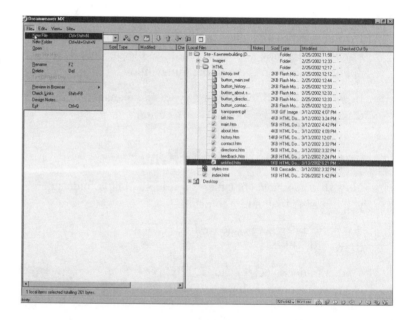

Opening Pages from the Site Window

Once you have an HTML web page file in your site menu, you can open it in the Document window by double-clicking on it. The Document window is where you will edit your HTML files, and I'll be spending most of this book explaining how to do that. But for now, you can experiment by opening HTML files you created in the Site window in the Document window.

For example, if you created a file called index.htm in the Site menu, you can double-click on it to open that file in Dreamweaver's Document view.

Press the F8 function key to return to the Site window. Or, choose **File, Close** in the Document window to close a file.

Once back in the Site window, you can always reopen, or return to an open HTML web page in the Document window by double-clicking on that file in the Site window.

The Least You Need to Know

◆ Websites contain many files, and many types of files. In addition to HTML web page files, they include image files, media files, script files, as well as other files that you'll learn about later in this book.

◆ Before you start your Dreamweaver site, collect all the files you already have in a folder.

◆ Even if you don't have any files prepared in advance, it's necessary to create a folder on your local computer before you define a site in Dreamweaver.

◆ The Dreamweaver Site window is one of the most important parts of Dreamweaver; it's where you organize, name, create, and delete files from your site.

◆ You can open HTML files for editing in the Document window by double-clicking on them in the Site window.

◆ You can open the Site window from the Document window by pressing the F8 function key.

Getting Connected

In This Chapter

♦ Understanding local and remote websites

♦ Hooking up with a server

♦ Uploading files to a server

♦ Maintaining local and remote sites

Once you've created a site on your local computer, the next step is to publish that site to a web server (or sometimes to a more restricted intranet server).

Sending, or uploading, these files to a remote server requires that *all* the files are sent to the server, and that the relationship between those files is preserved. Otherwise, browsers won't be able to find the pictures embedded in your pages, the targets of your page links, and so on.

Dreamweaver's Site window manages all the tricky file management involved in keeping your site together as it is transferred to a server. In this chapter, I'll show you how that works.

Local Sites and Remote Servers

Unless you are content to simply gaze upon your lovely website on your own (local) computer, you'll want to upload (send) your files to a remote server.

In order to expose your awesome site content (or even your humble beginnings of a site) to the world, you need to *upload* the site content to a *server*. Once it's there, it can be viewed by others.

The basic process of sending a website to a server, and accessing the site content in a web browser is illustrated in Figure 3.1.

Figure 3.1

From your local computer to the web.

The World Is Watching

Server

Local Site

Internet and Intranets

Servers fall into two basic types. *Internet* servers allow your content to be accessed by anyone in the world, assuming they can break through whatever roadblocks have been erected by their companies, by big-brotherish governments, and so on.

Intranet servers are accessible to a more limited, authorized audience. For instance, most large corporations, organizations, and educational institutions have intranets that share files, records, and other data *only* within the organization. These intranet servers are protected by security software called *firewalls*, and of course they are defended against hackers by legions of nerdy techie guys.

> **Definition**
>
> The **Internet** is the global network of servers that makes your website available to people around the world.
>
> An **intranet** is a more restricted network of connections that make your site accessible to people in your company or organization.
>
> A **firewall** is software that protects a server from unauthorized access (hackers).

Often, the decision of where your site content will be posted has been made for you. If your boss or your client has already secured server space—either on the Internet or an intranet, then all that's left for you to worry about is getting the necessary login information that is required to connect to the site. I'll address that process in detail later in this chapter.

In other cases, you, or your client, will have to procure web server space from a web presence provider. In spite of the industry shakeout of recent years, or perhaps in part because of it, server space is fairly easy and cheap to obtain, relative to other costs of web design and implementation. You can contract for server space for a small site (one without large media files) for about $5 a month, and small business sites are available in the $25 to $50 per month range.

Because your site lives and dies based on whether or not your server works well and supports the features on your site, I'll provide some shopping information in the next section.

Shopping for a Remote Server Host

There is a rather bewildering array of web presence providers out there, and often their ads aren't that helpful in figuring out what package you need.

Let's deconstruct a couple server space ads, starting with the current listings from Yahoo's Geocities hosting service. Geocities has the advantage of being reliable, affordable, and easy to use. It does have disadvantages, too, which I'll come back to shortly. Figure 3.2 shows the current set of hosting packages available through Geocities.

How *Much* Server Do You Need?

The most basic feature offered by a web presence provider is server space for your files, and access to those files by you (so you can upload files) and by visitors. These three elements are all measurable.

Figure 3.2

Geocities sites cost more if you want more server space.

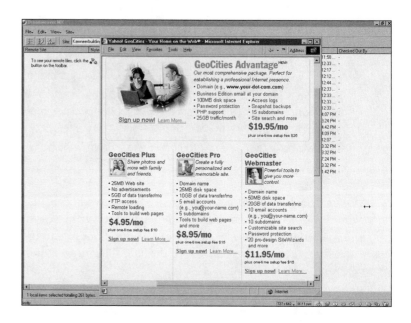

Definition

Bandwidth is measurement of the capacity for transferring information to and from the server.

Definition

Browsers use something called an **Internet Protocol (IP) address** to locate websites. The IP address is a set of numbers. Since these numbers are hard to remember, the domain name system associates easy-to-remember domain names (like ppinet.com) with these IP addresses, and allows visitors to find a site by typing in a domain name instead of a number.

The amount of space a site provider sells you is measured in MB, or megabytes. I wish Dreamweaver had a button you could press to quickly calculate your total site file size, but alas, not yet. You can estimate (or even total) your file size by looking at your Site window, and seeing roughly how many KB (kilobytes) are listed for your files in the Size column. 1000 KB equals one MB. If your site has 10 MB, make sure you purchase a site plan that provides at least that much MB.

The other essential feature is permission to send files to your server, and the ability of visitors to access the server. Sometimes these elements of a site are referred to as *bandwidth*. If your site will be getting a zillion hits a month, you'll need large amounts of bandwidth. If your site will get hundreds of hits a month, minimal bandwidth will do fine.

Other Site Features

Site providers offer additional features, along with server space and bandwidth. Some will register a *domain name* for you.

This is a valuable service. Registering domain names can be a hassle if you've never done it before, and after you register your name, you need to direct that domain name to your server. If you find a web presence provider who will do that for you, lucky you. In fact, I often find deals where a site provider will register your domain name free if you commit to a year of service.

Most site providers give you at least five e-mail addresses linked to your domain name, so if you desire, you can be me@mysite.com, your site administrator can be siteadmin@ mysite.com, and so on.

More advanced site features are required to host a live, interactive database on your site. I'll explain how to hook up a live database with Dreamweaver in Chapter 15. But if you plan to connect a database to your website, and allow visitors to search that data through your website, you'll need to find a server package that supports *one* (not all) of the server scripting languages used by Dreamweaver to create an online database. Those languages are: ColdFusion, ASP, ASP.NET, JSP, or PHP.

Perhaps you're saying to yourself, "Yeah, that's nice Dave, but I see these sites cost *at a minimum* about $9 per month." I hear you, and I've been there. If you're teaching yourself Dreamweaver you don't need a commercial site.

The list of providers of free web hosting continues to shrink. In April of 2002, Yahoo's free Geocities sites stopped supporting the Site window features of Dreamweaver (boo!). At this writing, you can still get a free website that supports Dreamweaver's Site features at www.freewebhosting.com. You have to put up with ads, but the sites work, and you'll be able to enable and test 90 percent of the features I cover in this book with your free site.

By the Way

A good way to shop for a site is to make a list of features you'll need. How much server space do you need? Do you need your domain name registered? How many e-mail addresses do you need? And will you be featuring an interactive database on your site? Once you know what you need, you can shop for a provider that supports your site.

Caution

Rates and options for web hosting vary considerably. You might want to spend a bit more for a site provider who will answer your phone calls and provide helpful advice. You'll find links to site providers I like at my site—www.ppinet.com.

Hooking Up Your Remote Server

Once you locate a deal for server space (or elect to start with free space), get out your pencil and notepad, and prepare to record some info that you'll want to keep in a safe place! When you sign up for web space, you'll need the following information:

- The URL (domain name) for your site.
- The type of access (this is usually FTP, unless you are publishing your site to an intranet, in which case your server administrator will tell you the type of site access to use).
- The FTP host address. This is something like *ftp.yoursite.com*.

- A host directory if necessary. Most sites do not require this. If this information is required, it will be supplied by your web server provider.
- Your login name. This is your user name, and is required to access your site.
- Your password. This, too, is required. Make sure you get a login name and password from your site provider.

Caution

I'll repeat my warning: *Write down this information and store it in a safe secure place where you can find it but others cannot access it!* Without your site access information, you're locked out of your site. And don't let your site provider set you up without providing the required information listed here.

Other information might be required before you can access your server in Dreamweaver. For example, if you are working in an organization that protects your computer with a firewall, you'll need firewall settings from your site security supervisor.

Uploading to a Remote Site

If you have accumulated basic login information from your site provider, you can make a connection between your local site and your remote server, and upload your site content.

I'm also assuming that you have already set up a local Dreamweaver site. If not, flip back to Chapter 2 and define a local site before you attempt to connect to a remote site.

Making the Site Connection

With your login info (which you got from your site provider) handy, follow these steps to connect your site to your server:

1. In the Site window, Choose **Site, Edit Sites.** Click on your new Fair site, and click the **Edit** button in the Define Sites dialog box. The Edit Sites dialog box will appear. Select your site (if there are more than one listed), and click the **Edit** button in the Edit Sites dialog box. The Site Definition dialog box appears.

2. The Site Definition dialog box has a list of categories on the left side. The first in the list is Local Info. This is where you start. Enter your URL in the HTTP Address area of the Local Info tab, as shown in Figure 3.3.

Figure 3.3

Define your URL in the Site Definition dialog box. In this case, I'm using one of the free sites available at Geocities.

3. Click on **Remote Info** in the Category list, and choose **FTP** from the Access drop-down list. As you do, other areas of the dialog box become active.

4. Enter the FTP address (like ftp.mysite.com) in the FTP Host area.

5. Enter your username in the Login area.

6. Enter your password in the Password area. The dialog box should look something like Figure 3.4.

By the Way

In the overwhelming majority of cases, you'll want to use the FTP access option for Internet sites. However, if your server provider or your intranet administrator tells you to use another form of access, follow his or her instructions instead of selecting FTP.

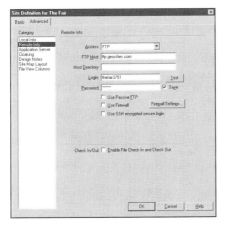

Figure 3.4

Login and password information must be obtained from your site provider.

7. Click **OK** when you've finished defining your remote hookup information. You'll return to the Edit Sites dialog box.

8. Click **Done** to close the Edit Sites dialog box and return to the site menu.

> **By the Way**
>
> Other, and less frequently used, Remote Information includes passive FTP, firewalls, and SSH (used for high-security servers). If your server utilizes these features, use the appropriate checkbox, but they are not required for most basic websites.
>
> Also, you can select the Check In/Check Out checkbox if you are working on a large project with an incalculable number of co-developers, and you need to ensure that multiple developers aren't changing a file at the same time. Not an option a small-scale developer needs to worry about.

By completing the local and remote site areas of the Site Definition dialog box, you've given Dreamweaver instructions on where to look for your remote site, and you've provided login information so Dreamweaver can unlock your site. You're now ready to make "the connection."

To connect to your remote site, choose **Site, Connect** from the menu. You'll see an interactive icon while Dreamweaver attempts to connect to your site. When the connection is successfully made, you'll see a second site display on the left site of the Site window.

If you're opening a new site, there will likely be no, or just a few files on the remote site. Often site providers supply an initial home page (an index.htm or index.html page). You'll want to get rid of that eventually, and replace it with your own content.

Uploading Sites and Files

Once you establish a connection to your remote site, you can upload selected file(s), or your entire site.

To upload all the files in your local site, select the root local folder, and choose **Site, Put** (or click the **Put** icon—an up arrow at the top of the Site window) to upload your site to your remote server. Figure 3.5 illustrates the process of uploading an entire site.

Figure 3.5

Because the root folder is selected, the entire site will be uploaded (Put) to the server.

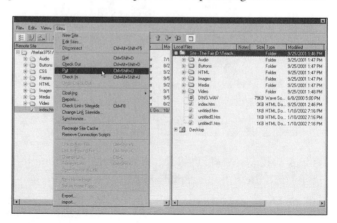

In the remainder of this book, you'll be spending most of your time using the Document window to edit individual pages. Even in the Document window, you can choose **Site, Put** (or click the **Put** icon) to upload the open page to your site.

As you begin to embed files (like images) on your pages, Dreamweaver will prompt you to upload dependent files when you upload a web page. You'll see a dialog box like the one in Figure 3.6.

Figure 3.6

Dreamweaver has determined that the page I'm uploading requires other files to work right, and wants to upload those files along with the one I selected.

You almost always want to accept that offer and upload all files associated with the one you are sending to the remote server. Associated files often include embedded images, and by uploading those images, you ensure that the latest version of your image is included in your page.

Downloading Files

There are a couple of reasons why you might want to download files from your remote server to your local computer. One reason is that you might have wiped out or corrupted one or more files on your local computer. Your remote server can function as a backup computer, and you can restore lost files by downloading them back from the server.

The other reason to download files is that you might want to change the computer you are using as your local computer. In that case, define your site in your new computer (as described in this chapter), and then build a local site by downloading the files already posted to your server.

To download a file, or an entire site, select the file(s) or the site root folder on the right side of the Site window. Then click the **Get** icon at the top of the Site window (a down-pointing arrow), or choose **Site, Get.**

The Least You Need to Know

◆ You generally create a Dreamweaver site on your local computer. To make it accessible on the web, you upload it to a server.

◆ Dreamweaver allows you to define the connection between your local site and your remote site in the Site window.

◆ Dreamweaver's Put feature manages the process of making sure your files are properly transferred to your remote server.

◆ You can also download (get) files from a remote server and copy them onto any computer using the Site window.

Part 2

Adding Pictures and Text

Once your site structure is in place, it's playtime. In the following chapters, I'll show you how to create, format, and lay out text for your web pages, and how to add images to your site. I'll also walk you through all the tricks for including useful links to pages within and outside your site.

4

Formatting Web Pages

In This Chapter

◆ Editing text

◆ Formatting text

◆ Formatting paragraphs

◆ Defining page properties

The single most widely used element of website content is text. And much of the work you do as a web designer involves importing, editing, formatting, and laying out text.

Dreamweaver makes it easy to apply fonts, type sizes, attributes like boldface or italics, and text coloring. You also have limited control over paragraph attributes, like indenting.

Creating Page Content in the Document Window

In the preceding chapters, I've dragged you through the details of the Site window. I know it was rough, but you needed to go through that boot camp experience to understand how the various files in your website were organized.

Now comes the fun part. The Document window is where you create, edit, and format actual page content. About time!

You can open a page in the Document window from the Site window by double-clicking on the filename. Or, you can create a *new* web page in the Document window by choosing **File, New.**

To save a file, or save changes to a file, choose **File, Save.** If you're saving a page for the first time, you'll be prompted to define a filename. Make sure you include an .htm or .html file name extension to the file as you save it, so Dreamweaver (and web browsers) will know this file is coded in HTML.

Once you've opened or created a file in the Document window, you can add and edit text.

Just Like Your Word Processor—but Different

The key to editing text in Dreamweaver is to not edit text in Dreamweaver, or at least not much. Dreamweaver comes with all the normal basic word processing tools like cut and paste, find and replace, and spell checking. But your word processor does a better job handling these tasks (while Dreamweaver does a *much* better job designing web pages!).

There are a couple of ways to prepare text for importing into Dreamweaver: You can simply open a text file in your word processor and copy and paste into Dreamweaver. Or, you can use your word processors limited export to HTML feature, and import the generated HTML into Dreamweaver. I'll walk you through the do's and don'ts of both of these options in the next section of this chapter.

While you want to edit text elsewhere, formatting text is best done in Dreamweaver. I'll return to that in the last half of this chapter.

Copying and Pasting

Since you'll usually want to prepare most of your text in a word processor, let's start with how to get that content into a Dreamweaver web page.

Once you copy text from your word processor into your operating system clipboard, you can paste it into Dreamweaver in one of two ways. You can simply choose **Edit, Paste** in the Dreamweaver document window to paste text. This preserves some minimal text formatting attributes—like paragraph and line breaks.

If you want to paste text with less preservation of attributes like paragraph breaks (in other words, if you want to paste text as one big paragraph), choose **Edit, Paste as HTML** when you paste text into the Document window. I know, you're not *really* pasting text as HTML, but this trick works for when you want to manage paragraph breaks in Dreamweaver.

Inside Info

There is actually a *different* logic to paragraph breaks in web pages than there is in printed text. In general, you'll want shorter paragraphs in your web page. One reason for this is that you often use larger fonts on a web page to compensate for the lower screen resolution that makes type harder to read. Another reason to manage your paragraph breaks in Dreamweaver is so you can flow text around images—something you don't do as often in a word processor. I'll return to flowing text around images in Chapter 5.

Editing Text

I'll assume that you're comfortable with the cut, copy, and paste features of normal text editors in the Mac and Windows environments. And yes, Dreamweaver supports click and drag to move or copy text.

The spell checker in Dreamweaver isn't as robust as the one in your word processor, but if you do *any* editing of text in Dreamweaver, you'll want to recheck your spelling before sharing your pages with the world. To check spelling, choose **Text**, **Check Spelling.** Then follow the prompts in the Check Spelling dialog box.

Dreamweaver's Find and Replace feature is cleverly hidden outside of the Text menu. To quickly replace all instances of "our president" with "our all-knowing, all-seeing master," for instance, you should choose **Edit, Find and Replace.** Use the prompts in the Find and Replace dialog box to search for and change instances of text.

The Find In drop-down list in the Find and Replace dialog box allows you to choose between applying find and replace to the open web page (choose Current Document), in the Entire Current Local Site, in Selected Files in Site (click to select files in the Site window before using this feature), or in a Selected Folder (if you choose this option, a Folder icon will let you navigate to a specific folder). The Find and Replace dialog box, with Find In options is shown in Figure 4.1.

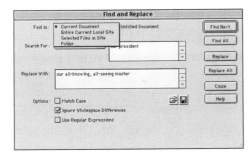

Figure 4.1

Dreamweaver allows you to search for or replace text in any selected page(s) or over an entire site.

Formatting Text

If you're new to web design, let me downsize your expectations a bit. You *don't* have the same freedom to format text for the web that you do with a desktop publishing program, or even a word processor.

On the web, your options are more limited. Do you just love using Tempus ITC font? Start thinking about Courier, Times Roman, or Helvetica and Arial. Like applying one and a half line spacing to text (I do!). That you *can* do, but it takes more advanced formatting skills than you'll learn in this chapter. We'll get to features like that when we explore cascading style sheets (referred to as CSS) in Chapter 9.

Why is it so difficult to assign formatting to text on the web? Two reasons: First, due to the low resolution of monitors compared to print (something like 72 dots per inch for monitors compared to 600 dots per inch on a typical desktop printer), intricate fonts often don't look very good on monitors.

The main reason why font options are so limited is that you must rely on your visitor's computer to supply fonts. So, if you assign Tempus ITC font, and your visitor's Mac, Windows, web TV, or whatever doesn't have that font, he or she will see text converted to a different font. That's okay; they'll still see the font. But by converting type to a different font, your page size, line breaks, and so on will be distorted.

To further press this point, formatting text for web pages is formatting for a moving target. Visitors will have different resolution monitors, different size monitors, and will have the type size settings in their browser software set to anything from small to large. Again, this is much different than formatting type for print, where you know exactly how large the page size will be, and how the type will appear to the reader.

With all that as a warning, let's now explore all the things you *can* do to type.

Assigning Fonts

Since, as I just explained, font display on the web depends on the visitor's set of fonts, Dreamweaver actually assigns sets of fonts to text. That is, you assign one font, but you also assign "backup" fonts in case the one you assign is not supported.

You can assign font attributes from either the Properties panel, or from the Text menu. Since the Properties panel is easier to access, I'll show you how to format text using it except when it's necessary to jump to the Text menu for formatting features not found in the Properties panel.

To assign a font to text, select the text and choose a font set from the Font drop-down list as shown in Figure 4.2.

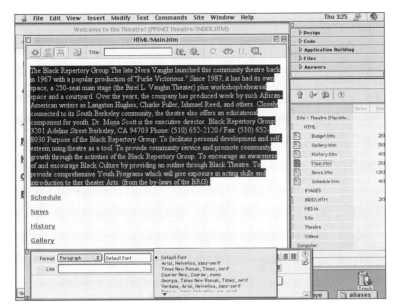

Figure 4.2

Assigning font to selected text.

What if you want to take a chance that visitors will have a font not already on the Dreamweaver font list? You can add fonts by choosing **Edit Font List** from the Font drop-down list in the Properties panel. This opens the Edit Font List dialog box.

To make new fonts available for formatting in Dreamweaver, select the font on the right side of the Edit Font List dialog box. Then, use the "<<" symbol in the Edit Font List to copy that font from the list of Available Fonts (on the right) to the list of Chosen Fonts (on the left), as shown in Figure 4.3.

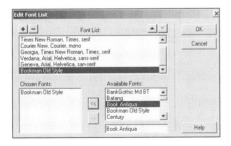

Figure 4.3

Adding new fonts to Dreamweaver's available set of formatting fonts.

Once you add a font to the Chosen Fonts list, you should also add one or two "backup" fonts in case a visitor's system doesn't support your chosen font. At least one backup font should be one of the three most universally supported fonts—Courier, Times Roman (or some variant of that, like Times), Helvetica (on a Mac), or Arial (in Windows). Add these additional fonts to your set by selecting them in the Available Fonts list, and then clicking the "<<" button again to add them to your font set. You can remove a font from a set by selecting it in the Chosen Fonts list, and clicking the ">>" button in the Edit Font List dialog box.

To create additional sets of Chosen Fonts, click the + sign at the top of the Edit Font List dialog box. After you define all the font sets you need, click **OK**. The newly defined font sets will now be available from the Font drop-down list in the Properties panel, and from the Text, Font menu option.

Changing Font Size

The Properties panel offers only seven sizes for text. And it doesn't even tell you what those sizes are! Again, this is a reflection of the fact that your visitors will have different system and browser settings that in many cases override the font size you define.

> ### Inside Info
>
> You *can* define set font sizes, even to the half point (like 11.5 points). To do this, you need to use cascading style sheets, which are covered in Chapter 9.

So, the sizes you choose from the Size drop-down list in the Properties panel are *relative* sizes, with 1 being smallest, and 7 largest. You can increase the size of selected text by choosing one of the values in the Size drop-down list with a "+" in front of it, or decrease size by choosing a value with a "-" in front of it, as shown in Figure 4.4.

Figure 4.4

Making text smaller.

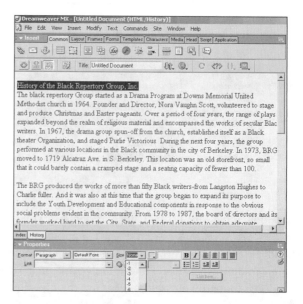

Changing Text Color

You can assign colors to selected text by clicking on the **Text Color** swatch in the Properties panel. The palette that opens when you click the Text Color swatch gives you a choice of any of 216 colors that are considered "browser-safe." These browser-safe colors are supported by a wide variety of operating systems.

You'll have a better chance of having your text colors reproduced on a visitor's monitor if you stick to these colors. Figure 4.5 shows color being applied to selected text.

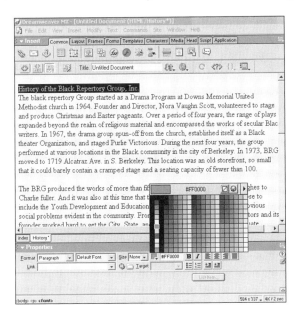

Figure 4.5

Assigning color to text.

Looking At HMTL

When you format text in Dreamweaver, you're *really* assigning HTML tags to that text. As I explained in Chapter 1, HTML is the language of web page design, and Dreamweaver generates HTML for you while you apply formatting in the friendly, word processor-like environment of the Document window.

Many Dreamweaver developers know HTML. Others don't. For those who are HTML coders, Dreamweaver gives you the option of looking at the HTML it generates, editing that code, or even writing all your HTML right in the

Inside Info

While you can apply colors to text, if your text has a *link* assigned to it, the text will change color in a visitor's browser depending on what *state* the link is in—never used, visited, or active. I'll explain links in detail in Chapter 6. Later in this chapter, I'll explain how to change default link colors for a page. And, in Chapter 9, I'll show you how to use Style Sheets to change your site's link colors.

Document window using HTML view. Even those of you who have no intention of spending time pouring over a hand-coding book will want to occasionally take a look at the HTML generated by Dreamweaver.

By the Way

Taking a peek at Dreamweaver's generated code is a good way to painlessly soak up at bit of knowledge of HTML code. For those of you who want to study HTML coding, there are many good HTML books around. My favorite introductory-level book is "HTML for the World Wide Web" by Elizabeth Castro (Peachpit Press).

Dreamweaver calls the normal Document window Design view. To see both the Design view and the HTML code on your page, choose the **Show Code** and **Design Views** button at the top of the Document window, as shown in Figure 4.6.

You can switch back to Design View by clicking the **Show Design View** icon at the top of the Document window.

Hardcore coders will want to hit the **Show Code View** icon at the top of the Document window to view just HTML. This turns the Document window into a fairly full-featured HTML editor. Since editing HTML is beyond the scope of this book, I'll drop you off here if you're about to start writing your own code.

Figure 4.6

Dreamweaver can display HTML as well as how that HTML will look on a page.

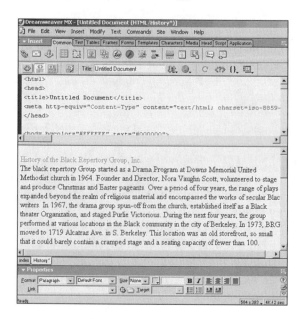

Formatting Paragraphs

Short of applying cascading style sheets, Dreamweaver doesn't provide too much in the way of paragraph formatting. But you can define paragraph alignment, indentation, and you can apply bullet list and automatic numbering to paragraphs.

The default spacing for paragraphs is one line in between each paragraph. A "cheap and easy" way to change paragraph spacing from the default double-spacing to single-spacing is to hold down the **Shift** key while you hit **Enter.** This creates a line break instead of a paragraph break, and avoids the line spacing that separates paragraphs. However, keep in mind that line breaks do not create new paragraphs. That means that any attribute you apply to a single paragraph (like indentation for example, or bullet points), applies to the entire paragraph, even though it might have line breaks within it.

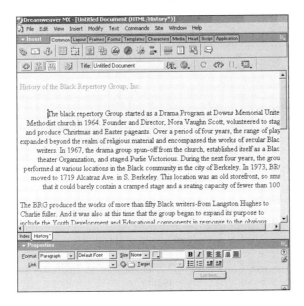

Figure 4.7

Right-aligning text.

You can align text left, center, right, or fully justified (stretching from one side of the page to another). To assign text alignment, click *anywhere* in a paragraph, click on one of the four alignment buttons in the Properties panel. In Figure 4.7, I'm aligning selected text right.

You can indent any selected paragraph(s) by clicking the **Text Indent** button in the Properties panel. Similarly, you can move indented paragraphs back to the right by clicking on the **Text Outdent** button. In Figure 4.8, I've indented a paragraph of text.

Dreamweaver will assign automatic numbering or bullets to selected paragraphs. Use the Ordered List button in the Properties panel to assign auto-numbering, and the Unordered List button to assign bullets.

Figure 4.8

Indented text.

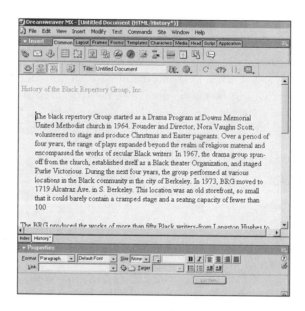

Defining Page Properties

Page properties include page background color, page margin size, page title, and elements called meta-tags which help search engines find and summarize your page content.

Page properties also include font color. Font color? Didn't we just learn that font color is applied to selected text within a page? Yup, sure did. But you can also define a default page font color (as well as change the default link text colors for a page).

When page font color, and selected text color (referred to as local formatting) conflict, the local font color prevails.

Color the Page

To define page background color, choose **Modify, Page Properties**. The Page Properties dialog box appears.

Click the Background color swatch to choose a page background color. Use the Text color swatch to define a default text color for your page. Use the Links, Visited Links, and Active Links color swatches to define link colors.

In Figure 4.9, I've assigned Black as the page background color, and White as the default text color.

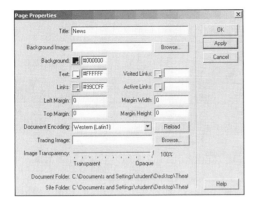

Figure 4.9

Since I'm using a black page background, I'm choosing a light color for the default page text color.

Since page colors apply the entire page, they are a quick way to assign coloring to a lot of text. They're faster and more efficient than assigning local text color by selecting text, and then applying colors. However, page color formatting is not used much by professional or experienced web designers. That's because Style Sheets (covered in Chapter 9) are an even better way to apply formatting not just to a page, but to an entire website. Page color settings are useful for small websites. For large sites, use Style Sheets.

Defining Margins

By default, web pages have a ten pixel margin around them. Sometimes this margin isn't noticeable. But sometimes, for design purposes, you will want to change the default margin. The most popular alternative to the default margin settings is to change margins from 10 pixels to *no* pixels. This setting is particularly effective when you use frames for page design.

To reset page margins, choose **Modify, Page Properties,** and enter values in the Left Margin, Top Margin, Margin Width, and Margin Height areas. Left Margin and Margin Width are the same thing, and Top Margin and Margin Height are the same thing. The difference is that one of them applies to Netscape Navigator and one to Internet Explorer. Which applies to which? Who cares? Just make sure you set identical values for Left Margin and Margin Width, and for Top Margin and Margin Height. Dreamweaver will generate two sets of HTML coding and *all* browsers will be covered. In Figure 4.10, I'm assigning a zero top and left margin.

Inside Info

Zero margin settings facilitate frame layout that appears "frameless"—where a visitor isn't even aware a page is broken into frames. I'll explain how this works in Chapter 10.

Figure 4.10

Assigning no top and left margin. By default, browsers do not display margins on the right or bottom of a page.

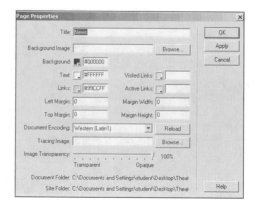

Adding Titles and Meta-Tags

Page titles provide the content that appears in a browser title bar. For that reason, you definitely want to assign titles to all your pages.

While page filenames should not have spaces, or multiple periods, page titles can have quotes, commas, spaces, or any other character. Figure 4.11 shows a page title appearing in a web browser.

Figure 4.11

This page title tells visitors what to expect on the page.

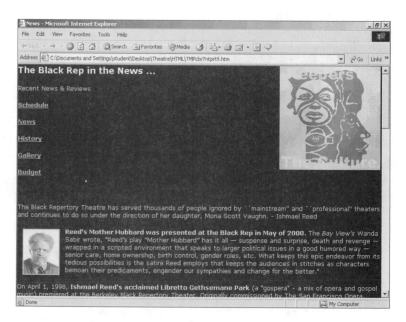

To assign a page title, enter a title name in the Title box at the top of the Document window. When you save your page, the title will be applied to the page.

Meta-tags provide additional information about your page that does not display in a browser, but is used by search engines to identify the content of your page, and to provide summaries of your page content when they list search results. Therefore, it's very valuable to have accurate and useful meta-tags.

The keywords meta-tag is used by search engines to categorize your site. The description meta-tag is used by search engines to summarize your page content when your page appears in a search results list.

To define keywords for an open page, choose **Insert, Head Tags, Keywords** from the menu. The Keywords dialog box appears.

Enter keywords, separated by commas, in the Keywords area of the Keywords dialog box as shown in Figure 4.12.

Figure 4.12

Keywords help search engines connect your page content with visitors.

To define a page description for search engines, choose **Insert, Head Tags, Description** from the menu. The Description dialog box appears. Unlike the keywords meta-tag, which is a list of words separated by commas, the page description should be a regular paragraph.

Styles for Beginners

Like many terms in web design, "style" can mean many things. One thing style refers to is the set of six heading styles, the Paragraph style, the None, and the Preformatted styles available from the oddly titled Format drop-down list in the Properties panel.

These heading styles (plus the other three) are all preformatted sets of font attributes. However, they are not a good way to apply local formatting to selected text, since they assign rather drab formatting (Times Roman font, black color, and font sizes that are more easily assigned from the Size drop-down list).

In short, the style options in the Format drop-down list in the Properties panel aren't very useful unless they are connected with cascading style sheets.

The Least You Need to Know

- You can easily copy and paste text into the Dreamweaver document window. But you have to apply text formatting in Dreamweaver.

- You have less control over font display in web pages than you do when you create printed content because you are depending on a visitor's system to provide fonts to display the formatting you assign.

- The Properties panel easily assigns text font, color, and size to selected text.

- You can align text left, right, centered, or full justified, and you can indent text or assign bullets in the Properties panel.

- As you define text properties, Dreamweaver generates HTML code "behind the scenes." You can see or edit this code in Show Code View.

- You can expand text formatting options by using cascading style sheets, which are covered in Chapter 9.

Adding Images to Your Site

In This Chapter

- ◆ Where do web images come from?
- ◆ Inserting, moving, and sizing images
- ◆ Aligning and spacing images
- ◆ Adding rollover text
- ◆ Creating a web photo album

Hardly a website exists that is devoid of images. While text suffers a bit in migration to web pages, pictures thrive on the web. Not many books are printed in full color, but nearly *every* website is viewed in color, making it fun and helpful to include color images.

You can use Dreamweaver to embed images, to resize them, and to move them around on your page. Dreamweaver also makes it easy to add rollover text to photos, to flow text around them, and to define spacing that prevents text from bumping right into a picture.

Where Do Web Images Come From?

Dreamweaver doesn't create images. For that, we have additional programs like Macromedia's Fireworks, Adobe's Photoshop, and a wide range of other graphics programs that can touch up photos, create drawings, and convert these images to web-compatible file formats.

Creating web graphics is beyond the scope of this book, and more to the point, it's beyond the scope of Dreamweaver. But it will be helpful to present the hard-core basics of web graphics so you understand the kind of graphic image files that will work in Dreamweaver.

Gifs, Jay-Pegs, and Pings

The two universally interpreted web graphic file formats are *GIF* and *JPEG*. GIF images have the advantage of allowing one color to be transparent, so the image appears to sit right on top of a page background. JPEG format does not support transparency, but does a better job presenting images with large numbers of colors, like photographs. GIFs are typically used for logos, graphical text, and navigation icons. JPEGs are typically used for photographs. The *PNG* file format is similar to the GIF format, and almost as widely supported.

Definition _____

JPEG stands for Joint Photographic Experts Group. As the name (*Photographic*) implies, this format was developed to present photos on the web. GIF stands for Graphics Interchange Format, and is reliably supported by every major operating system and browser. The **GIF** format supports primitive animation, and *animated GIFs* are the most universally accessible way to present animation on your site. GIF images are limited to 256 colors, and therefore not well-suited to the number of subtlety of photographic coloring. **PNG** stands for Portable Network Graphics, and provides more reliable cross-browser and cross-operating system color consistency than GIF images. However, **PNG** images are not supported by all older browsers.

Almost every graphics program has the capability to export images to either JPEG or GIF format. You, or your collaborating artist, should convert all images to JPEG or GIF (or PNG if you elect to narrow your site's audience to those with recent version browsers).

You *can* include images in a web page that are not supported by browsers. However, when you do, your visitors must have plug-in software installed with their browser in order to see your images. For instance, if you include images in Flash (SWF) format, visitors will need the Flash Viewer (which they can download for free) to see your images.

The folks at Macromedia integrated a very truncated version of their Flash package in Dreamweaver, enabling us to create some navigation graphics without leaving Dreamweaver (or buying Flash). I suppose the theory is that we'll be impressed with the interactive navigation graphics we create and then go out and buy Flash. Fair enough.

I'll show you how to generate Flash navigation buttons using Dreamweaver in Chapter 16.

Hooking Up Images with Your Page

When you place an image on a web page, you are actually embedding a separate image file in that page. In essence, the HTML code Dreamweaver generates for you tells a visitor's browser, "when you get to this point on the page, stick in this picture."

The big danger in embedding image files on your page is that they can get lost. If the instructions you embed in the page tell a browser "go look for the picture file over here," but the picture isn't there, then all visitors will see is a blank box with a little "X" in it, telling them you goofed up in embedding your image file on your page.

Dreamweaver takes care of making sure that image files are where they are supposed to be. But it can only do this if you are working in a defined Dreamweaver site. If you skipped Chapter 2, where I walked you through the process of defining your site, I strongly advise you to detour back there before proceeding to add images to your pages.

As you insert images into a web page in the Document window, from time to time you'll see prompts from Dreamweaver to copy the image file into your site. Say, "Yes!" when prompted to do this. That way, Dreamweaver will make sure that no matter how much you move, rename, or upload your image file, the link between the picture and the page will not get corrupted or broken.

Inserting, Moving, and Sizing Images

To insert an image in a web page, click to create an insertion point in the Document window and choose **Insert, Image** from the menu. The Select Image Source dialog box appears.

Since you want to insert an image, not a database element, choose the **File System** radio button in the Select File Name From area of the Select Image Source dialog box.

Use the Look In drop-down list to navigate to a folder on your local computer, and select an image to import. If you select the Preview Images checkbox, a preview appears in the Image Preview area when you click on an image file, as shown in Figure 5.1.

Inside Info

The Image Preview area also displays the size of the selected image in pixels, and the file size. The displayed download time is calculated based on the download speed you define. The default setting is 28.8 Kilobits per Second (KPS). To change this, choose **Edit, Preferences** in Windows or Mac OS9, or choose **Dreamweaver MX Preferences** in Mac OS X. Select **Status Bar** in the Category list of the Preferences dialog box, and choose a modem speed in the Connection Speed drop-down list.

Figure 5.1

You can preview an image before deciding to plug it into your page.

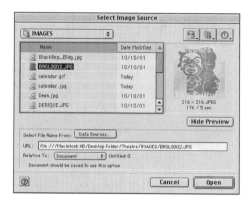

The Relative To drop-down list in the Select Image Source dialog box allows you to decide if you want Dreamweaver to keep track of the path to your embedded image relative to the Document (your saved web page), or relative to your Site. The Document option is more efficient. Just make sure that *before* you embed your image, you have saved your file so that Dreamweaver can connect your image with a stable, saved document (HTML file).

Once you find the image you want to embed, click **OK** in the Image dialog box to place the picture in the Document window.

If the image file you chose is not yet in your site folder, Dreamweaver will prompt you to copy the file to your site folder. The prompt dialog box looks like Figure 5.2. When you see this dialog box, click **Yes** to copy the image file into your site.

Figure 5.2

Copying images into your site folder helps Dream-weaver help you keep from losing image files, or having their links to your pages corrupted.

When you select an embedded image, the Properties panel displays a thumbnail of the image. The Properties panel also displays the image file size. The image file name, and path to the file are displayed in the Src area of the Properties panel.

You can assign a name to an image if you wish by entering the name in the filed in the Image area of the Properties panel. Image names are *not* the same as the image file name; in fact, they have no connection to each other. And, image names are not required. Image names are useful if you are going to implement animation or interactivity using

JavaScript, or using Dreamweaver Behaviors. In that case, image names will help you program your animation or interactive behavior. Image names should not contain spaces or any characters except letters and numbers (and cannot start with a number). If you're an ambitious web designer, it's not a bad idea to get into the habit of naming your images.

Sizing, Aligning, and Spacing Images

You can define image size and alignment for a selected picture in the Properties panel, or you can use your mouse to move and size an image interactively. Image spacing—the buffer space between an image and other images or text on the page—is set in the Properties panel.

You can move an image on the page by clicking and dragging on it. The easiest way to resize a selected image is to click and drag on a side or the corner handle. To retain the original height-to-width ratio as you resize an image, hold down the Shift key as you click and drag on the corner handle that appears when the image is selected, as shown in Figure 5.3.

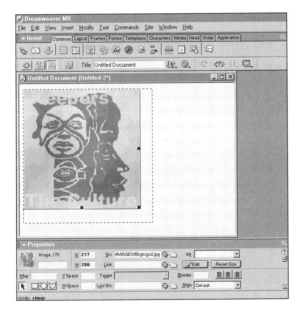

Figure 5.3

Usually, you will want to maintain the height-to-width of an image as you resize. Otherwise the image will distort.

As you resize an image interactively with your mouse, the W (width) and H (height) values change in the Properties panel. The changed value(s) will appear in boldface. You can reset an image to its original size by clicking the Reset Size button in the Properties panel.

Inside Info

It's best to size images in image editing software, not in Dreamweaver. Images that are enlarged in Dreamweaver will tend to look grainy, since the number of pixels is not increased as the image is expanded. Images that are made smaller will look OK, but they will retain the same (larger) file size of the original since they are not resampled. This means that they retain the same number of defining dots and thus the same file size as the larger version of the picture.

The Edit button in the Properties panel opens a selected image in your defined image editor. To change image editor settings, choose **Edit, Preferences (Dreamweaver MX, Preferences** in OS X), and choose **File Types/Editors** in the Categories list of the Preferences dialog box. Here, you can custom define image editing applications for different graphic file formats (like GIF, JPEG, and PNG).

After you edit an image with image editing software, save and exit the application to return to Dreamweaver. Dreamweaver will automatically substitute the updated, edited, saved image for the original picture.

Inside Info

There are other alignment options in the Align drop-down list, but they're not really useful for aligning text flow around images. The Middle option is not useful aesthetically since you rarely want to separate sentences with an image. The other options are used for formatting tiny, symbol-sized images that you want to align closely with text characters.

Flowing Text Around an Image

Unless you are placing images on a page using tables or layers (both covered in Part 3 of this book), you will almost always want to align images so that text flows around them—either to the right or the left.

To align an image, select the picture and choose either **Left** or **Right** from the Align drop-down list in the Properties panel. In Figure 5.4, I've aligned an image left, and text is flowing around the image to the right.

After you align an image, a placeholder icon appears on the page at the point where the image was inserted. You can click and drag on this placeholder to move an image.

Giving a Picture Some Space

Pictures need space to breath! They rarely look good with text bumping right up against them. Image spacing is defined in pixels, and can be set for both height and width.

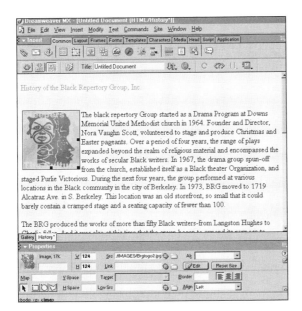

Figure 5.4

By aligning the image "Left," I'm defining the text flow around the right side of the picture.

In my surveys of web pages, I've noted that the average image spacing seems to be five pixels of horizontal spacing, and three pixels of vertical spacing. I tend to like to use even more spacing than that—often as much as six or eight pixels of horizontal spacing to give my pages and pictures a clean, airy look.

To define spacing around a selected image, enter values in the H Space (for horizontal spacing) and V Space (for vertical spacing) areas of the Properties panel. Figure 5.5 shows one image with eight pixels of horizontal spacing.

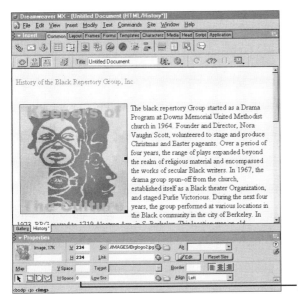

Figure 5.5

The image has eight pixels of horizontal spacing and is nicely separated from the surrounding text.

Enter value in the H space area.

On the Border

You can assign borders of various thicknesses to a selected image by entering a value in the Border area.

Border coloring is determined by surrounding text. Or, if the image is a link, by the link color defined for your page or site.

Figure 5.6 shows an image with a two-pixel border.

Figure 5.6

Image borders can sometimes help set off a picture and emphasize it on the page.

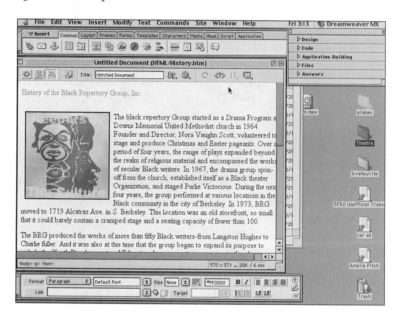

Adding Alt Text

The Alt area in the Properties panel defines text that is associated with an image in several ways:

◆ The text displays in a browser if a visitor has turned off images.

◆ The text displays in a browser if an image link is broken.

◆ The text can be read by software that makes websites accessible to blind people.

◆ The text displays in Internet Explorer when a visitor rolls over (moves his or her mouse over) the image.

In short, Alt text is a handy thing to add to an image. Just type in a description of your image in the Alt area of the Properties panel for a selected image, and you've associated that text with the picture.

You won't see Alt text unless you test your page by previewing it in Internet Explorer (choose **File, Preview** in Browser, and select **Internet Explorer** if you have that browser installed on your system). Figure 5.7 shows Alt text being displayed as a mouse scrolls over an image in Internet Explorer.

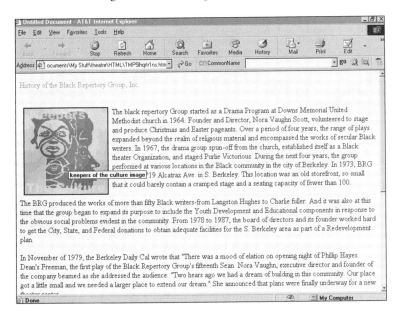

Figure 5.7

Many website visitors expect to see text when they roll over an image.

Avoiding Frustration with Image Placeholders

Often, too often actually, you'll be designing a site, but your client, your supervisor, or your colleagues in the art department haven't provided you with all the images you need to finalize a page.

Instead of pacing the room, or banging your head against the wall, you can design pages using Image Placeholders until the real images are provided. Image Placeholders can have a defined size (which can match the artwork you are patiently awaiting), allowing you to finalize text layout.

To insert an Image Placeholder, click to define an insertion point in the Document window, and choose **Insert, Image Placeholder**. In the Image Placeholder dialog box, you can name the placeholder in the Name area, you can choose a color for the box using the Color swatch, and you can define alternate text that will display in browsers in the Alternate Text area, as shown in Figure 5.8.

You can define the size of the placeholder in pixels by using either the Width and Height areas of the Image Placeholder dialog box, or by clicking and dragging to change the size right in the Document window.

Figure 5.8

The alternate text in this Image Placeholder simply tells viewers that a final (real) image will be substituted later.

Later, when the real image arrives, you can substitute the picture for the placeholder using the Browse for File navigation icon (looks like a folder) in the Properties inspector for a selected Image Placeholder.

Using Images as Page Backgrounds

In addition to embedding images within a page, you can use them as page backgrounds. You can *also* use images as table cell backgrounds to create interesting layered effects. I'll explain how to use images as table backgrounds in Chapter 7.

Images that are used as page backgrounds will *tile*—that is, they will repeat themselves to fill an entire page. Keep in mind that you don't know what monitor width will be used by a visitor to see your page. He might be looking at your page through an older 640 pixel monitor, a new 1280 pixel wide screen, or something in between. That makes using page background images a bit dicey; they have to be images that tile well. Figure 5.9 shows a page with a tiled background as viewed in a browser.

Figure 5.9

Tiled images repeat as necessary to fill a browser window.

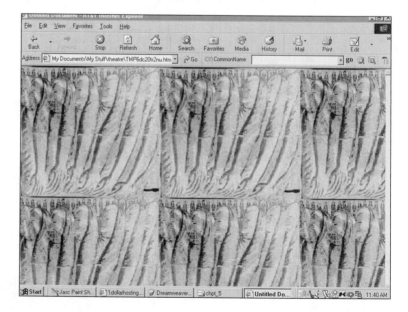

Tiled page background images have a couple distinct disadvantages:

♦ They add to page load time.

♦ They are often distracting and make it difficult to read text placed on top of a tiled background.

Creating tiled images is a specific skill, and requires carefully designed images that mesh together seamlessly in a program like Photoshop. If you have such a background image (or found one in a clipart collection), insert it in your page by choosing **Modify, Page Properties**. Click the **Browse** button next to the Background Image area to browse your local site for an appropriate tile image. Use the **Select Image Source** dialog box to locate a background image, and then click **OK.** Click **OK** again to close the Page Properties dialog box, and view your new background image tiled across the page in the Document window.

Using a Tracing Image as a Design Template

If you have an image, like a photo or a sketch, that you want to use as a guide to laying out your page, you can embed that image as a page background. However, if you place the image as a Tracing Image, the picture will be visible in the Document window, but will not be visible when visitors see your page in a browser.

To load a Tracing Image for an open page, choose **View, Tracing Image, Load,** and then navigate to and select an image.

Once you've loaded a Tracing Image, you can change where the image appears on your page by choosing **View, Tracing Image, Adjust Position.** You can then use the arrow cursor keys on your keyboard to adjust where the Tracing Image appears, as shown in Figure 5.10.

To hide a Tracing Image, choose **View, Tracing Image, Hide.** You can change or remove a Tracing Image in the Tracing Image area of the Page Properties dialog box.

Figure 5.10

Tracing Images are helpful layout tools, and they won't show up in a browser.

The Least You Need to Know

◆ Dreamweaver places images on a page, but you need separate graphics software to create web graphics, and save them to GIF, JPEG, or PNG format.

◆ Images on a web page are separate files. Dreamweaver keeps track of where those files are stored on your local site and maintains the integrity of the links between those images and your page so long as you are working in a defined Dreamweaver site.

◆ By aligning images left or right, you can flow text around them on the page.

◆ Image spacing improves the appearance of your pictures and your page layout. You assign spacing in the Properties panel.

◆ Alt text displays in Internet Explorer when a visitor rolls over (moves his or her mouse over) the image.

Chapter 6

Getting Linked

In This Chapter

- ◆ Linking text
- ◆ Creating links to e-mail addresses
- ◆ Linking images
- ◆ Creating image maps
- ◆ Controlling link targets
- ◆ Navigating with named anchors

One of the great wonders of web design is the ability to allow visitors to your site to instantly jump to any other place on your site, or jump to any location on the web.

You can use Dreamweaver to assign links to text or images. You can open links in your site's browser window or in a new browser window. And you can easily define clickable hotspots (also known as image maps) anywhere on a picture.

Site-Wide Linking

Any text or image can be used as a link to any location within or outside of your site. Is there such a thing as too many text links? Perhaps, but in general you can never provide too many link options for visitors.

It's often helpful to draw a flowchart of your site before you even begin to design pages. That way, you can make conscious decisions about the kinds of options you want to provide for visitors.

Link Strategies

There are two basic ways to organize a link structure for your site. A linear link structure works like a guided tour, or a slideshow. Visitors start at your home page, and are provided with something like "next" and "previous" links that lead them on a structured journey through your site. Linear site structures have the advantage of allowing you to strictly control when visitors see your site content. The disadvantage to a linear link structure is that a visitor who gets frustrated with your preordained path through your site will exit the site.

The other basic approach is what is sometimes called a hierarchal structure. This method of assigning links uses a model that looks something like a branching tree, where the home page provides links to a handful of pages, and each of those pages then has links to other pages. This method of organizing links is useful when your site is divided into different sections. For example, a company that markets a product might have links at the home page to a catalog, an order page, a shipping information page, and a contact page. The catalog page might then have links to several products, the order page might have links to order forms and information, and so on.

You can adopt one of these structured approaches to defining links, or you can try a more flexible link strategy that allows visitors more freedom to navigate your site. However, you still might want to consciously divert the discovery path. For example, if you are providing visitors with an order form, you might want to force them to read some preparatory information that will help them fill out the form correctly. In that instance, you would *not* want to provide a link directly from your home page to the order form.

In short, you'll want to think consciously and strategically about what kinds of links to place where on your site. And then, make sure you've implemented that strategy by providing clearly marked, necessary links on your pages.

Generating Links in the Site Window

Dreamweaver makes it easy to apply a site-wide link strategy by letting you generate links right in the Site window. You don't have much control over where these links are placed; Dreamweaver places them on the bottom of pages to which they are assigned. But you can ensure that a basic set of essential links is in place to guide visitors around your site.

To define links for an open site in Site view, start by viewing your site in the Site window (press the F8 function key). Use the Expand/Collapse icon at the top of the Site window if necessary to expand the Site window (the Site window is hardly usable in the collapsed view!).

With the Site window expanded, your local site is visible in the right side of the window. Then, use the following steps to generate a site map and define links.

1. Click on your site's home page (it should have the filename index.htm or index.htm).

2. Choose **Site, Set As Home Page** from the Site window menu. This defines your selected file as the home page and helps Dreamweaver generate a graphic display of your site's links (a Site Map).

3. Click on the **Site Map** icon in the Site window. Dreamweaver will generate a graphic display of your site links, as shown in Figure 6.1.

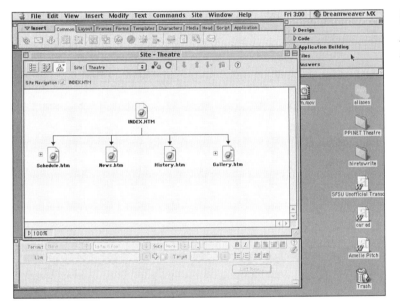

Figure 6.1

A generated picture of your site links.

4. Click on the **Home Page** icon in the Site Map (on the right side of the Site window). As you do, a Point to File icon appears next to the selected file. Click and drag from the icon to a file in your local site to generate a link on the home page to the selected page, as shown in Figure 6.2.

5. You can continue to click and drag from any page in the Site Map view to any file to generate additional links. Figure 6.3 shows a site with a basic navigational structure defined, a set of pages linked to the home page, and additional pages linked to those pages.

Figure 6.2

Creating a link to your home page in the Site window.

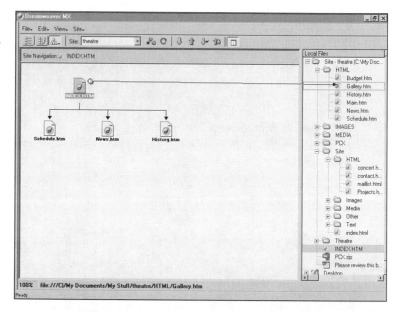

Figure 6.3

This Site Map provides links from the home page to four "child" pages, each of which has its own links to other pages.

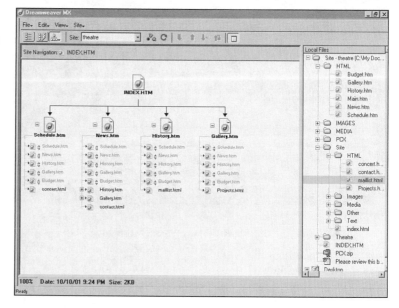

After you finish generating links in the Site window, you can double-click on any HTML files in the local site view to open that page and inspect the generated links. The generated links can be formatted and edited in the Document window.

Generated links are a quick and dirty way to ensure that a link structure binds your site together. But you will almost always want to supplement generated links with customized linked text and images on each page.

Linking Text

You can assign a link to any selected text in the Properties panel. If the link is an external URL, that is, a page or file in another website, simply type the full URL (starting with http://) in the Link area of the Properties panel.

If the link is a file in your open website, click the **Browse for File** icon to the right of the Link area. This opens the Select File dialog box. Navigate to and select the file to which you are linking the selected text.

In most cases, you will want to leave the Relative To drop-down list set to "Document." This makes it easier for Dreamweaver to ensure that your link connection is not broken when you edit or move files.

Once you've selected a file to which you want to link the text, click **OK** to define the link.

Definition

The links you define using the Browse for File icon in the Properties panel are referred to as **relative** links. Rather than keep track of the entire location of those links, Dreamweaver simply records directions to the selected link from the current page. Relative links help ensure that Dreamweaver will change the path to a defined link if you make changes to a file's folder location or filename in the Site window.

Absolute links are links where you enter the entire URL (starting with http://) in the Link area. These links are *not* defined relative to the current page, and instead a browser "starts from scratch" to go look for these links on the web. Absolute links do *not* update if there is a change to a filename or location. Absolute links tend to go bad over time, as their targets change. Therefore, you need to periodically test the absolute links in your site.

There are online sites that provide link-checking for free. At this writing, my favorite is http://validator.w3.org/checklink. You enter your URL, and the site checks out your links and identifies ones that are broken.

Linked Images

You link an image to a file pretty much the same way you link text. Select the image, and define a link target in the Link area of the Properties panel.

One frequently used technique in displaying large photos is to link a small, thumbnail version of the image to a larger version of the image. This requires that you (or your illustrator) create two versions of an image—a small version that will be displayed on the page, and a large version that will display when a visitor clicks on the small image.

To be clear, the target of a link does not need to be an HTML file. Link targets can be any file that opens in a web browser, including a text file (with a TXT filename extension), or a JPEG, GIF, or PNG file. If an image is the target of a link, that image will open in the browser window.

> **Caution** _____
>
> One concern in opening an image file through a link is that your visitor might get stranded in the browser window with the link. Of course he or she can use the Back button in their browser to return to your site. But if you want to provide clear instructions, you might include a "click the back button in your browser" message in the actual large version of the image, as a guide to visitors.

Creating Image Maps

Image maps are sets of clickable hotspots within a single image. One of the more frequently used implementations of hotspots is on actual maps that people use to get directions. An _image map_ on top of a map allows a visitor to click on a spot on the map and open an associated web page or see an associated photo.

To define an image map for a selected picture, choose one of the three Hotspot tools in the Properties panel—the rectangular, oval, or polygon hotspot tools. Use any of these tools to draw an area on your image, as shown in Figure 6.4.

Figure 6.4

Drawing a hotspot for an image map.

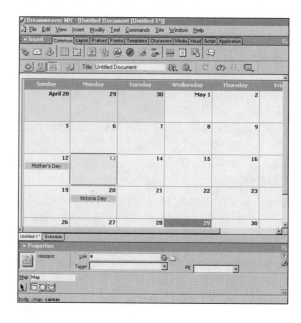

With the hotspot drawn, the Properties panel changes to allow you to define a link and unique Alt text for the hotspot. Enter a URL, or use the Browse for File icon to define a target for the link. (I'll explain how to use the confusingly named Target drop-down list a bit later in this chapter.)

In Chapter 5, I emphasized the usefulness of defining Alt text with each image. You can enter different Alt text for each hotspot within an image. So, it's possible that you would define Alt text for your image, and then a separate Alt text that would appear only when a visitor scrolled over a hotspot on the image.

To test your hotspot links choose **File, Preview** in Browser. Select a browser (if you have more than one defined), and test your hotspot Alt rollover text (this only works in IE), and your hotspot links.

Caution

One rather weird thing that happens when visitors follow hotspots in Internet Explorer is that the outline of the hotspot becomes visible. This isn't a major problem, but particularly if a polygon hotspot outline is drawn crudely, the outline can look somewhat tacky in IE. For this reason, I advise sticking to rectangular and oval hotspots, and avoiding polygons.

Defining Browser Window Targets

You can control whether a link opens in the current browser window or in a new browser window. This is done through the Target drop-down list in the Properties panel.

By default, links open in the same browser window that displays the current open page. That's very appropriate for visitors who are surfing and following links within your site. Hopefully, you've provided them with easy to access links on every page that return them to your home page and make it easy to continue to navigate around your site.

On the other hand, sometimes you don't want your page to close when a link is followed. This is often the case when you provide links to pages outside your site. For instance, you might provide visitors with a link to Yahoo! or Google, or to Amazon.com to purchase one of my computer books (just a thought!). In that case, you likely don't want to lose that visitor when he or she follows the outside link. Instead, you can define these links to open in a new browser window. When your visitor finishes shopping at Amazon, or getting directions at Yahoo! Maps, she can close the active browser window, and your site will still be open in the original browser window.

To define a link target to open in a new browser window, choose **_blank** in the Target drop-down list for the link, as shown in Figure 6.5.

Figure 6.5

Creating a link that will open in a new browser window.

Navigating with Named Anchors

Particularly when you are working with long pages, it is often helpful to provide named anchors (sometimes called page bookmarks). These named anchors allow you to define link destinations within your page.

A useful application of named anchors is to create several locations within the page to which a visitor can quickly jump. You'll usually want to include a link back to the top of the page, so that visitors can jump back and forth from navigational links on the top of the page, to places within the page, and then back again to the top of the page.

Defining such links within your page is a two-step process. First, you need to create some named anchors on your page. These named anchor spots won't be visible in a browser, but they will identify spots on your page that can be linked to.

The second step is to define links within your page to named anchors.

Inside Info

Using the Point to File icon to connect to a named anchor can be a bit tricky if the named anchor is not visible on the page. In that case, click and drag from the Point to File icon to either the up or down scroll arrow and scroll until your named anchor target is visible. Without releasing your mouse button, click on the named anchor.

To create a named anchor, it's easiest if you select a single word on your page. If you need an anchor in a place where there is no text (like the very top of your page), you can simply click without selected text.

With one word selected, or with your insertion point anywhere on the page, choose **Insert, Named Anchor.** The Named Anchor dialog box appears, as shown in Figure 6.6.

If you started with selected text, that text automatically appears in the Anchor Name area of the Named Anchor dialog box. If you didn't select any text first, type in a single-word anchor name, like **"Top".** Then click **OK** to define the anchor. Create as many anchors as you need on your page.

Figure 6.6

Defining a named anchor.

Once you define an anchor, the easiest way to create links within your page is to use the **Point to File** icon in the Properties panel. Do this by first selecting text (or an image). Then, click the Point to File icon to the right of the Link area in the Properties Inspector. Click and drag from the Point to File icon to the named anchor (represented by a cute little icon that looks like an anchor), as shown in Figure 6.7.

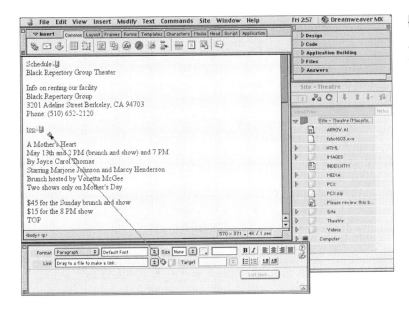

Figure 6.7

Linking to a named anchor using the Point to File icon.

After you define a link to a named anchor, that link will appear in the Link area of the Properties panel with a "#" symbol in front of it. This is how HTML identifies named anchor (or page bookmark) links within a page. You can test your bookmark links by previewing your page in a browser (**File, Preview in Browser**).

The Wide World of Links

More advanced chapters in this book will explore enhanced linking features. In Chapter 9, I'll show you how to alter the way links look when they are scrolled over, so they change appearance when hovered on. In Chapter 10, I'll show you how to define links in a frame that open pages in a different frame. And in Chapter 16, I'll show you how to create animated Flash buttons and text that serve as links. But the basic rules of generating links that we covered here apply to any link, no matter how "flashy."

I want to reemphasize a point I made earlier in this chapter: A link target does not have to be an HTML web page. Any URL will do. A link target can be an image, but it can also be just about any file—a sound file, a video file, an Excel spreadsheet, a Word document, or a Flash file.

Definition _____

URL stands for **Uniform Resource Locator,** and refers to the address or location of any file on the World Wide Web. A URL can point to a web page, an image, a media file, or any type of file accessible on the web.

Will that really work? Sometimes. Links to non-HTML files will work if your visitor has a plug-in to interpret the linked file. So, for example, if your visitor has Flash, you can link to a Flash file and he or she can see it. If your visitor has MS Word, you can link to a Word file and your visitor will see that file open in their own version of Word.

When you provide links to non-HTML-compatible files, you will often want to provide visitors with information on how to download the necessary player or viewer software required to hear or see that file. I'll return to these issues in depth in Part 6 of this book when we explore the process of embedding media in your site.

The Least You Need to Know

- Links can be assigned to any text or image on your page.
- Link targets can be any file in your site, or any file outside your site.
- Image and text links are defined in the Properties panel.
- You can create clickable hotspots inside any image, and each hotspot can have its own unique link target.
- Use the confusingly named Target drop-down list in the Properties panel when you want to open a link in a new (_blank) browser window.

Part 3

Tables, Layers, and Frames

Tables and layers are used to organize text and images wherever you want them on your pages. Layers can even be used to stack objects on top of each other.

In the following chapters, I'll show you how to lay out pages with tables and layers, as well as how to break your page up with frames.

I'll also show you how to apply powerful external style sheets to design and apply a site-wide color scheme.

Chapter 7

Table That—Using the Basic Page Layout Tool

In This Chapter

◆ Tables and layers as design tools

◆ Defining table properties

◆ Formatting table cells

◆ Using a table to define page width

◆ Using tables to present data

In my Dreamweaver classes, I inevitably encounter student outrage that there is so little control over where objects *go* on a page. Frustrated students demand, "But I want that picture to go *here!*" emphasizing the point by waving their arms at the monitor hoping to entice an image or block of text to the desired location.

In earlier chapters, I've explained how to align graphics to allow text to flow around them to the left or right. This is a basic form of combining images and text, but it does not provide the kind of control most of us want and need to design web pages.

The answer: tables!

Tables and Layers as Design Tools

One significant limitation of regular HTML layout is the lack of control over the placement of text, graphics, and other objects (like media plug-ins) on a page.

Tables are the basic tool for controlling page layout in web page design. Tables are used to create a layout grid for a web page, allowing you to closely define where objects sit on the page. Tables are a fundamental building block of web design.

A Look Under the Hood

Don't take my word for this, do some experimenting. Look at a page you like at a website, and then view the source code in your browser. You'll almost certainly see a complex set of rows and columns that govern the location of text and pictures.

> **By the Way**
>
> You can identify tables in the HTML source code you see when you choose View, Source from Internet Explorer. Look for the `</table>` tag that identifies the end of a table. You'll be able to spot other HTML tags that define table attributes like width, background color, spacing and padding between cells, and table alignment. The tag "`<TABLE WIDTH="467" BORDER="0" CELLSPACING="3" CELLPADDING="3" ALIGN="left">`" translates to a table that is 467 pixels wide, has no border, has cell spacing and cell padding of 3 pixels, and is left aligned.

Better still, once we start designing tables in Dreamweaver, you'll see table gridlines right in the Document window. Figure 7.1 shows a website with images spaced along the top, and a block of text on the right edge of the page.

Inside Info

Not only can images be placed in table cells, but some advanced site designers break large graphics into "slices" that are displayed in adjacent table cells for more efficient downloading. The images are "sliced" in programs like Adobe Photoshop and are then inserted in adjacent table cells for faster loading.

Let's take a quick look behind the scenes at this page in Dreamweaver. In Figure 7.2 you can see (if you look closely) that the images and block of text that seem to be "placed" on the page are actually located in table cells.

The Tables vs. Layers Controversy

Layers provide even more control over object placement, and layers can be overlapped, providing some 3-D layout capability, as you will see in Chapter 8.

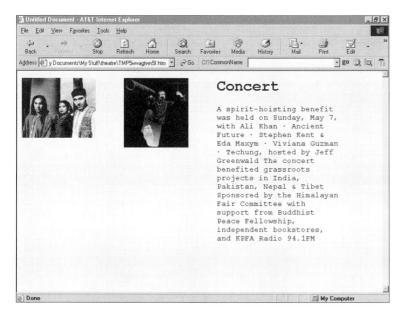

Figure 7.1

Behind the column of text on the right and the photos on the top of this page lies a table grid.

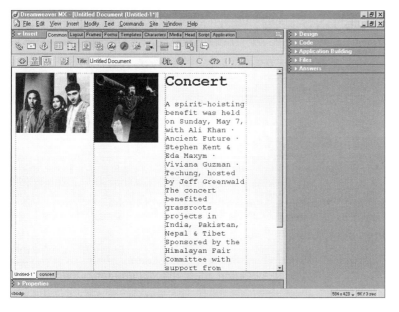

Figure 7.2

Table cells, visible in Dream-weaver, act as locators for text and pictures.

So why mess around with tables? Layers are less predictable than tables. Layers rely on browsers interpreting the latest version of cascading style sheets (CSS-2) to support absolute placement of objects.

Even those browsers (like IE 5 and higher) that do support CSS-2 do not always accurately support absolute positioning, especially when browser windows are sized at other than popular dimensions.

In short, tables are more reliable than layers for defining object placement and are supported by more browsers, more consistently.

Creating a Table

Now that I've whetted your appetite, let's break down how tables are created and defined.

Start out by choosing **Insert, Table.** The Insert Table dialog box appears, as shown in Figure 7.3.

Figure 7.3

The easiest way to define tables is with the Insert Table dialog box.

Inside Info

There is another approach to creating tables that involves working in something called "Layout View." This is a graphical approach to defining tables. Most of my students find Layout View pretty confusing, and since there's nothing there you can't do *without* Layout View, I advise staying clear of it. If you must tread down this dark and confusing path, choose **View, Table View, Layout View.** When you're done, choose **View, Table View, Standard View** to return to a more sane table-editing environment.

The Insert Table dialog box allows you to define how many rows and columns to include in your table, as well as the size of your table. Enter a number of rows in the Rows box, and the number of columns in the Columns box.

Cell padding is the space within a cell—between the cell content and the edge of the cell. Cell spacing is the space in between cells. Cell padding and spacing are defined in pixels.

Table width can be entered in the Width box and is defined either in pixels or as a percentage of the browser width. Generally, it's better to use pixels since that method provides much more control over how your table appears. Pixels provide a fixed size for your table, while percentage creates a table whose size changes depending on the size of a visitor's browser window.

The Border box in the Insert Table dialog box defines how thick a border appears around the table.

All the properties you define in the Insert Table dialog box can easily be changed later. So don't agonize too much over them when you first create a table. When you have defined the table, click **OK** and a table appears in your Document.

Tweaking Table Properties

When you select a table, table properties appear in the Properties Inspector. You can enter different values in the boxes of the Properties Inspector, and change the table appearance that way.

Selecting a table is easier said than done. The trick is to click right on the top left corner of the table. As you do, the cursor displays as a four-sided arrow, as shown in Figure 7.4.

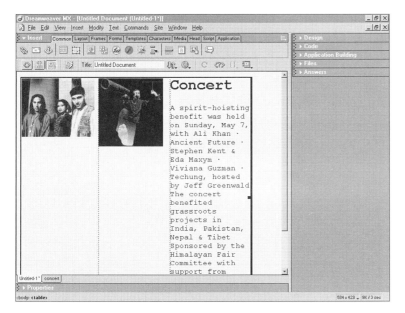

Figure 7.4

Before you edit table properties, you have to select the table.

If you're a bit klutzy, like me, there's another way to select a table. Just click anywhere in the table (now *that* I can handle) and press **COMMAND/CTRL A** until the whole table is selected (sometimes that happens the first time you press COMMAND/CTRL A, sometimes you have to repeat the process to select the whole table). Or, for the menu inclined, you can choose **Modify, Table, Select Table.**

Once you select a table, the Properties Inspector will provide you with just about all the table editing tools you could want. The table properties in the Properties Inspector include:

- ◆ **Table Name**   Used for JavaScript applications.
- ◆ **Rows and Columns**   Defines the number of rows and the number of columns in the table.
- ◆ **Width and Height**   Determines page space in pixels or percent of page space.
- ◆ **Padding**   Determines the spacing within a cell.
- ◆ **Spacing**   Identifies the spacing between cells.
- ◆ **Alignment**   Left, right, or center.
- ◆ **Border**   Determines the thickness of line around table (0 for no border).
- ◆ **Background Color**   Applies to entire table, but can be customized for individual cells.
- ◆ **Brdr Color**   Determines the color of a border around the table (if there is one).
- ◆ **Background Image**   Tiles to fill the entire table.

In addition, the Table Properties Inspector has icons that allow you to clear row and column sizing (returning to original shrink-to-fit sizing), or to convert a table size back and forth between pixels and percent.

Resizing a Table

To resize a table, click and drag on the side table handle to expand the width of the table as shown in Figure 7.5.

Figure 7.5

You can resize tables interactively in the Document window.

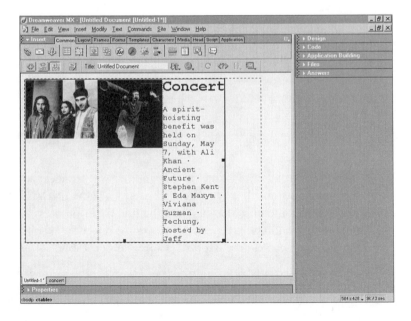

Or, you can resize the table in the Properties Inspector by entering a new value in the W (Width) box.

I find the easiest way to change the number of columns or rows in a selected table is to enter new values in the Rows or Cols areas of the Properties Inspector. If you enter a value with *fewer* rows or columns than the table already has, you'll delete columns starting at the far right, or rows starting at the bottom of the table.

Caution _____

When you delete rows or columns from a table, you also delete whatever *content* is in those rows or columns. If you want to delete the table rows or columns, but *not* the contents of those rows or columns, copy or move the contents *out* of the table first.

Getting Aligned

Tables can be aligned on the left or right side of a page, or centered. It's rare that it works aesthetically to align a table on the right side of a page. But there are times when that works, like when you want to flow text around a table, as shown in Figure 7.6.

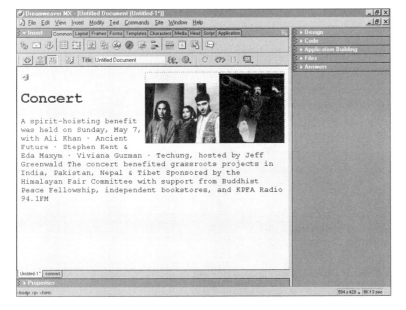

Figure 7.6

Here, text flows around a right-aligned table.

More typically, tables are aligned left, or centered.

To define table alignment, select a table and then choose **Left, Center,** or **Right** from the alignment list in the Properties Inspector.

The *Default* option in the alignment list in the Properties Inspector defines table alignment based on the previous paragraph.

Table Borders and Backgrounds

Tables can have borders with width defined in pixels, or they can be borderless.

Table border thickness is set in the Border box of the Properties Inspector for a selected table.

To change the *color* of table borders, choose a color from the Brdr Color palette in the Properties Inspector.

You can define a background color for a table, or even a background image. If you leave these settings untouched, your table background will be transparent, and match the background color of your page (if any).

Table background images can be rather cool. First, a word of warning: If the image you choose as a background is smaller than the table, that image will tile. Meaning, it will repeat itself. If you've designed a background tile image in a graphics program, that might be a good idea. If not, tiling can be tacky.

However, background images that are the same size as tables can produce a layered effect, where the table contents (images or text) sit on top of the table background. In the website shown in Figure 7.7, I used a table that matched the size of a photo, and then entered text in the table to produce the text-on-image effect.

Figure 7.7

The text was typed into the table, the image is actually the table background.

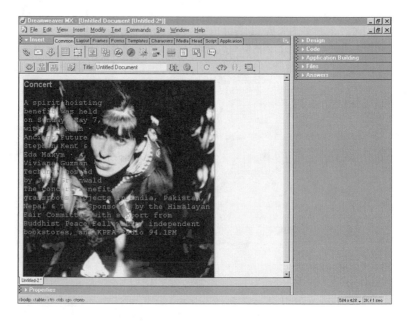

To choose a table background color, select the table and then pick a color from the Bg Color palette in the Properties Inspector.

To place an image in a table background, click the **Browse for File** icon next to the Bg Image box in the Properties Inspector, and navigate to the image to be used as the table background.

Using a Table to Define Page Width

Since visitors will see your page in a wide variety of browser widths, you can have more control over how your page looks if you define page width using a table. By defining your own page width, you can determine how line breaks will appear, how text will flow around aligned pictures, and you can make text more readable by confining it to a set column width.

In the following tutorial, I'll show you how to convert page content to display in a one-cell, 600 pixel width table. Ready?

Open a web page in the Document window. You have probably formatted this page already, and added text and images. The following steps will walk you through the process of constraining all your page content into a table.

1. At the top of the page, choose **Insert, Table.**
2. In the Insert Table dialog box, define a 1 column, 1 row table with cell padding of 6, a width of 600 pixels, and no border.
3. Cut and paste all of your page content into the new, one-cell table.
4. Format the table so it is centered on your page.
5. Assign a table background color.
6. Save your page.

Defining Cell Properties

Tables are a useful tool for page design in their own right, as is illustrated in the preceding tutorial for defining web page size.

The real fun, however, starts when you break a table into cells, and format each cell individually. You can change cell backgrounds, sizes, and alignment to gain much control over how objects appear on your page.

If cell and table formatting conflict, for example background colors, cell formatting takes precedence.

Formatting Cell Text

Before we explore formatting cells, a quick visit to the potentially baffling realm of formatting cell *text*.

Cell text can be formatted just like text not in a table. When you select text in a table, the top half of the Properties Inspector displays text formatting tools, while the bottom half displays cell formatting tools. This gets a little confusing, since some tools look alike. Here, we'll focus on formatting text in a table. Next we'll deal with cell properties.

1. Click at the top of the second column to select all the cells in that column.

2. Choose the **Right-Align** icon in the Properties Inspector to right-align the cell contents.

3. Choose the top row of the table, and assign boldface.

4. Click and drag to select all cells, and apply Arial size 4 to the text.

5. Select individual text, and apply color formatting (for example, you might want to make the bottom row a different text color.

6. Click and drag on the divider between the two columns to make the second column as narrow as possible without wrapping text.

Formatting a Single Cell

Cell properties can be formatted using the Properties Inspector. I'll show you how to use these features in the following tutorial, where I'll have you define cell background colors, and vertical alignment. First, refer to the steps at the beginning of this chapter to create a table with several rows and columns. Then, follow the steps below to explore cell formatting:

1. Click and drag on the divider under the top row to create a row that is about double the height of the other rows.

2. Select all cells, and change the vertical alignment to top using the Vert drop-down list in the Properties Inspector.

3. Change vertical alignment back to middle. Your options are: top, middle, or bottom for vertical alignment.

4. Change the background color of the selected cells to purple.

By the Way

You might assume that the default setting for cell alignment is *top*—that normally cell contents would start at the *top* of a cell, and fill the cell from top to bottom. Makes sense to me, but it doesn't work that way. Instead, the default vertical alignment for cell content is, oddly enough, centered. Part of my unconscious routine when I begin to work with a table is to quickly select all cells and change vertical alignment to top.

5. Assign background colors to other cells.

6. Save your page.

Formatting Multiple Cells

You can apply cell formatting to multiple cells simply by selecting them, and then assigning attributes from the Properties Inspector.

Caution _____

Be careful about making math errors when you define cell and table sizing. Math errors? Yup. What you want to avoid is defining cell widths that *total more than the table width*. For example, if you've defined a table to be 400 pixels wide, and you define three cells to be 150 pixels wide each, a quick check on my calculator tells me this is going to cause a conflict. When cell and table widths collide, the results are unpredictable.

You can both split and merge cells. Splitting and merging cells creates irregular, and interesting table grids useful for nonsymmetrical page layouts. For example, the layout in Figure 7.8 creates the illusion of irregularly placed, free-floating objects on a page.

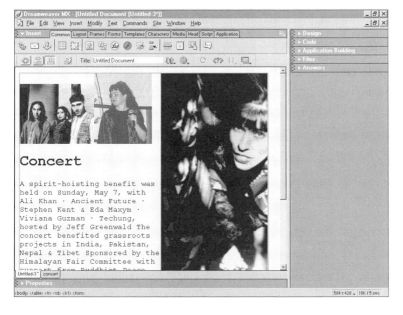

Figure 7.8

This layout was created by both merging and splitting cells.

By the Way

The Merges ... button in the Properties Inspector is only available when you have selected two contiguous cells. Otherwise, it is grayed out. The button is called the Merges Selected Cells Using Spans button because it uses the HTML *span* command. As if we were really that interested!

To merge two contiguous (touching) cells, select them both and click the **Merges Selected Cells Using Spans** button in the Properties Inspector.

To split a selected cell, click the **Splits Cell into Rows or Columns** button in the Properties Inspector. The Split Cell dialog box appears. Use the Rows or Columns radio buttons to split a cell horizontally (columns) or vertically (rows). Then enter a number of rows or columns using the split box, and click **OK** to change the table.

Using Tables to Present Data

While the main use of tables in web design is to create a layout grid for object placement, tables are also used to present data.

You can layout data in rows and columns just as you would in a spreadsheet program, or using the tables feature in a program like Microsoft Word.

Importing Data into Dreamweaver

To import data into a Dreamweaver table, it should be in a text file (such as Microsoft Word), with columns of data separated by tabs.

If you have some data to import, follow these steps:

1. Choose **Insert, Table Objects, Import Tabular Data** from the menu to open the Insert Tabular Data dialog box.

2. Use the Browse button to navigate to the text file in your local site.

3. Leave all the other settings to their defaults, as shown in Figure 7.9, and click **OK** to generate a table from text data.

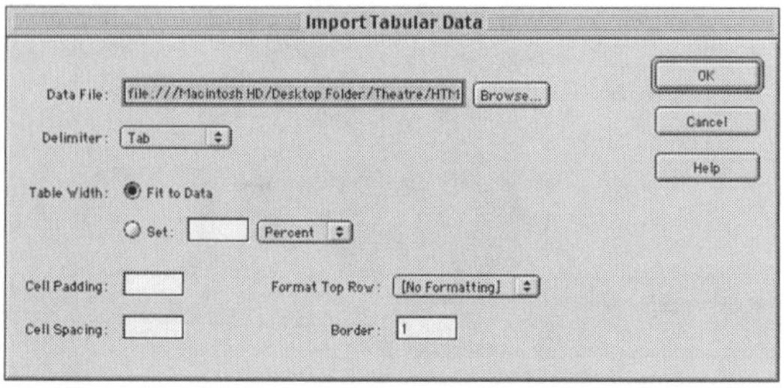

Figure 7.9

Preparing to dump data into a table in Dreamweaver.

Formatting Data Tables vs. Using Tables for Page Design

There are no special rules for formatting tables displaying data. However, from a design point of view, you will usually want to do some things differently when you create a table for displaying data. The following guidelines are, of course, flexible, but they should be helpful.

♦ Data tables often have borders. Design tables are often borderless, since they are supposed to be invisible placeholders for content.

♦ Data tables sometimes use spacing between cells, while design tables usually do not use spacing since it tends to "give away" that there is a table grid on the page.

♦ Data tables usually do not use merged or split cells, as the intent is usually to have symmetrical display of information.

Figure 7.10 shows a table displaying data. Note that the top row was created from merged cells, but other than that the table does not use merged or split cells.

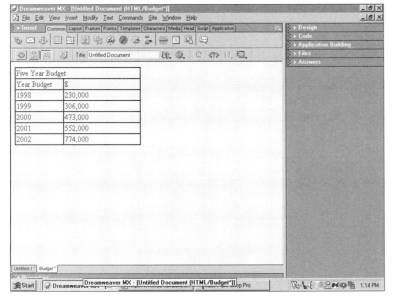

Figure 7.10

This table was created by importing a text file.

The Least You Need to Know

♦ Tables are the most reliable and widely used tool for placing objects on web pages.

♦ You can create a table by choosing Insert, Table, and defining table size, rows, and columns.

♦ Tables can have custom defined background colors, and even background images.

◆ Within a table, individual cells can be formatted. If cell and table formatting conflict, for example background colors, cell formatting takes precedence.

◆ Cells can be merged, or split, to create asymmetrical page layouts.

◆ Tables are usually used to provide a layout grid for objects on a page, but they can also be used to display tabular data.

◆ Dreamweaver will automatically generate a table from imported data.

Chapter 8

All Layered Up

In This Chapter

◆ Designing page layouts with layers

◆ Placing text and images in layers

◆ Converting layers to tables

◆ Overlapping objects with 3-D layers

Wouldn't it be nice if you could just click and drag to place blocks of text, or images, *anywhere* on a web page? You can. Kind of.

Layers allow you to interactively drag any object anywhere on a web page in the Dreamweaver document window. That's the good news. The limitation is that even in the most up-to-date browsers, layer objects are not guaranteed to appear where you positioned them in Dreamweaver.

Does that mean that layers are simply a cruel illusion? No. You can use layers to place objects with tremendous freedom, as long as you design your page in such a way that exact location isn't critical in your page display. One interesting application of layers is the ability to stack them on top of each other.

Designing a Page with Layers

Layers are used in page design in several ways:

- ◆ You can design a page by placing text and images (or even media content) in layers, and easily moving them around the page to locate them.

- ◆ You can stack layers on top of each other.

- ◆ You can combine layers with interactive programming tools like Timelines and Behaviors, which we'll explore in Chapter 19.

Although I cautioned at the beginning of this chapter that layer-based location is unreliable in browsers, you can use layers to place objects, and then convert them to tables to stabilize the page layout. Tables are supported by all recent and even not-very-recent browser versions.

Special Layer Tricks

Stacked layers are a fun way to pile objects on top of each other. If you keep your page design simple, you can create effective stacking layer presentations that are flexible enough to work in different browsers and browser window sizes.

Finally, the ability to "float" objects on your page in layers becomes especially useful when you start working with animated Timelines and other animated and interactive Dreamweaver Behaviors. You can use these Behaviors to control the location and activity of content placed in layers.

In short, layers can be used to layout a page, and then converted to tables. Or, in specific instances, they can be left unconverted as cutting edge design tools. Browser support for layers is unpredictable, but that doesn't mean you can't use them at all in final page design.

Need a Headache? Design with Layers for Netscape

In the course of this chapter, I'll note layer features that are not supported by (still widely used) Netscape Navigator 4.7. In addition, Netscape Navigator 6 offers less reliable support for layer features than Internet Explorer.

Netscape's lack of support for layers provides a special challenge to designing pages for visitors using that browser.

Older versions of Dreamweaver provided a feature to use different, proprietary HTML code to help Netscape recognize layers. However, in MX that option (using the <layer> tag) has been removed.

Inside Info

Dreamweaver MX provides an option to add JavaScript code to a page that helps Netscape maintain layer position. From the Document window menu, choose **Edit, Preferences** and click on the **Layers** category. Select the **Add Resize Fix When Inserting Layer** checkbox to have Dreamweaver automatically add this code in pages.

The added JavaScript forces the page to reload each time the browser window is resized, re-assigning the layers to the correct position.

You can also add or remove the JavaScript code to an individual page by choosing **Commands, Add/Remove Netscape Resize Fix,** and clicking the **Add** button in the dialog box.

If you *are* designing for a significant Netscape audience, you'll probably want to use the convert layers to tables feature in Dreamweaver after you design with layers. I'll explain how to do this later in this chapter.

Defining Layers

You can define, move, format, and name layers in the Document window.

To create a layer, choose **Insert, Layer.** A Layer icon appears at the insertion point, and the layer itself appears in the Document window, as shown in Figure 8.1.

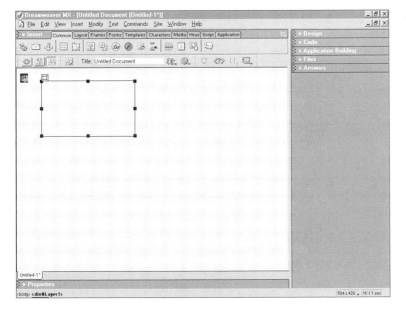

Figure 8.1

Creating a layer in the Document window.

By the Way

By default, new layers created in Dreamweaver are 200 pixels (px) wide, and 115 px in height. You can change this by choosing **Edit, Preferences** (Illustrator, Preferences in OSX), and choosing **Layers** in the Category list. In the Layers section of the Preferences dialog box, you can edit default layer size and other default layer attributes. I'll show you how to resize a layer shortly.

You can select a layer by either clicking on the border, or clicking on the *layer anchor*—the icon associated with each layer. Selected layers display eight sizing handles on the sides and corners, as well as a special *selection handle* in the upper left corner of the layer used to move a layer.

As you create a layer, you can see (and change) layer properties by viewing the Properties panel with a layer selected.

You'll almost always want to see the borders around your layers as you work with them. But if you want to see layers as they will appear in a browser window (without outlines), you can choose **View, Visual Aids,** and deselect Layer Borders as shown in Figure 8.2. Choose **View, Visual Aids,** and select Layer Borders to make layer borders visible again.

Figure 8.2

Displaying borders around layers in Document view helps you as you lay out a page.

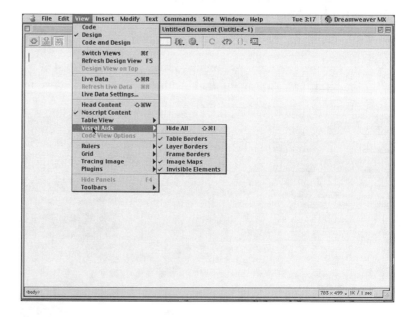

Using Layers to Hold Images and Text

You can place images or text in a layer by inserting these objects in a layer or by dragging them into a layer from elsewhere on your page.

In the Document window, simply click in a layer and start typing to place text in a layer, or you can copy and paste text into a layer. Just make sure you have the layer selected before you paste if you want the text to fall inside the layer.

Similarly, you can place an image in a layer by clicking inside the layer, and choosing **Insert, Image** (and then navigating to and selecting an image). Or, you can click in a layer, and paste an image from the clipboard.

Moving Layers

You can move a layer by clicking on the selection handle, and simply dragging to a location on the page. You'll notice that the layer *Anchor* doesn't move as you move the layer. This can be handy at times if you are searching for a lost layer on a crowded page. Since you can select a layer by either clicking the selection handle *or* the anchor, you can select lost layers by clicking on their anchor.

You can resize a selected layer by clicking and dragging on any of the side or corner handles, as shown in Figure 8.3.

Inside Info

If you use a lot of layers, you might find the screen getting a bit cluttered by too many layer markers. You can hide them by choosing **Edit, Preferences** (Illustrator, Preferences in OSX) and selecting the **Invisible Elements** category. Deselect the **Anchor Points for Layers** checkbox in the Preferences dialog box to hide these markers.

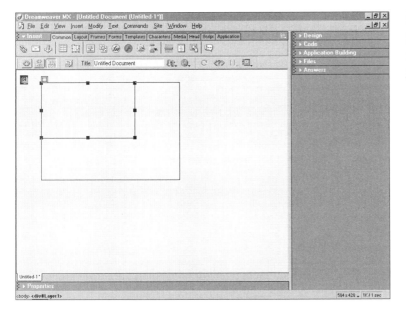

Figure 8.3

Resizing layers the easy way—by clicking and dragging on a handle.

Setting Layer Properties

You can easily, and roughly resize or move a layer right in the Document window. Or, you can more precisely size and locate a layer using the Properties panel.

You can also use the Properties panel to define layer background color, name, as well as more complex attributes, like how a layer handles text that is too large to fit inside the layer.

The Layer ID area of the Layer Properties panel assigns a name used in advanced applications like JavaScripts or Dreamweaver Behaviors. Names should not have spaces or non-letter/number characters to avoid conflicts with scripting languages. Even if you don't know a Behavior from an ice-cream flavor yet, naming layers is a good practice to get into.

Layers can have background images or background colors—much like tables or table cells. You can use the BG Image area in the Properties panel to define a background image for your layer. The best way to do this is to use the Browse for File (folder) icon to navigate to and select a background image.

You can set a background color for a layer by choosing a color from the Bg Color swatch.

You can locate a selected layer by entering values in the L (distance from left) and T (distance from top) areas of the Properties panel. You can specify an exact size for the layer by entering values in pixels in the W (for width) and H (for height) areas.

Figure 8.4 shows a layer defined at 100 pixels square, with a yellow background, and placed exactly 100 pixels from the top and 100 pixels from the left edge of the page.

Figure 8.4

Defining the exact size and location of a layer in the Properties panel.

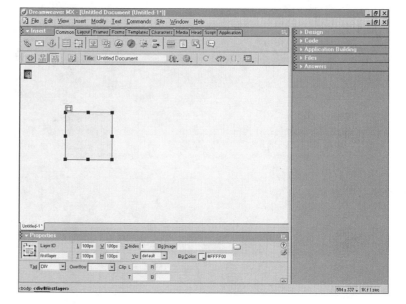

Squeezing Text Into or Out of a Layer

What happens if you put a page worth of text into a 100 pixel square layer? Or a 400 pixel square image? Obviously in both cases, the content won't all fit in the layer!

Or, what happens if your text fits just fine in the Dreamweaver document window, but doesn't squeeze into the layer when viewed in a browser with the font size set to "Largest."

To deal with these scenarios, it's important to define how you want overflow layer content handled. By default, Dreamweaver will extend the height of your layer to accommodate all the text you place in that layer. However, you can also elect to display only the amount of text that will fit in the layer, or to provide horizontal and vertical scrollbars so a visitor can read all the text by scrolling across or down the layer.

The options in the Overflow drop-down list in the Properties panel control how overflow text is controlled. The default, Visible, setting expands the layer to display all text. The Hidden option is kind of the opposite of the slogan of *The New York Times* ("All the news that's fit to print"). This option hides all text that doesn't fit. The Scroll option provides scrollbars at all times. And the Auto option displays scrollbars as needed. Figure 8.5 shows a text layer in a browser with scrollbars.

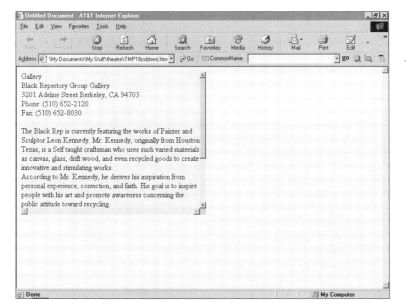

Figure 8.5

If the content does not fit, you can use scrollbars to display the text.

Additional fields in the Layers Properties panel control whether or not a layer is visible (The Viz drop-down list), and allow you to clip (crop) layer content. You can enter pixel values in the L(left), R(right), T(top), and B(bottom) areas of the Properties panel to crop layer content.

Converting Layers to Tables

You can combine the flexibility and ease-of-use of layers with the reliability of tables by first using layers to design your page, and then converting those layers to tables.

Converting layers to tables resolves any browser compatibility issues, because even old versions of all browsers support tables.

Before converting layers to tables, you need to make sure that none of your layers overlap. You can guarantee that you don't create overlapping layers by viewing the Layers panel (choose **Window, Others, Layers**). Select the **Prevent Overlapping** checkbox in the Layers panel, and Dreamweaver will prevent you from overlapping layers.

To convert layers to a table, choose **Modify, Convert, Layers to Table.** As you do, the Convert Layers to Table dialog box appears as shown in Figure 8.6.

Figure 8.6

Converting layers to a table—let Dreamweaver do the work.

Usually, it's sufficient to simply select the Most Accurate radio button in the Convert Layers to Table dialog box. But if you want Dreamweaver to avoid generating *too* complex a table, you can choose the **Smallest: Collapse Empty Cells** checkbox, and enter a minimum cell size in pixels in the Less Than area of the dialog box.

The Use Transparent GIFs checkbox automatically creates invisible images for the last row in the table that prevent the table from being resized in browsers. Use this option to fix the width of the generated table.

By default, tables created from converted layers are left aligned. Use the **Center on Page** checkbox to center the generated table.

Frustrated Photoshop, PageMaker, or Illustrator designers might want to experiment with the different grid checkboxes in the Convert Layers to Table dialog box.

After you define how you want your table created from your layers, click **OK** in the Convert Layers to Table dialog box to convert your layers to a table.

If you run into error messages converting layers to a table, here are the most common trouble-shooting solutions:

- ◆ If you get a message that your layers overlap, locate and move overlapping layers.
- ◆ If you get a message that you have nested layers, locate any layer located *within* a layer, and move it outside of the layer within which it was placed.

Drawing Layers

In Chapter 7, I briefly noted the fact that Dreamweaver has a Layout view that can be used to "draw" tables. I find that attempting to "draw" tables is pretty frustrating and unintuitive for students. On the other hand, drawing layers is more intuitive, and kind of a helpful design feature.

To change to Layout view, choose **View, Table View, Layout view.** As you do, the Common tab of the Insert Panel group appears in the Document window. Use the Draw Layer tool in the Common tab of the Insert panel to draw layers wherever you want them, as shown in Figure 8.7.

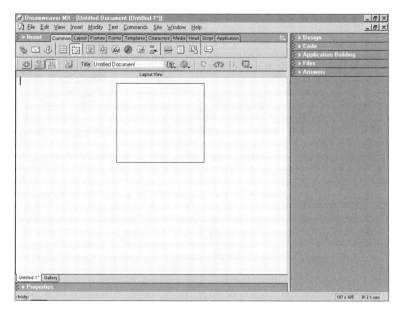

Figure 8.7

Creating layers just by drawing.

By the Way

If you plan to convert your layers to tables, check the **Prevent Overlaps** checkbox in the Layers panel. The F2 function key is a shortcut to display (or hide) the Layers panel.

When you switch to Layout view, you also activate the Draw Table button in the Insert panel. Just as I advised against using the Draw Table tool to create tables, I even more strongly advise against *mixing* drawing tables and drawing layers. If you want to design a page by drawing layers (and then, for reliability, converting them to tables), go for it. This is a nice way to design pages—especially for folks coming from desktop publishing or graphic design backgrounds who find tables just too weird.

Using Layers for 3-D Overlapping

In addition to their role as a 2-D design tool, layers can be used to stack objects on top of each other. For example, in Figure 8.8, I've placed a text layer on top of a picture.

Figure 8.8

The layer with the higher Z-Index value appears on top of a layer with a lower Z-Index value.

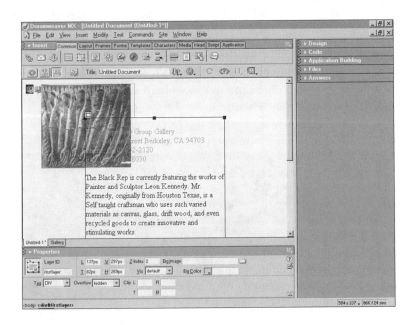

Stacking order is defined by the Z-Index value for each layer. The higher the Z value, the more an object is moved to the top of the stacking order. So, for example, a layer with a Z-Index value of 2 will appear *on top of* another object with a Z-Index value of 1.

If a top layer does not have a background image or background color, the content of that layer will appear on top of the content of lower layers.

In Figure 8.9, the image has a lower Z-Index value, and therefore the text appears on top of the image.

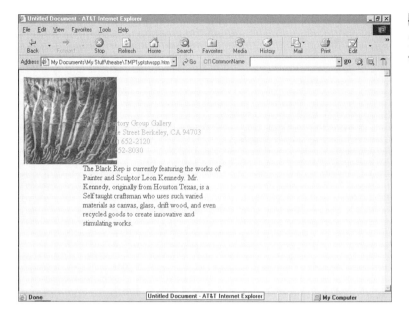

Figure 8.9

Testing stacking layers—they work in Internet Explorer.

The Least You Need to Know

◆ Layers are an easy way to design page layout, but they are not reliably supported by all browsers.

◆ You can layout a page using layers, and then convert the layers to tables for a more consistent page display in browsers.

◆ If you plan to convert layers to tables, make sure your layers do not overlap in the Document window.

◆ Layers function something like little windows in a browser, and can have their own backgrounds, and even scrollbars.

◆ Layers can be stacked on top of each other for effect. The Z-Index value determines which layer displays on top, with higher Z-Index values moving layers "to the top" of layers with lower Z-Index values.

Getting Stylish

In this Chapter

◆ Understanding local, page, and external styles

◆ Defining page styles

◆ Creating external styles

◆ Applying styles to web pages

External (aka cascading) style sheets (CSS for short) are one of the most powerful tools in Dreamweaver. You use external style sheets to define formatting like text size, color, and font, and then you can apply those formats *globally* across your entire website.

Style sheets give a website a coherent, consistent look. Visitors feel "at home" at any page in your site since they encounter a similar look and feel as they navigate from page to page.

CSS—the Good Side

Style sheets are also an important productivity tool in large-scale web development projects. Page designers can quickly create pages without having to do much in the way of formatting, and then simply attach a style sheet to bring the page into conformity with the formatting of the rest of the site.

Finally, external style sheets are easily revisable—a change to a style sheet is *automatically* applied throughout your site, to every page to which the style sheet was attached.

Style sheets save time in formatting page text, allow centralized design control in large projects, and are easily updated. So what's the downside?

CSS—the Evil Side

Before I lead you into the universe of external sheets, I'll warn you in advance of the pitfalls. First, my students tend to find style sheets tricky to define and apply. In part, it's because the concepts involved are a little complex, and require that you step back from thinking just about *page* design and think about *site* design.

Also, style sheets are one of the unintuitive (that's a nice way of saying confusing) features of Dreamweaver. I'll address both these hurdles by spending some time explaining the concepts involved in applying style sheets, and then walking you through the process of using them in detail.

There are also more objective challenges in using style sheets. Browser support for cascading style sheets is uneven. This becomes a particularly big problem when or if you try to stretch the limits of the latest CSS specifications (CSS-2).

My approach in using style sheets is to apply them in such a way that they enhance site appearance, but site appearance is not dependent on a visitor's browser supporting style sheets. For example, even though it is technically possible to format a style with an applied shading color, I usually avoid this. And I definitely avoid creating a style with a dark shading color and light colored text. If a visitor's browser doesn't support all the style attributes, he or she might end up "seeing" (or more to the point—not seeing) white text on a white page.

On the other hand, if you stick to features that enhance text, but aren't required to view the text, the "worst case" scenario is that some visitors will see your pages without some text formatting features.

Local, Page, and External Styles

External style sheets are called cascading style sheets because there are actually three basic levels of formatting that you apply to a website. And these three levels "cascade" over each other in this way:

- ◆ **Local formatting** that you apply on a page to selected text takes precedence over all other formatting.
- ◆ **Page formatting** that you apply to an entire page, takes precedence over formatting applied to an entire site.

◆ **Site wide formatting** (through an external style sheet file) is overruled by any local or page formatting you apply.

When all three types of styles are applied to a page for example, the first priority goes to the locally defined styles (sometimes called "inline") styles. Second priority goes to page-wide styles. And, only if there are no conflicting inline or page-wide styles, the formatting attributes of an external style sheet are applied to text.

A Detour—Quick Note on Page Styles

In between local style formatting and external style sheets is page formatting. Page formatting is overridden by local formatting, but supercedes external style sheets. If all this is beginning to sound like a law class, I sympathize.

Page styles are defined by choosing **Modify, Page Properties** with a page open in the Dreamweaver Document window. As you can see, the Page Properties dialog box allows you to define a default text color for all text, as well as three states of links (normal, visited, and active).

Because the accessible options for page properties are limited in Dreamweaver, and because they fill a rather niche role in web design, we'll simply note them here and focus on external style sheets.

How External Styles Work

The "external" in "external styles" does not mean that style sheets come from another planet (that's extraterrestrial). Instead, it means they applied from another file. That file is called a CSS (again, for cascading style sheets) file, and is attached to a page. Most of this chapter will involve showing you just how to do that.

The extraterrestrial thing, while not literally applicable to style sheets, can be helpful if you've seen one of the many remakes of the old movie about how space creatures take over the minds of humans. In a somewhat similar way, CSS (external styles) attach themselves to a page, and take over the attributes of one of the basic HTML styles.

HTML styles? Just how many "styles" are there in web design? Too many! *HTML styles* refers to the set of six heading styles (Heading 1, Heading 2, and so on), and the Paragraph style that are accessible from the Format drop-down list in the Properties panel.

These HTML styles have built-in formatting: Times font, black color, and different relative sizes (with Heading 1 being the largest and Heading 6 the smallest).

Definition

Inline formatting is just another way of saying formatting you applied to selected text. When you select text, and apply a font type, font color, font size, or any other font attribute, you are applying an inline style.

I briefly noted these HTML styles in Chapter 4, where I advised you not to worry about them until you got to the style sheet chapter. Well, now you're here so it's time to take note of these HTML styles.

Since the built-in preformatting of these HTML styles is so dull and dreary, they don't have much use on their own. Their usefulness comes when you redefine them using external style sheets. Once you redefine HTML styles through external style sheets, they take on a whole new set of formatting attributes, and become much more useful.

External vs. Inline

At this point I have to emphasize again that external styles are overruled by any *inline formatting* you've applied on a page.

What this means is that if you have extensive inline/local formatting on your pages (and you probably do!), you will want to strip that formatting from text that the external style sheet will be applied to.

Stripping Local Formatting

Before you finish nice wood floors, you strip off all the old dirt and wax. Before you detail a car, you wash off all the dirt. And … before you begin to apply style sheets to your site, you'll want to strip most of the local formatting from your pages.

You can do that by following these steps:

1. Select all the text on a page by choosing **Edit, Select All** in the Document window.
2. In the Properties panel, select **Default Font** on the Font drop-down list.
3. In the Size drop-down list, choose **None.**
4. In the Color palette, select **Default Color,** as shown in Figure 9.1.
5. Delete attributes like boldface and italics as well if they have been applied.

After you have stripped all local formatting in this way, it is probably helpful to select Paragraph from the Styles list. You're now ready to apply HTML heading styles to text.

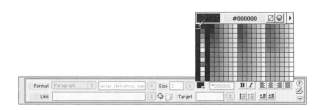

Figure 9.1

Stripping colors from text.

Creating External Style Sheets

External style sheets are saved to files in your website with a CSS file name extension. They are similar to HTML pages, and the style definitions are created using coding *similar* to HTML. I emphasize *similar* because CSS coding actually has its own syntax which is different than HTML code.

Enough of the techie talk. Luckily, we don't need to worry about that coding. Dreamweaver will generate CSS files for us, and allow us to easily edit the styles within them.

Creating an External Style Sheet (CSS) File

The CSS Styles panel is not one of Dreamweaver's more intuitive features. Oddly enough, the first step is to create a style, and then you generate the external style sheet file.

Further, applying styles is rather nonintuitive as well. For most style sheet applications, the CSS Styles inspector appears to be empty, even when you have applied a style to a page.

So … expect things to be a little counter-intuitive in the following style sheet tutorials. Have faith that it will all make sense by the end of this session!

Defining a New HTML Style

The basic and most powerful way to use external style sheets is to redefine the default six heading styles (Heading 1, Heading 2 … Heading 6), and the normal paragraph style. By supplying your own formatting definitions for these styles, you can quickly and easily apply formatting to many pages across a website.

As we create a new style sheet, we'll start by redefining the standard HTML styles.

The first step in defining a new CSS is to open a web page in the Document window and view the CSS Styles inspector (choose **Window, CSS Styles**). With a page open in the Document window, and the CSS Styles panel active, follow these steps to define styles:

1. Somewhat buried on the bottom of the inspector is the New CSS Style icon that creates a new style, shown in Figure 9.2. Click the **New CSS Style** icon.

Figure 9.2

Defining a new external style sheet.

2. The New Style dialog box appears. In the Type area, click the **Redefine HTML Tag** radio button.

3. In the Tag drop-down list, choose **h1.** This is the HTML tag for Heading 1.

4. In the Define In area, select the **(New Style Sheet File)** option. Your New CSS Style dialog box should look something like the one in Figure 9.3.

Figure 9.3

Defining a new CSS style.

5. Click **OK** to close the New CSS Style dialog box. The Save Style Sheet File As dialog box will appear. This is the point where you generate a new CSS style sheet·file. Navigate to the folder with your Site (it may already be selected by default), and name your file *style*.css, where *style* can be any file name. Your Save Style Sheet File As dialog box should look something like Figure 9.4.

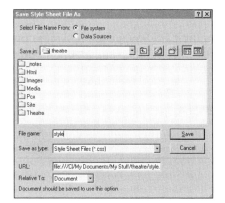

Figure 9.4

Saving a style sheet file.

Caution

If you're just experimenting here, or want to play it safe, feel free to copy me and name your first style sheet *style.css*. You *do* need to type the CSS filename extension. Otherwise Dreamweaver will get confused and might not be able to find your style sheet file.

Also, at the end of this chapter, I'll note some of the things that can go wrong with style sheets. One of them is that some browsers can only detect a CSS file if it is in the *root* folder for your site. So, it's safest to navigate to your root folder before saving your CSS file.

6. Click **Save** to close the Save Style Sheet As dialog box. The Style Definition for h1 in *style*.css (or whatever file name you chose) dialog box opens. Here, you define the font style, color, size, and so on for Heading 1 in this style sheet. In Figure 9.5, I'm assigning 18 point Courier font, with purple color as the definition for Heading 1 in my style sheet.

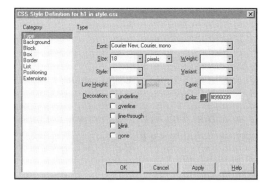

Figure 9.5

Defining a Heading 1 style.

7. When you've finished defining the first style in your CSS file, click **OK.**

8. Click the **New Style** icon again in the CSS Styles inspector. This time, the New Style dialog box opens with your CSS file listed in the Define In drop-down list, as shown in Figure 9.6. And, the Redefine HTML Tag radio button is selected. Pull down the Tag drop-down list, and choose **h2.**

9. Define additional styles, like h2, h3, h4, h5, h6, and p (paragraph) styles.

Figure 9.6

Defining additional styles in an existing CSS file.

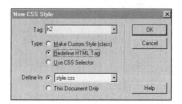

At this point, you have defined as many as six HTML heading styles (Heading 1 through Heading 6), as well as custom font formatting for paragraph text. Nice work!

If all this has your head spinning a bit, you might want to skip the next section of this chapter. If, on the other hand, you're fascinated by the new horizons opened by style sheets, you might want to check this next section out. In it, you'll define styles that apply to different link states.

Defining Link State Styles

Links in browsers can (basically) display in four states: untouched (normal), hovered over, active (clicked), and visited. Normally, browsers (by default) display links as underlined text in blue. Visited sites are displayed in purple (with underlining). And active links are displayed in red (with underlining).

You can change these default formats, including getting rid of the underlining. And, you can define a link state for links that are rolled over by a mouse cursor. That link state is called "hover."

To define link state styles, follow these steps:

1. Click on the new style icon in the CSS Styles panel.

2. The New Style dialog box appears. In the Type area, choose the **Use CSS Selector** radio button.

3. In the tag drop-down list, choose **a:link.** This is the tag for normal links.

4. In the Define In area, your currently active CSS file should be selected. The New Style dialog box should look something like Figure 9.7.

Figure 9.7

Defining a link style for an existing CSS file.

5. Click **OK** to open the Style Definition dialog box for this tag (normal links).

6. Choose font attributes for normal link text. You can remove underlining by choosing the None checkbox in the Decoration area of the dialog box, as shown in Figure 9.8.

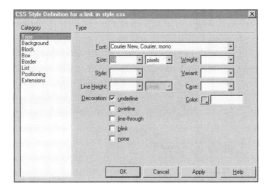

Figure 9.8

Getting rid of underlining for a link style.

7. Click **OK** to complete the definition.

8. Define additional link styles for the other three link states (active, hover, and visited).

Inside Info

One link formatting strategy you can apply is to use different colors, or other formatting attributes (like boldface) instead of underlining to identify links. This produces a nice, clean page look. You can make your links more animated and add energy to your page by assigning format changes to hovered links, like having them turn boldface or turn another color.

You can only test the effect of link styles when you actually view your page in a browser (choose File, Preview in Browser, and select a browser). Link states are not accurately displayed in the Dreamweaver document window.

A Quick Look at Custom (Class) Styles

You may have noticed that besides HTML tags and CSS Selectors, there is a third style type—Custom Style (Class) styles.

Custom or Class styles are nonstandard styles that are applied on top of the attributes assigned by other styles. So, for example, if you wanted to be able to quickly apply green coloring and italics to selected text throughout your website, you could define a custom style that did just that.

Oddly enough, these rather esoteric styles are the only ones that show up on the CSS Styles inspector!

Class styles are not a particularly effective tool unless you get into some pretty esoteric web design activity. If you want to apply local formatting in combination with using HTML styles, just select text and apply the formatting you need.

Saving and Applying a CSS File

As you add new styles to your CSS file, you automatically resave the CSS file with the new style definitions.

So, there's no special procedure for "saving" a CSS file. Each time you save a new style associated with a style sheet, Dreamweaver is cool enough to revise your CSS file.

Those of you who have studied hand-coding CSS can feel free to open the generated CSS file and add or edit the code there. The rest of us will be content to let Dreamweaver do that for us.

Applying an External Style Sheet to Web Pages

Once you've generated an external (CSS) style sheet with defined styles, you can apply that entire set of styles to any page in your site. To do that, follow these steps:

1. Open a web page in the Document window.

2. Select a line of text at the top of the page, and apply the Heading 1 style using the Properties inspector.

3. Strip all local formatting from the selected text by deleting anything from the Font, Font Size, or Font Color areas of the Properties inspector, and remove any other attributes such as boldface.

4. Select most of the text on your page, and apply the Paragraph style to that text using the properties inspector. Again, strip local coding from your selected text.

5. Apply Heading 2 and Heading 3 styles to some text on your page (you might have to create additional text to do this). Strip local formatting from this text as well.

Caution

If your styles did not apply, check again to make sure you've stripped all local formatting from styles.

6. With the CSS Styles inspector active, click on the **Attach Style Sheet** icon (shown in Figure 9.9), and double-click on your CSS style sheet file. The style definitions will be applied to the page.

Figure 9.9

Attaching a style sheet to a page.

Editing and Updating CSS Styles

Once you have created an applied style sheet, you can open the CSS file, change style definitions, and the changes will be applied to all changes to which the CSS file is attached. Follow these steps to edit a CSS file:

1. In Site view (press **F8**), double-click on your CSS file to open it. A dialog box appears listing defined styles for your site, as shown in Figure 9.10.

Figure 9.10

Editing an existing CSS file.

2. Select a tag and click **Edit.**

3. Change the attributes for your selected style and click **OK.**

4. Click the **Save** button in the CSS dialog box.

5. View your home page in the document window. The new style has been applied.

After you update a style sheet in your local site, select the CSS file in the Site window, and choose **Site, Put** to upload the revised CSS file to your remote site.

Final Warnings and Troubleshooting Tips

So, you say your beautiful styles aren't working in browsers? Here are a few things to check.

I mentioned in the beginning of this chapter that Netscape Navigator 4.7 and earlier browsers do not support all style sheet attributes. So, you should test pages in Netscape to make sure that missing formatting features don't destroy your page.

Another flaw in how Netscape handles CSS files is that version 4.7 at least (I haven't tested every version since) requires that the CSS file is located in the *root folder* of your site. While in general, tidy site management (refer back to Chapter 2 for more information on this) requires organizing files into folders within your site, you should break that rule if you plan on having Netscape 4.7 visitors see your styles. In short, save CSS files to your root folder in your site.

Finally, if you *change* attached style sheets, Dreamweaver doesn't do a very tidy job of fixing the HTML code. Changing style sheets is not a scenario I've explored in this chapter, but it can be done. If you have more than one CSS file in your site, you can change the associated CSS file for a page by attaching the new CSS file using the same technique I explained in this chapter for assigning an initial CSS file. If you replace one CSS file with another, Dreamweaver simply adds lines of HTML code to your page, instead of replacing the original HTML code. Having a stack of CSS files listed for your page can confuse some browsers. Therefore, if you replace one CSS file with another, I suggest you go into the Show Code view in the Document window, and locate out-of-date lines of code that refer to discarded style sheets. The HTML syntax will look something like this:

```
<link href="STYLES.CSS" rel="stylesheet" type="text/css">
```

Find the lines of HTML that refer to discarded style sheets. Select them in Show Code view and press the **Delete** key to remove them.

The Least You Need to Know

◆ External style sheets are a powerful way to apply global text formatting to an entire website.

◆ Text formatting can be applied to page text in three ways: through local formatting (to selected text), page formatting, and external styles.

◆ If you have already applied local formatting to text (such as font, font size, and font color), then external styles will have no affect on that text because local formatting "trumps" external styles.

◆ Dreamweaver will create a CSS file for you. The process isn't simple, but you can do it by following the steps in this chapter.

◆ Once you attach a CSS file to a page, the page adopts the formatting in the CSS file.

Chapter 10

I Was Framed

In This Chapter

◆ Designing with frames

◆ Understanding how frames work

◆ Preparing pages to get framed

◆ Designing a frameset to display framed pages

Don't believe all the stereotypes out there about frames. They've been given a bad rap. It all goes back to the days when inconsistent browser support, over-zealous designers, and tiny monitors combined to fill browser windows with crappy looking unreliable chunks of content.

Today, all current and even not-so-current browsers support frames just fine. Those frame-insane designers who had to put four of five frames on every page have grown up or moved on. And the proliferation of larger monitors has created more space in browser windows.

Designing with Frames

Frames are an especially nice way to provide a constant, static navigation section of a website that appears on screen at all times, while visitors view site content in other sections of the browser window.

In addition to using frames as a navigation tool, frames also allow you to surround content in a constant site environment. In some cases, it is appropriate to include outside content in your browser window.

Evil Frames

To provide comic relief and some perspective, let's have some fun looking at a "bad frames" page. The example in Figure 10.1 breaks many if not all of the rules that prevent annoying frame syndrome.

Figure 10.1

Ouch! Too many frames with distracting scrollbars.

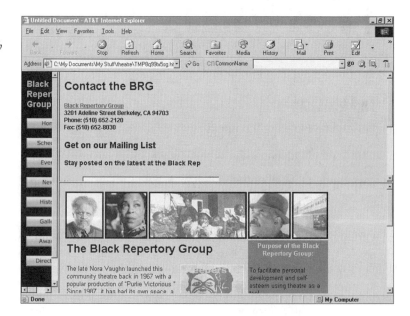

The site in Figure 10.1 has ...

◆ Too many frames.

◆ Content that doesn't fit within a frame.

◆ Too many frame scroll bars.

◆ Frame links that open in the wrong window (the bottom frame is displaying a link target that should be displayed in the main frame).

Good Frames

Now that we've dispensed with the "bad frame" example, let's explore good applications for frames.

The evolution of higher resolution monitors has opened the door to more effective use of frames. When monitor resolution was around 600 pixels in width, there wasn't much screen to be divided up between frames. However, a 1000 or 1200-pixel screen allows a nice, wide 600-pixel display in one frame, with plenty of space left over for a navigation frame. In fact, 1000+ pixels is often just *too* wide to effectively display content. I addressed this issue in Chapter 7 when I advocated using 600-pixel or 800-pixel tables to constrain page width. Frames can provide a similar function.

Frames can be used as a navigation structure for a site and as a way of framing content inside other content. For example, it's often effective to use a left or top frame as a navigation frame. That frame remains constant as visitors browse throughout a site, displaying content that you want available at all times, as well as providing consistent navigation links.

Figure 10.2 shows a site with a navigation frame on the left, and a content frame on the right.

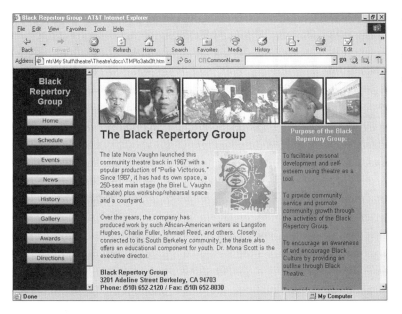

Figure 10.2

This basic frame design has wide applicability—a navigation frame on the left, content on the right.

Integrating Outside Content in Frames

Let me take a moment to discuss when it is appropriate to include content from other sites in a frameset.

It is not appropriate (and sometimes not legal) to take content from another site, and make it appear in your site's frameset so that you mislead visitors about who owns that content.

On the other hand, if you have required permissions, you can include outside content within a site through frames. For example, I designed a site for an insurance broker, who wanted visitors to be able to view frequently updated policy and rate information supplied by the insurance carriers. At the same time, my client didn't want visitors to *leave* his site to view that content, because he wanted to be sure that when they decided to purchase a policy, they purchased from him.

In this situation, I designed a site where both my client's content (order forms, contact information, and so on), as well as content from insurance carrier's sites appeared in frames in his site. Visitors aren't conscious that they're viewing content from another site, and when they click the "order insurance" link, the outside content is replaced within the frame.

How Frames Work

"Frames" are more accurately referred to as "framesets." That's because every "frame" is really made up of a *set* of frames. Each page that is embedded within a frameset has its own frame. And an additional frame is used to define how all the other frames will fit together. Every frameset, therefore, is made up of at least three HTML files. One of these HTML files does not display any content of its own. It is simply an HTML file that defines the structure of the frameset, as illustrated in Figure 10.3.

Figure 10.3

The anatomy of a frame.

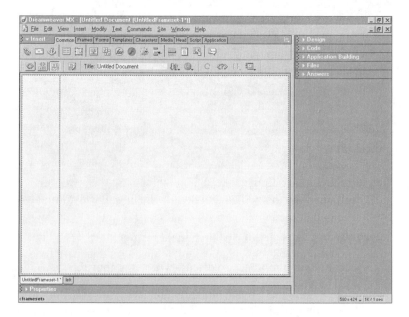

Dreamweaver helps manage the potentially confusing process of keeping track of all these HTML pages. We'll walk through that process in the tutorial at the end of this discussion. But you'll keep yourself more oriented if you keep in mind that each time you "save a frame" you are actually saving the frameset file that defines the structure of the frames, as well as embedded HTML pages within that frameset.

Navigation Issues with Frames

Since framesets are composed of multiple HTML pages, you need to take that into account when you define target pages for links in your frameset. The diagram in Figure 10.4 illustrates the point.

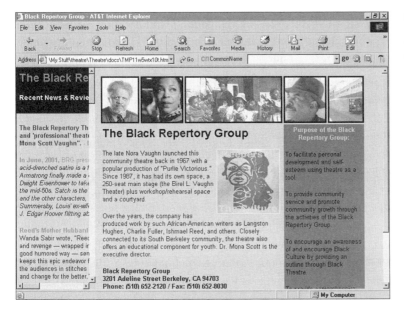

Figure 10.4

Links must open in an appropriate frame.

Usually, one frame acts as a navigation area for a frameset. You don't want links in that frame opening in the same frame; you want them to open in another frame. Again, we'll walk through this when we start the tutorial. But it will be helpful to keep in mind that when you create links in a frameset, you have to define the target of those links in a different HTML page.

Making Frames

Now that I've issued necessary warnings and provided you with some background information, I'll walk you through the details of creating a frameset.

The process can get a little confusing, but if you follow the steps in the remainder of this chapter, I think you'll be fine. Keep in mind that frames combine pages with a defining frameset. Which comes first? Either one. But I find it easier—especially when teaching— to start with pages, and then combine them into a frameset.

In the rest of this chapter, I'll use as an example a simple, two-frame design using the left frame as a navigation frame, and displaying content in the main (or right) frame. You can feel free to apply what you learn to create more complex framesets, but I find that the basic two-framer is very effective and is appropriate for a vast majority of frame design applications.

Preparing Pages for a Frameset

Since framesets serve as a design structure for HTML pages, I find it easier to first create the HTML pages that will be plugged into a frameset. Then, those HTML pages can be plugged into distinct frames within the frameset.

So, the first task is to create the two HTML pages that will be embedded in our frameset. You can do this on your own since you already know how to create new web pages in Dreamweaver.

In the following steps, I'm going to provide rather detailed instructions, including providing file names for you to use. Of course you can adapt this by using your own file names, but because framing can get confusing, I suggest using my file names the first time through.

Caution

Be sure to save your file as left.htm when you're done. And, just to keep things from getting too confusing, I recommend closing this file after you create it.

Inside Info

Again, I recommend closing this file after you name it (main.htm).

To prepare pages for framing, follow these steps:

1. Create a page called left.htm. Include navigation text (*Don't* define the links yet), so the page looks something like Figure 10.5.

2. The next step is to create the page that will serve as the main home page for the frameset. Create a page that looks something like the one in Figure 10.6 (feel free to embellish it—I'm keeping it simple so I don't get distracted from the frames point).

3. Before moving on, make sure you have saved your new pages. Closing them will make it easier for you to keep track of your files as you plug them into a frameset in the next section.

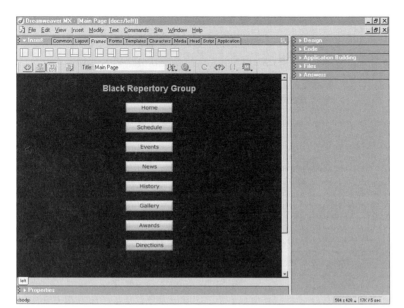

Figure 10.5

Creating a page that will plug into a frameset as a left-side navigation frame.

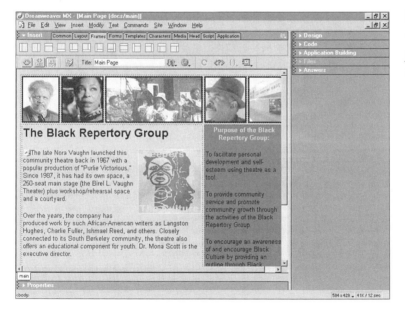

Figure 10.6

This page will be the main frame in the site and display content.

Defining a Frameset HTML File

Now that you've defined the pages that will become the embedded content of our frameset, it's time to define the HTML file that will serve as the frameset itself. Here's how:

1. Open a new file in the Dreamweaver document window.

2. Give this page a title. This is the information that will appear in a browser title bar.

3. Save the file as **frameset.htm.**

4. Choose **Modify, Frameset, Split Frame Left** from the menu.

5. Click and drag on the frame divider so the left frame is about one fourth of the page, as shown in Figure 10.7.

Figure 10.7

Resizing frames.

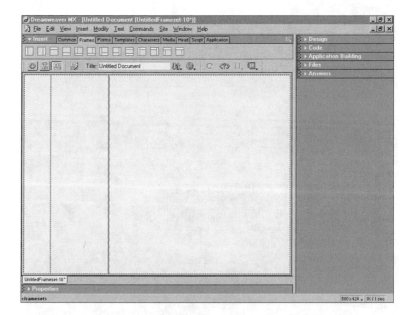

6. Click on the left side of the frameset and choose **File, Open in Frame.**

7. Navigate to, and double-click on **left.htm** to embed that file in the left frame.

8. Embed **main.htm** in the right frame—your frameset should look something like the one in Figure 10.8.

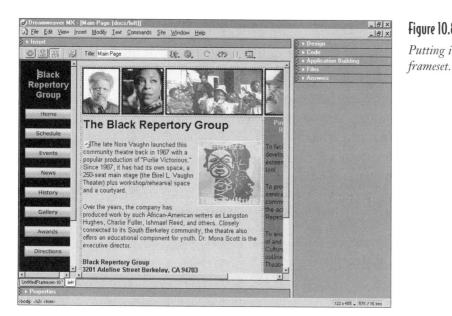

Figure 10.8

Putting it all together in a frameset.

Managing Frameset Files

Let's review where we are. We created a file to hold our frameset (frameset.htm), as well as two HTML files that are embedded within that frameset.

When you save a frameset, you save changes to any HTML file within the frameset that has had changes made to it. Your save options will differ each time you save a frameset, depending on which frames you have edited.

Sometimes Dreamweaver does not prompt you to resave frameset files with their original file names. Don't be disoriented by this. You need to do a little of your own work to keep track of which file is which.

When you choose **File, Save all Frames,** you'll be prompted one-by-one to save HTML files within your frameset.

You can tell which file you are saving by looking at which section of the frameset is outlined in dashed lines.

For example, in Figure 10.9, the frameset itself is outlined in dashed lines. That's how I know that the file I'm saving should be frameset.htm.

Figure 10.9

Look closely: The dashed line defines the selected file in a frameset.

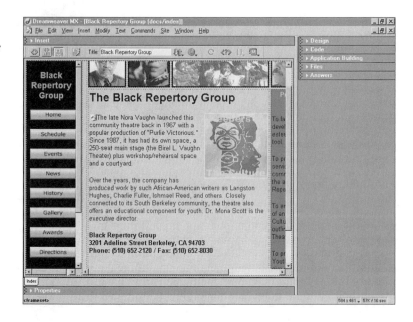

Defining Frame Links

When you create a link in a navigation frame, you almost always want that link to open not in the navigation frame, but in the other frame in your frameset.

To ensure that links open in the right frame, you need to associate each frame with a frame name, and then use those frame names as link targets.

Naming Frames

To assign a name to each frame, you'll use the Frames panel. Choose **Window, Others, Frames** to display the Frames panel.

Inside Info

Don't confuse a frame name with a frame file name. Frame names are defined in the Frames panel, and are used to define link targets. Even though you have assigned file names to frames, you still need to assign names to them.

When you click in a frame in the Document window, that frame is selected in the Frames panel, as shown in Figure 10.10.

You can also select a frame by clicking on it in the Frames panel. With a frame selected in the Frames panel, open the Properties panel. The Properties panel displays with a Frame Name area. Enter a name for your frame, as shown in Figure 10.11.

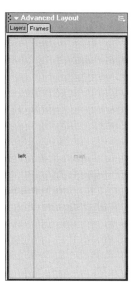

Figure 10.10

Choosing a frame in the Frames panel.

Figure 10.11

Naming frames.

Assign a frame name in the same way to your other open frame(s). You're now ready to define link targets.

Assigning Link Targets

Now that you have named your frames, you can use those names to define a link target.

To assign a link target in a navigation frame that will open in a main frame, follow these steps:

1. Click on text or an image in the navigation frame to which you will assign a link.

2. In the Link area of the Properties panel, define the target for the selected text or image.

3. In the Target area of the Properties panel, select the name of the frame in which the link should open. In Figure 10.12, the target link is the Main frame.

By the Way

You can review the basics of linking in Chapter 6. There, I explain other link target options, like opening a link in a new browser window.

Figure 10.12

Defining a frame target for a link.

When you test your page in a browser, *make sure* that all links open in the appropriate frame.

Formatting Frames

Dreamweaver allows you quite a bit of control over how frames will look. Frames can display with thick, colored borders or no borders at all, with resizable dividers between frames or with locked frame sizes, with scrollbars or without.

Some frame properties are defined for individual frames (like scrollbars). Others, like border width, are defined for an entire frameset. I'll walk you through this process in the next sections.

Formatting Frame Borders (or Making Them Disappear)

By default, visitors can see borders between your frames. You can change the width and display of those borders. Or, you can just hide them. Many attractive sites employ hidden frame borders, to create a clean, uncluttered page look. Figure 10.13 shows a borderless frameset in a browser.

Figure 10.13

Look ma! No (visible) frame lines.

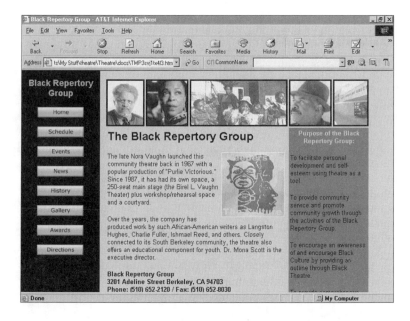

To define frame border properties, follow these steps:

1. Before you can define frameset properties, you need to select the entire frameset, not any one frame. I find this easiest in the Frames panel. Click on the outside border of the frameset in the Frames panel to select the entire frameset, as shown in Figure 10.14.

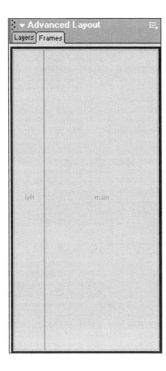

Figure 10.14

Selecting the frameset is easiest in the Frames panel.

2. With the entire frameset selected, the Border Width area appears in the Properties panel. Enter a value in pixels to define the width of the border. For a borderless frameset (with no visible border), enter 0 (zero) in the Border Width area.

3. Use the Border Color palette in the Properties panel to define a color for the border.

Hiding Scrollbars and Locking Frame Sizes

Scrollbar properties (hidden or visible), and visitor-enabled resizing is defined in the Properties Inspector for specific frames within a frameset. You can, for example, allow a vertical scrollbar in your content frame, while defining your navigation frame to never show a scrollbar.

On the other hand, if you want to prevent visitors from changing the relative sizes of your frames, you should select the No Resize option in Dreamweaver for *both* of the related frames.

To set resizing and scrollbar properties for a frameset, follow these steps:

1. Select a single frame, not a frameset in the Frames panel.

2. Select the **No Resize** checkbox in the Properties panel to prevent visitors from resizing the selected frame.

3. The default scrollbar option (Default) uses the browser default, which usually displays scrollbars as needed. Use the Scroll drop-down list to change this to Yes (to display scrollbars all the time), or No (never display scrollbars). The Auto option is similar to the Default option and displays scrollbars as needed.

Saving Frameset Changes

As I've mentioned, saving frames and framesets can be confusing. Sometimes it seems like Dreamweaver keeps prompting you to save a frameset, when you've already saved it.

The confusion comes from the fact that when you save a frameset, you are saving at least three HTML files, one for each embedded frame, and one for the frameset itself. The frameset HTML file saves such important information as the frameset properties (such as border size and page title). Other border attributes (such as scrollbar settings) are saved with individual embedded frames.

Caution

Make sure you assign a page title to the frameset. It is a good idea to assign page titles to individual frames in case they are opened independently in a browser window. But it's most important to assign a title to a frameset file, because this is the title that will appear in your visitor's browser title bars. And you don't want that tacky "Untitled" message to appear in their title bars. Assign a title by entering a page name in the Title area at the top of the document window of an open page (or frameset).

The easiest way to make sure you're saving all your editing changes is to save *everything* after you edit a frameset. After you change frameset properties, choose **File, Save All** to save both edited frames, and the frameset file.

The Least You Need to Know

◆ Frames are an effective way to narrow the page display and provide navigation sections of your website.

◆ Avoid more than three frames in page design, they make pages look too crowded.

◆ An easy way to create frames is to first design the pages that will go inside the frame, and then define the frameset.

◆ Links in a navigation frame should almost always be opened in another (main page) frame.

Part 4

Managing Your Assets

Dreamweaver MX includes potent tools to help loosen your page design juices, including preformatted template pages.

Dreamweaver also provides tools for organizing and reusing page design elements.

In the next chapters, I'll show you how to let Dreamweaver help you create good-looking pages in a hurry.

Chapter 11

Page Design Shortcuts

In This Chapter

◆ Organizing your assets

◆ Storing dynamic page content as library items

◆ Designing custom page templates

◆ Orchestrating a site with templates

As I gaze across the chaotic expanse of my office, I often wish for a genie to appear who would gather up all the stacks of junk, make lists of what's in each pile, and produce the file or book I need at my beck and call.

While real life isn't so accommodating, I get Dreamweaver to do that work for me, and so can you. As you design a website, unbeknownst to you, Dreamweaver has been carefully cataloging every picture, every Flash object, every URL you've included, every color you've applied, and more! All this information is stashed in, and available from, the Assets panel.

Counting Up Your Assets

As your site grows in size, you'll find it helpful to use the Assets panel to embed pictures, videos, and other objects into pages. The Assets panel organizes all the objects in your site, and makes them easily accessible.

Using the Assets Panel to Organize and Insert Objects

The Assets panel is an alternative to looking for files in the Site window. The Assets panel organizes and displays all the elements you've used in your website, so you can easily grab them and drag them into a page.

The Assets panel organizes your objects into the following categories:

By the Way _____

There is a special category of assets called Library items. When library objects are plugged into a page, they cannot be edited in the page itself. Instead, they are edited in a special version of the Document window. And, after you change a library object, that object is updated in every page. We'll explore library assets later in this chapter.

◆ **Images**

◆ **Colors**   All the colors you've used in your site—very handy for maintaining a consistent color theme

◆ **URLs**   All the website addresses used in your site, both internal links and external websites

◆ **Flash movies**

◆ **Shockwave files**

◆ **Movies**   (other than Flash)

◆ **Scripts**   JavaScripts, for example

◆ **Templates**   Pages you use to design other pages from

◆ **Library**   Holds library items—a special type of revisable, embedded object

Those categories are displayed (and selected) from a strip of icons on the left side of the Assets panel, shown in Figure 11.1.

Grabbing Assets off the Panel

Many assets can be applied by simply clicking and dragging from the Assets panel into the Document window. For instance, you can drag an image from the Images category of the Assets panel onto a page, as I'm doing in Figure 11.2.

By the Way _____

If a recently added asset does not appear in the Assets panel, click the **Refresh Site List** button in the bottom of the Assets panel.

Similarly, you can drag Flash objects, Shockwave objects, and movies onto your page.

Other assets, including colors, links, and some scripts, are applied to existing text or other objects. To associate one of these assets with an object, select the object (like text or a picture), choose a color, a URL, or some other asset, and click on the **Apply** button in the Assets panel.

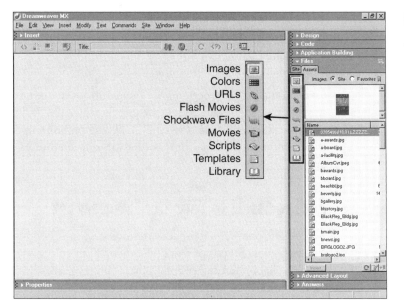

Figure 11.1

Asset categories.

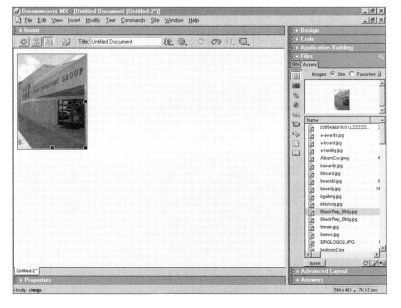

Figure 11.2

Dragging an image from the Assets panel onto a page.

Organizing Assets

Since selected objects in the Assets panel are displayed clearly in the top area of the panel, the Asset panel is often a more convenient way to find files than digging around in the Site menu.

Inside Info

At times, the Full Path column in the Assets panel is helpful in identifying exactly where a file is stashed on your site. However, it's rarely that useful to sort your assets with this column.

Inside Info

The Templates and Library categories do not have a Site and Favorites radio button option. They are different from other assets in that they are user-defined. We'll explore them later in this chapter.

If, for example, you're looking for just the right image to stick on a page, it's usually easier to find it in the Assets panel (Images category) than it is to browse around your site window.

You can make this process easier by taking advantage of the fact that the Assets panel will sort files by name, size (file size), and type (file type). Clicking on either of these column headings will sort files for a selected category.

Adding Assets to Your Site Favorites Set

The Assets panel has two radio buttons on top—Site and Favorites. Since your site may easily have an uncontrollable number of total objects in any category (like hundreds of images, links, or colors), you can refine the set of objects that is displayed by assigning some objects Favorite status.

To make an object a Favorite, click on that object, and click on the **Add to Favorites** icon at the bottom of the Assets panel, as shown in Figure 11.3.

Figure 11.3

Adding an asset to your list of favorites.

You can display your list of favorites by clicking the **Favorites** radio button.

Using the Favorites List to Create a Color Scheme

One of my favorite uses of the Favorites feature (and I favor using this!) is creating a list of (I won't say *favorite*) frequently used colors. This set of colors can function as a color scheme for your site.

To define a four-color color scheme for a site using the Favorites feature in the Assets panel, follow these steps:

1. View your Assets panel.

2. Assign four colors (only) that are used in your site as "favorite" colors.

3. Reformat text color on your Performers page, using all of, and only, the four colors you made favorites. (Assign colors from the Favorites by first selecting text, then dragging a color onto that text, as shown in Figure 11.4).

> **By the Way**
>
> Dreamweaver MX allows you to choose from several sets of prefab color schemes. In most cases you'll want to create your own, but I'll introduce you to the preset color schemes in Chapter 12.

Figure 11.4

Creating a customized color scheme in the Assets panel.

Once you define this color scheme, you can access it easily in the Assets panel from any page in your site.

Libraries—A Special Kind of Asset

Most of the asset categories simply list objects already in your site. Library assets are different. If you've worked with symbols in Flash, you have a good idea how Library assets work.

Library assets are objects that can be embedded many times in a website. If the Library asset is changed, that change is automatically updated throughout the site. Examples of objects that are well suited to being Library assets are:

◆ Company logo

◆ Contact information

◆ Recent news

With any of these examples, the object in question can be placed many times throughout a website, and then revised once. After the Library asset is revised, that change takes place throughout the site.

Creating Library Items

Library items can include images, and also blocks of text. You can create a text library item from scratch right in Dreamweaver. That text block is then "replaceable" throughout the site as needed. Like when your company gets swallowed up by a bigger company and you need to replace 4,987 instance of contact info throughout your site!

Follow the following steps to create a couple of text library items that you can use in your site. In these steps, I'll use the examples of a "contact us" block of text, and a "what's new" block of text. But of course you can substitute other blocks of text.

1. On a blank page, create two paragraphs, a "Contact Us" paragraph providing contact information for your organization, and a "What's New" paragraph updating visitors as to what's new at your organization.

2. In the Assets panel, choose the **Library** category.

3. Click and drag to move the first (Contact Us) paragraph into the Library. Name the Library asset (Contact is a good name).

4. Click and drag to move the second (What's New) paragraph into the Library, and name it as well. Your Library Assets panel should look something like Figure 11.5.

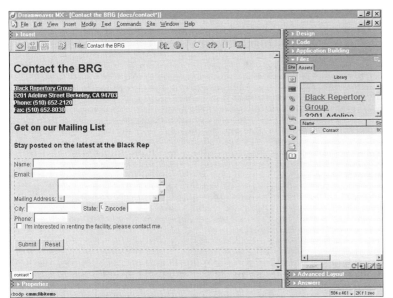

Figure 11.5

Adding text to your Library.

Now you're ready to embed your new Library assets in your site.

Embedding Library Assets

Once you have created Library assets, you can open any page in the Document window, and drag these assets onto those pages.

Any object that has been saved as a library item can be dragged into a page, just like any other asset.

In Figure 11.6, I'm dragging library text onto a page.

> **Inside Info**
>
> You cannot edit the Library assets in the Document window in Dreamweaver. These objects can only be edited in a special Library window. As part of your assignment, do that next.

Changing Library Assets

The real fun in using Library assets is that you can change them *globally* throughout a site.

To change a Library asset, double-click on it in the Assets panel. As you do, you'll open the asset in a special editing window. This window has a gray background, as shown in Figure 11.7.

Figure 11.6

"Borrowing" text from the Library.

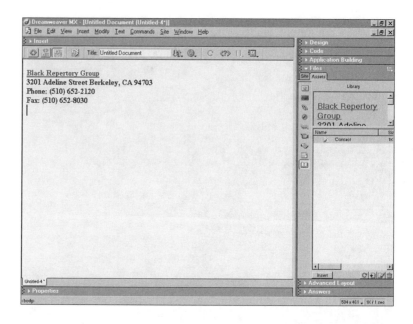

Figure 11.7

This special document window allows you to edit Library text.

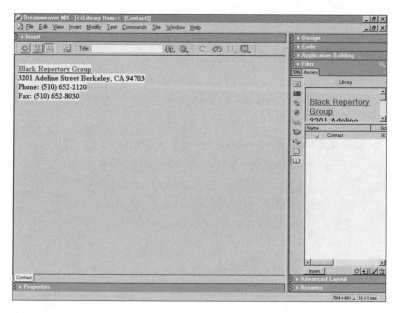

Edit your Library asset, and press **Ctrl+S** to save the changes. You'll be prompted to apply changes you've made to each instance of the Library asset with an Update Library Items dialog box, as shown in Figure 11.8.

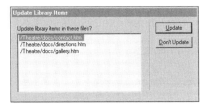

Figure 11.8

Dreamweaver is bragging about all the work it did for you by updating a changed library item.

Click **Update** in the dialog box to update the Library asset throughout your site. The Update Pages dialog box then displays a log of all the pages where the embedded asset has been changed. Click **Close to Then,** close the special editing window (the one with the gray background).

Check out your pages. Note how the assets have changed on all the pages in which they were embedded!

Defining and Using Templates

Templates are useful when you are working on a site that will include many web pages with a similar format. For example, I recently finished a site for a literary agency with a large number of clients. Each client got his or her own web page within the site, and each of those pages had some common elements:

- ◆ A title
- ◆ A photo of the author
- ◆ A photo of the author's most recent book
- ◆ Bio information
- ◆ Contact information

I can create a template page with areas for each of these elements to speed up the process of creating these pages, and to maintain a consistent look and feel. Further, if I elect to turn over some of the page design to an assistant, I can define how the page will look, while entrusting my assistant to plug in content in appropriate places.

By the Way

If you're looking for a way to get Dreamweaver to help you with page design, you're in the wrong chapter. Jump ahead to Chapter 12 where I show you how to use Dreamweaver MX's set of prefab page design templates. The templates we're exploring here are ones you make yourself.

Creating a Template Page

Before you start to apply a page template, you must create one. In the following steps, I'll walk you through the process of creating a simple page template with a few headings, some text, and an image. Feel free to wander from the well-marked path here, and create different or additional template objects.

Follow these steps to create a template:

1. Open a blank page, and choose **File, Save as Template**. From the Site drop-down list, choose a site to which you'll save the template. Enter a name for the template in the Save As area of the Save As Template dialog box, as shown in Figure 11.9.

Figure 11.9

Saving a page as a template.

2. Type a heading at the top of the page, "Heading" and assign **Heading 1** style to this text.

3. Under the top heading, create three Heading 2 style headings: **About This Page, Latest News, Contact Info**.

4. Under each of the three Heading 2 headings, type the words **"text goes here,"** as shown in Figure 11.10.

By the Way

Note that your template shows up in the Assets window, Templates section.

Figure 11.10

Preparing to define an editable region.

5. Select the Heading 1 text at the top of the page and choose **Modify, Templates, New Editable Region.** In the New Editable Region dialog box that appears, enter **"Name"** as shown in Figure 11.11.

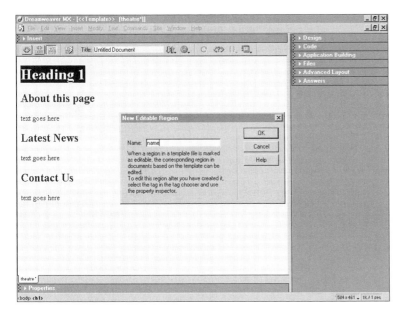

Figure 11.11

This editable region can be changed by other page designers.

6. Define all the other paragraphs on the page as editable regions, and save the page. Your page should look something like Figure 11.12.

7. Add one or two photos to the page layout, and make them editable regions.

Feel free to apply page formatting and design elements to your page. For instance, you could place all the page content in a 600-pixel-wide table. Or, define a page background color (choose **Modify, Page Properties** to do that).

Creating New Pages from Templates

Once you create a template page, you can generate pages from that text. Follow these steps to create one such page, and then try some on your own:

1. Close your template page (saving changes if necessary).

2. Choose **File, New.** In the New Document dialog box, select the **Template tab.** Double-click on the template you just created in the Select Template dialog box, as shown in Figure 11.13.

Figure 11.12

A template page.

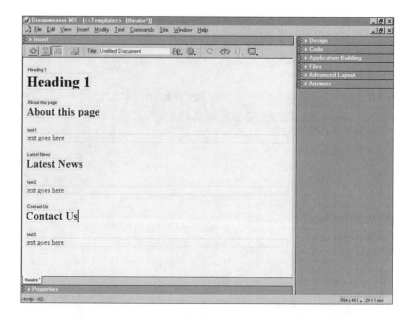

Figure 11.13

Choosing a template page.

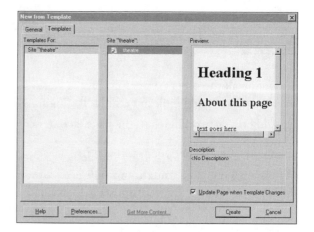

3. Enter text into the template areas.

4. If you included image template objects, replace the images in the template with ones relevant to the page content.

5. Assign a page title in the Title box at the top of the Document window.

6. Save the new page with an .html or .htm file name extension.

Revising a Template Layout

After you use a template to create many pages, you can edit the template, and automatically revise the format of all the pages to which that template was applied.

To revise a template (and all the pages generated from that template) Follow these steps:

1. In the Assets panel, double-click on the template. This opens the template for editing.

2. Change the page format.

3. Save your page. You'll be prompted to update all the pages created with this template (do so).

4. Examine the pages generated from your template. They should all be updated.

The Least You Need to Know

♦ Every color, image, and URL you add to a page is saved by Dreamweaver. You can view this list of saved objects in the Assets panel.

♦ You can drag images, or apply colors and URLs from the Assets panel.

♦ Library items are special assets that can be updated or revised throughout a site.

♦ Dreamweaver comes with a set of prefab template pages. But you can define your own template pages, with editable regions where other designers can plug in text and images.

Automated Web Pages

In This Chapter

◆ Grabbing color schemes from the pros

◆ Designing web photo albums

◆ Recording and playing commands

◆ Saving commands to create a set of macros

◆ Using Dreamweaver commands to format and sort tables

Dreamweaver MX has some handy features that provide assistance in designing web pages. You can rely on expert advice for a page color scheme. You can automate keystrokes to make repetitive tasks easier, and you can use the new Web Photo Album feature to easily display a whole batch of photos.

Picking color schemes from a prefab list, automating tedious commands, and whipping up photo displays automatically might not please hard-core HTML purists, but it *does* make it easier to design pages.

Using Color Schemes

In Chapter 11, I explained how to use the Assets panel to create and store a *color scheme*—a set of colors that you use (and restrict yourself to) as you design a site.

By constraining your colors (for text, background colors, and so on) to a defined set, you provide a global look to your site. Visitors feel like they are gracefully being shuttled from room to room in a house as they navigate your site—encountering the same color scheme in every room.

> **By the Way**
>
> For those who want to dig deeply into the do's and don'ts of web colors, the ultimate guide to managing colors on the web remains *Coloring Web Graphics* by Lynda Weinman and Bruce Heavin.

Why Web-Safe Color Schemes?

The next problem is figuring out a set of nicely matching colors that are also *browser safe*. Browser safe colors are the 216 colors that are reproduced faithfully on the overwhelming majority of operating systems and browsers.

Many modern monitors support millions of colors. Other, older monitors support only the browser-safe set. Therefore, professional web designers restrict themselves to the browser-safe set.

The folks at Macromedia hooked up with web color gurus Lynda Weinman and Bruce Heavin to develop a set of color schemes made up of attractive, browser-safe color sets.

Assigning a Color Scheme

To assign one of the preset color schemes to an open page in the Document window, choose **Commands, Set Color Scheme.** The Set Color Scheme dialog box opens, as shown in Figure 12.1.

Figure 12.1

Choosing from one of Lynda and Bruce's color schemes.

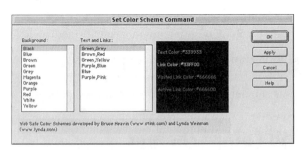

Start by selecting a page background from the Background list in the Set Color Scheme dialog box. As you do, a selection of text and link color sets appear in the Text and Links column of the dialog box. Choose one of the matching text and link color sets. You can use the Apply button in the dialog box to see exactly how the color scheme will appear when applied to your page. Click **OK** to assign the new color scheme.

Cooking Up Web Photo Albums

The Web Photo Album feature in Dreamweaver MX is pretty powerful, and does a lot of work for you. In return, it requires you turn over your first born son. Well, no, not quite, but you do need to purchase another Macromedia application—Fireworks MX—in order to make the Web Photo Album work.

If you're willing to shell out for Fireworks (or you already have it), the Web Photo Album will:

◆ Convert a folder of image files into web-compatible graphic file formats.

◆ Create small *thumbnail* images based on each of your (full size) photos.

◆ Create links from the generated thumbnails to the full sized images.

◆ Lay all your photos out in an attractive web page.

That's quite a bit of work. The Web Photo Album is a nice feature for laying out a family photo album, but it also has commercial use when your web design project requires converting massive numbers of photos to web-ready images.

> **Inside Info**
>
> The color scheme you select is applied (and can be altered) in the Page Properties dialog box. To see page properties, choose **Modify, Page Properties.** The page background, text, and link colors you selected from the color scheme list will be applied to the page properties.

> **Inside Info**
>
> The Web Photo Album works by running a program in the JavaScript language to open Fireworks MX, and to generate both a small (thumbnail) version of each image, as well as a web-compatible duplicate of each image in the selected file. Dreamweaver generates a web page displaying all the thumbnails in a table layout, with links to the larger images.

Organizing Your Files for the Web Photo Shoot

Before you can generate a Web Photo Album, you have to move *all* the image files you want to use into a folder on your local computer. This folder should not contain any additional photos.

You also need a folder to hold the new, generated files that are produced when you create a Web Photo Album. You can create that folder during the process of defining your Web Photo Album, but I find it less confusing to create this second, empty folder in advance.

The photos you place in the first folder (the one you create the Web Photo Album from) can be in any of the following graphic file formats:

- GIF (One of the universally supported web-compatible image formats.)
- JPEG (The other universally supported web image format—can use the jpg or jpeg file name extension for these files.)
- PNG (A format similar to GIF, and widely supported on the web.)
- PSD (Photoshop's proprietary format.)
- TIF (A widely used format for photos and scanned images—files should have a .tif or .tiff file name extension.)

Generating a Web Photo Album

Once you've collected and organized files of supported formats into a folder, you're ready to generate your Photo Album.

To create the Web Photo Album, follow these steps:

1. Choose **Commands, Create Web Photo Album.** The Create Web Photo Album dialog box appears.

2. In the Title area of the dialog box, enter a title for your photo album. This title will appear when your photo album page is generated. You can add extra text to the page by entering it in the Subheading Info and Other Info areas.

3. Click the **Browse** button next to the Source Images Folder area, and navigate to the folder that has the images you collected to use in your photo album. Select the folder with your images.

4. Click the **Browse** button next to the Destination Folder area, and navigate to the folder where Fireworks and Dreamweaver will save the files created for your photo album. Select the folder. The Create Web Photo Album dialog box should look something like Figure 12.2.

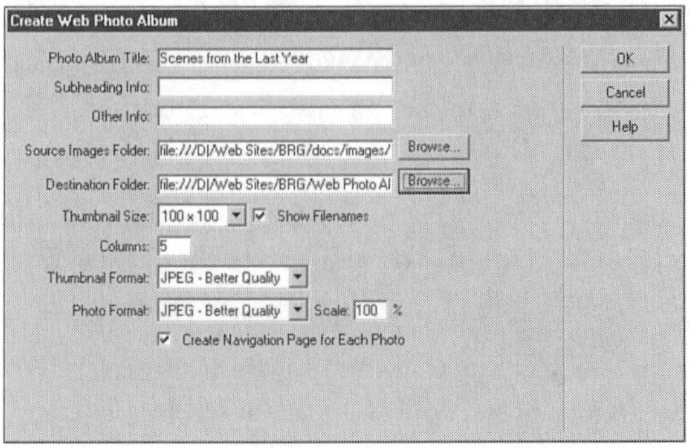

Figure 12.2

Defining a generated photo page display.

5. The Thumbnail Size drop-down list is set by default at 100-pixels square—a good size for thumbnail images. The Show Filenames checkbox will display the name of your image file, and you should leave this selected *only* if you have descriptive file names you want to display.

6. Use the Columns area to define how many table columns you want Dreamweaver to generate to display your photos. For instance, if you have eight photos, it might work well to generate four columns (which would include two rows) to display your pictures.

7. Use the Thumbnail Format and Photo Format drop-down lists to choose a graphic file format for your images. The default JPEG setting is almost always best for displaying photos.

8. It's best to leave the Scale percent set to 100%. This maintains the original size of your full-sized photos.

9. The Create Navigation Page for Each Photo checkbox generates a new web page with each full-sized photo. These generated web pages come with links to help a visitor navigate back to the website.

10. Click **OK** to generate a Web Photo Album. Fireworks will launch (if it is not already open), and you'll see each of the images in your folder open quickly while Fireworks reformats them and creates a thumbnail. After the photo album is generated, you'll see a dialog box telling you the photo album is finished. Click **OK.** The resulting page layout will open in Dreamweaver, and look something like the one in Figure 12.3.

Caution

The folder you specify in step 3 should not have any files in it. Fireworks and Dreamweaver will create files for this folder, and potentially overwrite any existing files.

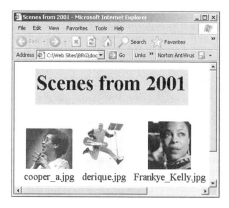

Figure 12.3

This page layout, including the thumbnails, was generated by Dreamweaver and Fireworks.

You can format the table that displays your Web Photo Album—change the table or cell background colors, border thickness and color, spacing, and so on.

Recording and Playing Commands

Recorded commands help you automate sets of steps you repeat often. I often use recorded commands, for example, to assign similar attributes (like size, border, alignment, and so on) to a whole bunch of pictures on a page. Rather than go through the tedious task of defining these attributes over and over, I record a set of commands, and then blast through my page automatically applying the same set of formatting attributes to each image.

It's also possible to save a set of recorded commands, and keep it "on file" for use whenever you need it. In this section, I'll show you how to both record a set of commands, and also to save a set of commands once you've recorded them.

Recording Steps

As I mentioned, I often use recorded commands to format images on a page with the same attributes. Recorded commands can also be used to apply sets of text formatting, or any task you repeat often.

In the following set of steps I'll use the example of applying a set of formatting commands to a bunch of images on a page. Feel free to copy my application of this feature, or adapt the steps to a different use.

1. On a page with a bunch of images, select one of them. Then choose **Commands, Start Recording.**

Inside Info

All the steps you perform from now on will be recorded, until you stop recording. If you leave Dreamweaver, the recorder will "pause" until you return to Dreamweaver. Some procedures are not supported by the recording feature, and if you attempt them, you'll see a dialog box warning you that the step you attempted is not available in (or allowed in) Recording mode. You will be given the option to stop recording or to try a different step.

2. Assign a set of attributes to the image in the Properties panel, like size, border size, a link target, vertical and horizontal spacing, or other features.

3. After you define these image attributes, choose **Commands, Stop Recording.**

4. Select a different image, and choose **Commands, Play Recorded Command.** The steps you recorded will be applied to additional images.

Saving Recorded Keystrokes

The Recorded Command feature just saves one set of commands at a time. If you've recorded a helpful set of keystrokes, you might want to save them, and use them in other documents.

To save the current set of recorded keystrokes, follow these steps:

1. Choose **Window, Others, History** to display the History panel.

2. **Shift+click** to select the set of steps you want to save in the History panel, as shown in Figure 12.4.

Figure 12.4

Selecting steps to save as a command.

3. Click on the **Save Selected Steps as a Command** icon in the bottom of the History panel.

4. The Save As Command dialog box appears, as shown in Figure 12.5. Enter a command name in the dialog box and click **OK.**

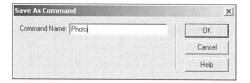

Figure 12.5

Naming a customized command.

Apply Commands

Saved commands appear in the Commands menu, and can be applied to a selected object (like an image or a block of text) by choosing **Commands,** and then clicking on the command. In Figure 12.6, I'm applying a command I defined by recording and saving keystrokes.

Figure 12.6

*Recycling keystrokes with a
saved command.*

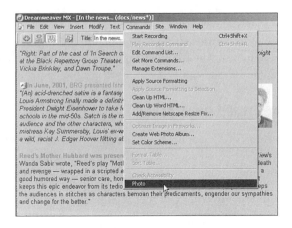

To delete a saved command, choose **Commands, Edit Command List**. The Edit
Command List dialog box appears with a list of all your saved commands.

To delete a command, select it in the Edit Command List dialog box and click on **Delete**.

Formatting Tables—the Quick Way

The Commands menu includes some built-in commands. The most useful of them apply
predefined formatting to tables, and sort tables.

To choose from a variety of nicely designed table formats, choose **Commands, Format
Table.** This opens the Format Table dialog box shown in Figure 12.7.

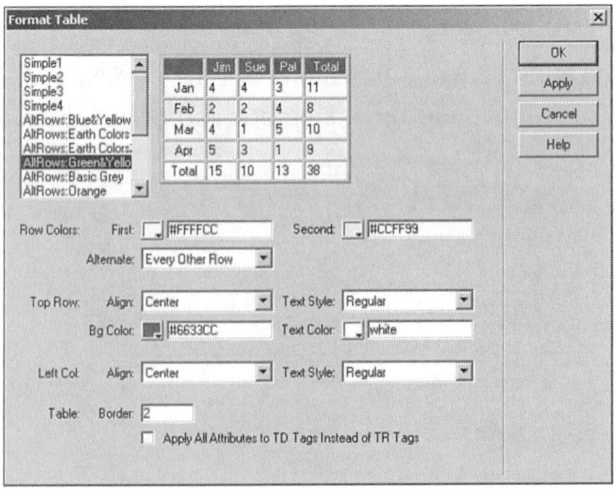

Figure 12.7

*Picking from the set of
predefined table formats.*

From the Format Table dialog box, choose one of the formats from the list in the upper
left corner of the dialog box. You'll see a preview of the table format in the top right section of the dialog box.

Use the color palettes and drop-down lists in the Format Table dialog box to change or fine tune the colors and fonts that come with the preset format you chose. You can test the selected formatting by clicking **Apply,** which displays the selected formatting attributes right on the table in the Document window.

Sorting Tables

Dreamweaver goes well above and beyond the basics of page formatting with its sort tables feature. Sure, one might expect that the folks who send a table over to you for display would have sorted it first. But if they missed the boat on that, you can cover for them by sorting tables right in Dreamweaver.

To sort a selected table, choose **Commands, Sort Table.** This opens the Sort Table dialog box, as shown in Figure 12.8.

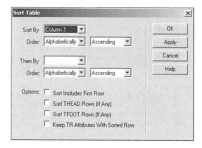

Figure 12.8

Sorting a table.

The Sort Table dialog box allows you to define how you want a table sorted. Use the Sort By drop-down list to choose a column to sort by. Select the Sort Includes First Row checkbox *only* if you do not have a heading row in your table, and you want to *sort all rows* in your table, including the top row.

Use the Order drop-down list to elect to sort Alphabetically or Numerically.

If you want to further sub-sort your selected table by a different column, you can define the second sort options in the Then By area of the Sort Table dialog box. Use a second (Then By) sort criteria, for example, if you want to sort a company directory first by department, and then by employee last name. In that example, you would select the department column in your table in the Sort By drop-down list, and last name in the Then By drop-down list.

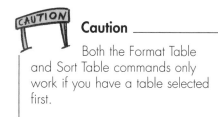

Caution

Both the Format Table and Sort Table commands only work if you have a table selected first.

The Least You Need to Know

◆ Dreamweaver's preset color schemes are attractive and browser safe—so they will display reliably on any browser or operating system.

◆ You can have Dreamweaver create a page layout for a set of photos. You must have the photos in JPEG, GIF, PNG, TIFF, or Photoshop's PSD format first, and you must have Macromedia's Fireworks installed on your computer to use this feature.

◆ You can save yourself repetitive keystroking by recording and playing back sets of keystrokes as commands.

◆ Dreamweaver comes with built-in commands to sort or format a table.

Part 5

Good Form (Input Forms)

Dreamweaver forms can be used as jump menus to let visitors pick a link from a drop-down list. They can also collect data and send it to you via e-mail, or store it in a server database.

MX has massively bulked up what you can do with online data in Dreamweaver. These tools allow you to connect your website to live (constantly updated) data in a database.

In the following chapters, I'll introduce you to all these form-handling and database-managing features.

Chapter 13

May I Have the Input, Please?

In This Chapter

♦ Connecting input to a server

♦ "Borrowing" input forms

♦ Creating your own input forms

♦ Attaching input forms to CGI scripts

♦ Preparing input forms for a server database

Input forms allow you to interact with visitors in a way that turns your website into a two-way street. Not only can you share information with visitors, visitors can share information with you. You can use forms to collect feedback from visitors, to get folks to sign up on your mailing list, or to take orders for a product.

Data collected by your input form can be sent to your server, where it can be relayed to you as an e-mail, or stored in a file on your server. This kind of server information management is called server-side data handling. The advantage of handling data at a server is that it can be stored permanently, while client side data is never sent to a server for permanent storage. Data collected for mailing lists, ecommerce applications, feedback forms, and so on is best managed in a server.

Connecting Input to a Server

When a visitor fills out a form at your site telling you he or she wants to get on your mailing list, share some feedback, or order some bird toys, that information is collected not on your visitor's computer, but on *your* remote web server. That information is then shared with you by e-mail, or by saving the collected data in a file or database.

By the Way

The scripts (small computer programs written in languages like PERL) that manage form data are called CGI scripts. CGI stands for Common Gateway Interface.

Let me emphasize this point, because it's a new concept. Up until now, every Dreamweaver feature we've explored in this book works pretty much the same on your local computer, and on a server. It has not been necessary to even *have* a server connection; you can create a local site and teach yourself Dreamweaver without ever connecting with a server. Of course, nobody could see your site unless you invited them into your home or office, but nevertheless, most features in Dreamweaver work fine on your local computer.

Not so with server-processed form data. The CGI scripts that manage form input data that you want to save are stored on your server. There's no way (setting aside scenarios where you have your own local web server software) to use (or test) CGI scripts on your local computer.

You *can* design forms on your computer. And you can test them in a browser window to the extent of making sure your checkboxes check and your text fields accept text. But you can't actually submit data in a form and collect it without connecting your input form to a server script that will manage the data.

If you have not contracted for server space on a remote server, you will want to do that before you develop input forms for your site. Every web-hosting company provides unique information that is required to connect your forms to CGI scripts at their server. And in several places in this chapter, I'll itemize the information you need from your site provider to connect your form to their CGI scripts.

"Borrowing" Input Forms

Because input forms are one of the more complicated elements of designing web pages, and because they need to be connected with CGI scripts, many web-hosting providers offer preconfigured forms that include all necessary CGI connection information. Web-hosting providers often supply you with a selection of preset forms.

If so, you can simply copy the HTML code they provide you with into Dreamweaver, using the **Edit, Paste HTML** menu option in the Document window.

Figure 13.1 shows a sample input form supplied by Geocities. When you copy the HTML provided for this form into a page, the connection to a server CGI script is already embedded in the HTML code.

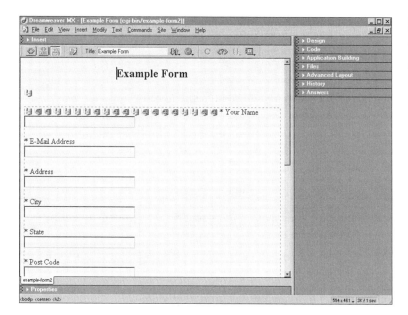

Figure 13.1

This feedback form can be altered in Dreamweaver.

You can do *some* editing to a copied input form. You can change formatting, change field names, and change label text that displays next to fields. Just be sure *not* to change any of the coding that connects the form to the CGI script.

In the next section of this chapter, I'll walk you through creating your own input form. Once you learn to do that, you'll recognize, understand, and be able to edit the form elements that come with prefab forms supplied by web-host providers.

Inside Info

It isn't necessary to switch to Show Code view to paste HTML into Dreamweaver. You can work right in Design view. Just remember to paste HTML, don't use the regular Edit, Paste command to insert copied code.

Creating Your Own Input Forms

Input forms are made up of three main elements:

- ◆ The form
- ◆ Form fields
- ◆ Submit (and Reset) buttons

All three of these elements are required for a form to work. If you place form fields on a page in the document window, and they are not in a form, they won't work! I know, my students have tried that many times. Similarly, a form without fields is no fun either. And no form will work without at least a "Submit" button.

In this section, I'll show you how to create these three elements, one by one.

Creating a Form

Forms appear in the Document window as dashed red lines. You can place a form anywhere in a page in the Document window, but I suggest not placing them at the very top of the page—they're harder to delete up there. And, usually, you'll want some introductory text anyway, like "Thanks for taking the time to tell us how you feel," or "Fill out this form to place an order," and so on.

To create a new form in an open page in the Document window, follow these steps:

1. Near (but best not at) the top of your page, enter some text explaining your form, and inviting a visitor to fill the form out.

2. Choose **Insert, Form.** Dashed red lines appear. These define the form. All form elements must be inside the form lines.

3. Feel free to use tables, either inside the form, or outside the form to control the placement of form objects. I'll return to the use of tables in form design at the end of this chapter.

4. It's easier to define a form if you press Enter once or twice to create some paragraph breaks inside the form. Now you have space to begin adding form fields.

Adding Fields to a Form

Form fields are the way that you actually collect information in a form. Visitors type their name, choose a location from a drop-down list, and click a checkbox (to take examples of three types of form fields) as they provide you with data.

There is a whole psychology to designing forms. And it's a bit beyond the scope of this book. But I'll share a few tips with you:

◆ Keep forms as small as possible, after all, nobody *has* to fill out your form.

◆ Keep options clear.

◆ Whenever possible, collect data in a form field like a drop-down menu or checkbox, instead of having visitors type in data. This allows you to constrain the type of information you collect to that which is going to be useful. And, it helps avoid spelling mistakes (better that *you* let a visitor choose Katmandu from a drop-down list of cities than ask him or her to spell it themselves).

The main form fields used to collect data are text, radio buttons, check boxes, and a drop-down list. Figure 13.2 illustrates all four of these types of form fields.

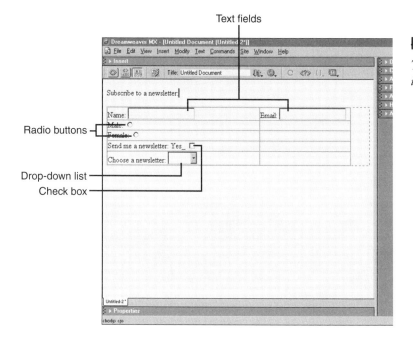

Figure 13.2

This form uses four types of input form fields.

Field Names and Values

I'll go into a little detail on the various types of form fields next, but first, it will be helpful to explain the two things that *all* form fields have: a field name and a value.

The field name is something like "Name," "E-mail," "Country," or "Contact_Me." The field name tells *you* what information you are looking at when you get data input into a form.

The field value is something like "Dave," "dkar-lins@ppinet.com," "USA," or "Yes." This is the information a visitor submits into the form field.

Caution

Remember, form fields only work if they are inside a form! If you don't see dashed red lines (and aren't keeping your form fields inside those dashed red lines) your form isn't gonna work!

Because form data is processed at a remote server, the rules for form field names are strict. Avoid spaces and anything but alphanumeric characters (A-Z, 0-9).

I'll explain how each type of form field is used next.

Types of Form Fields

Different types of form fields are used to collect different types of information. For instance, a text field is good for collecting an e-mail address, but if you want to find out which credit card a visitor is using, you might want to provide a drop-down list instead. Below, I've listed the available types of input form fields.

- **Text Fields** are used to collect either one line of text (like a name or e-mail address).

- **Text Areas** are used to collect multiple lines of text, like comments, complaints, and other freestyle submissions from visitors.

- **Check Boxes** have two states—checked or not checked. You can have as many check boxes as you wish in a form, and they have no connection to each other (so visitors can check or uncheck any checkbox).

- **Radio Buttons** must be created in groups. The best way to do this is to create one radio button, and then copy it several times. The radio button name must be the same for every button in the group, while the checked value should be different. Dreamweaver MX has a nice feature that generates radio buttons in groups.

- **List Menus** are like navigation jump menus, except that they collect data and send it to a server. Insert a List Menu, and click on List Values in the Properties panel to define menu options.

- **File Field** form objects allow visitors to navigate to a file and upload it along with the rest of the form data. Note: These fields are *not* supported by the Geocities CGI scripts and will cause your input form to not work.

- **Hidden Fields** are a way for you to embed information in a field that will be sent to the server without any input from the visitor.

Inserting Fields

Regardless of the type of field, you insert them from the menu into the form. In the scenario below, I'll walk you through the process of building a sign-up form that uses some, but not all of the available types of form fields.

Follow these steps to add form fields to a form, creating a sign-up form:

1. With your cursor inside the form, choose **Insert, Form Objects, Text Field.**
2. Type the text "**Name**" to the left of the new text field.
3. Click on the new text field, and view the Properties panel.
4. In the Properties panel, enter **Name** in the text field area.
5. Create a similar text field but name it E-mail.

6. Choose **Insert, Form Objects, Check Box.** Use the Properties Inspector to name this field Contact.

7. Type "**Contact me**" to the right of the checkbox.

8. Enter **Yes** in the Checked Value area of the Properties Inspector.

9. Type "**Comments**" inside your form and press **Enter.**

10. Select the new text field, and use the Properties Inspector to select the **Multiline** radio button. Name the field Comments, and change the Char Width to 60 and the Num Lines to 3.

By the Way _____

This is the information that will display in your database, or e-mail message, when a visitor selects the checkbox.

If you followed these steps, you'll have a form that looks something like the one in Figure 13.3.

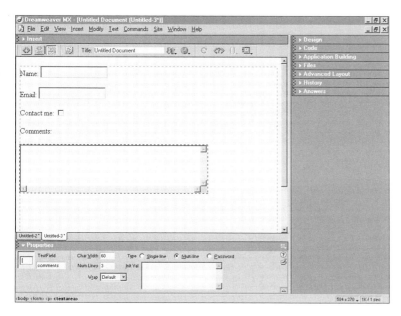

Figure 13.3

A typical sign-up form.

Radio Buttons Travel in Groups

Radio buttons are an odd type of form field in that they must be grouped to be useful. Think of the buttons on your car radio. You can only choose one button (station) at a time. Thus, the "radio button" metaphor.

Use radio buttons when you want to restrict a visitor to choosing just one from a set of options. Can't you do that with a drop-down list? Yes, you can! And therefore radio buttons and drop-down lists are similar.

Examples of using radio buttons include when you want a visitor to rate your site on a scale of 1-5 (but to just choose one value), or when you want a visitor to tell you if he or she is using MasterCard, VISA, Diner's Club, or American Express.

Inside Info

This group name will be the same for each radio button. Later, if you view (or edit) a radio button in the Properties panel, you'll see that each button in the group has the same name. This is necessary to make the radio buttons function together.

To add radio buttons to a form, follow these steps:

1. Choose **Insert, Form Objects, Radio Group**. The Radio Group dialog box appears.

2. Enter a name in the Name area of the Radio Group dialog box.

3. Double-click on the first radio button label, and enter a new label.

4. Double-click on the first radio button value, and enter a new value. Each radio button within a group will have its own unique value, which can be a number or text.

5. Enter a label and value for the second radio button.

6. Use the "+" sign to add additional radio buttons.

7. After you've defined all the radio buttons for the group, choose either Line Breaks or Table from the set of radio buttons at the bottom of the Radio Group dialog box. Line breaks separate radio buttons into separate (single spaced) lines, and the Table option lays out your group of radio buttons in a vertical table.

After you generate a group of radio buttons, you can edit the generated labels right in the Document window, and you can edit the checked Values in the Properties panel, as shown in Figure 13.4.

You can also elect to make one of the buttons in a group of radio buttons selected by default. To do that, select the checked radio button in the Initial State area of the Properties Inspector for a selected radio button.

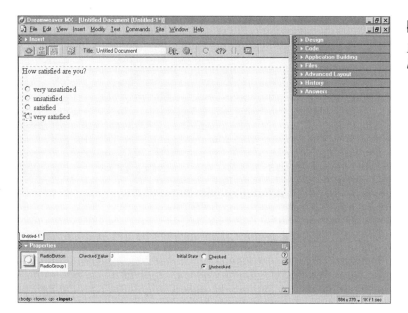

Figure 13.4

Editing a generated radio button.

Adding Buttons

One more step before your form will work! You have a form, and form fields. But you need a submit button before the data will go anywhere.

Forms often contain a second button—a *reset* button. This button clears all existing form content, and allows a visitor to "start over" filling out the form.

To add submit and reset buttons to an existing form, follow these steps:

1. With your cursor inside your form (and almost always at the bottom), chose **Insert, Form Objects, Button.** By default, this button is a submit button, with a label that says "Submit."

2. Insert a second button, and use the Properties panel to change this to a Reset Form button, as shown in Figure 13.5.

3. You can customize the label on your button if you wish in the Label area of the Properties panel for any selected button.

Now that you've created a form, inserted form fields, and added a submit button, your form is finished. But you still need to make it work with a CGI script at your remote server if you actually want to collect and store any data.

> **Inside Info**
>
> In many environments, the work of the web designer is done at this point, and database specialists take over and configure the form to connect with a CGI script. In other cases, where you are managing site development from beginning to end, you will need to configure the CGI connection yourself.

Figure 13.5

Adding a submit and reset button to the form.

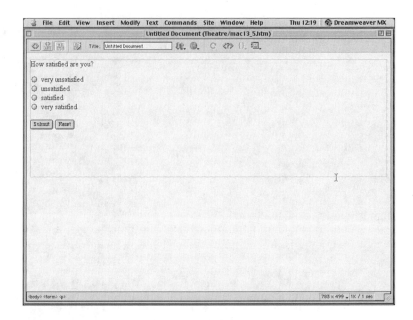

Connecting Your Form to a Server CGI Script

The information you need to connect a form to a server-side CGI script is provided by your server provider. Or, in some cases, they will provide you with instructions on how to add your own CGI scripts to your site.

Inside Info

There are many sites on the Internet that provide free CGI scripts that can be copied and pasted into a folder at your server. Some of these folks have additional services you can pay for where they connect the CGI scripts for you.

The CGI script itself is either provided for you by your web-host provider, or your web-host provider will give you information on how to copy CGI scripts available on the Internet into a special CGI folder at your site.

To be clear: *You* don't write CGI scripts. Techies do. If your web-host provider is worth much, they will have some CGI scripts already set up that you can connect to. If they're not worth much, they'll supply you with instructions for copying CGI scripts you get on the Internet into a folder at your site.

When you connect to a CGI script in Dreamweaver, you don't need to know diddly about CGI, or what kind of code is in your script. All you need to know is the folder at your site that contains the CGI script. That is the information you want to get from your web-host provider.

Once you know where your CGI script is stored at your server, you can direct the form to that script. I'll walk you through that in the following steps:

1. Click on the form tag selector for the form (<form>) at the bottom of the document window to select your form.

2. In the Form Name area in the Properties panel, type a name for your form. This information will appear when you get e-mail with form submissions.

3. In the Method area, choose **POST.** This is almost always the method used to upload data to a server. If your web-host provider has given you other instructions for connecting to your CGI script, follow those instructions.

4. In the Action area, type the path to your script. My path looks like Figure 13.6.

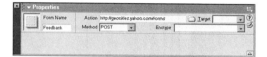

Figure 13.6

Entering CGI script information in the Form Properties panel.

After you define the CGI script connection, save your page and upload (PUT) it to your server.

You can't test your input form by previewing your page, you will need to Put (upload) your page to the server, and test the form there.

If your form uses a simple script to send data to your e-mail address, you'll get input data sent that looks something like what I got in Figure 13.7.

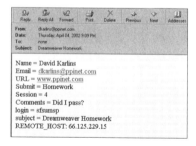

Figure 13.7

Data collected in a form, and sent via e-mail.

Form Design Tips

Good looking forms use table rows and columns to align form fields and labels.

By placing labels and form fields in cells, you can have them line up evenly, and provide even spacing between labels and form fields.

Use color in your table background, cell backgrounds, and cell borders to liven up your form. Forms have a rep for being a bit dull, so use creative coloring to make your form inviting.

Figure 13.8 shows a form where table cells control field location and add color.

Figure 13.8

Forms look neater when you align form fields with table cells.

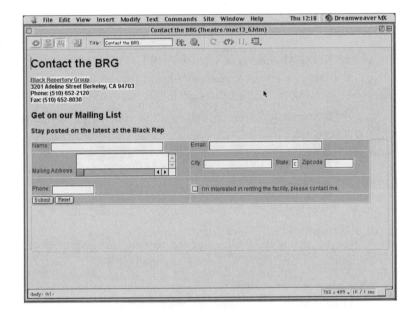

The Least You Need to Know

- ◆ To collect data in a form, the form must have a form defined, at least one (and usually several) form field, and a submit (and usually a reset) button.
- ◆ Form fields must be inside the form or they won't work. If you don't see a dashed red line on your page, you aren't putting fields in a form properly.
- ◆ Form field types include text boxes, text areas, radio buttons, check boxes, and drop-down lists.
- ◆ Forms are connected to a server using information provided by your web-host provider.

Chapter 14

Jump Around with Forms

In This Chapter

- ◆ Using scripts to process form data in a browser
- ◆ Validating form input
- ◆ Creating jump menus
- ◆ Tweaking jump menu behaviors
- ◆ Using jump menus with frames

In Chapter 13, I showed you how to create forms that collect data that is sent to a server. The server then sends that data to you in an e-mail or saves it in an online data file.

In this chapter, I'll show you how to use forms to process data right in a visitor's browser. This data is not saved permanently on a server, but is used to produce "instant results." We'll explore two examples of processing data in a browser—validation scripts that test data before it's sent to a server, and jump menus that work as navigation tools.

Client-Side What?

In Chapter 13, the emphasis was on collecting valuable data like sign-up lists, visitor feedback, or orders for products and services. It's obvious that you might well want to save some of that collected data and reuse it—to fill orders, to respond to feedback, etc.

In this chapter, I'll show you how to collect data in a form that you will never see. This process of collecting temporarily data is called *client-side* form processing.

Why Would You Want to Throw Away Valuable Data?

Why would anyone in their right mind want to collect data in a form and then "forget" it right away? Let's look at two examples, validation forms and jump menus.

Client side processing is used for validation forms that test form data before it is submitted to a server. If you want to make sure that every submitted form has the e-mail address filled out, you can test the form right in a visitor's browser and make sure that he or she has filled out the e-mail form before that data is submitted. If there is no e-mail address in the form, a client-side script can reject that form. This isn't information you really need to save, or even know about. But it will act on form data to ensure that forms that do get submitted are complete.

In Figure 14.1, a visitor has filled out a form incorrectly. The warning that appears is a result of client-side form processing.

Figure 14.1

Rejected! This form was busted by a validation script.

Another example of client-side data processing is a jump menu. A visitor chooses a web page from a drop-down list (which is a type of *form*), and zap—he or she *jumps* to a new web page. Again, it's not critical that their selection be saved for eternity, the point is to get them from page A to page B.

Figure 14.2 shows a jump menu at work.

Figure 14.2

Using a jump menu to navigate a site.

How Does Client Side Processing Work?

The short answer to this question is, "who cares, that's what I spent all that good money on Dreamweaver for." And that's a *good* answer.

The longer answer is that when you create a jump menu or a validation script, Dreamweaver generates JavaScript code.

JavaScript is a programming language supported by all modern web browsers. It's a language that runs right in the browser, as opposed to the PERL based CGI scripts I touched on in Chapter 13, which run on a server.

Inside Info

Some very old web browsers do not support JavaScript, and so Dreamweaver created jump menus and validation scripts will not work on those browsers. Out-of-date browsers that fail the JavaScript test include AOL's browser up to version 3, and Internet Explorer versions 1 and 2. The installed base of those prehistoric browsers is so low that web developers generally feel save including JavaScript elements in all sites.

Why Learn JavaScript?

Millions of people were endowed by their creator with the inclination and aptitude to study this wondrous scripting language, and I wasn't one of them. That's why I let Dreamweaver generate JavaScript for me.

Still, it's kind of fun to take a look at the JavaScript that gets generated when you create a jump menu or validation script. If you want to peruse the JavaScript you produce, click on **Show Code** view to see what it looks like. Figure 14.3 shows some generated JavaScript from a validation script. And that's the *last* you and I are going to talk about JavaScript.

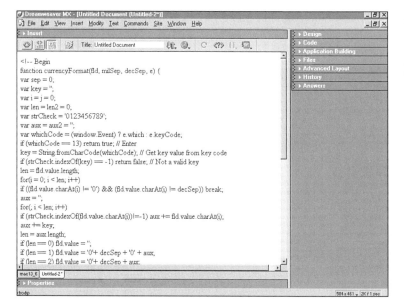

Figure 14.3

You don't need to learn JavaScript—Dreamweaver will create it for you.

Figure 14.4

The Behaviors panel can be used to assign validation scripts.

Adding Validation Scripts to a Form

Validation scripts prevent visitors from submitting data that isn't going to be very helpful. After all, do you really want to get an order from a client who hasn't provided a shipping address?

If an order requires a VISA number, or if visitor feedback requires an e-mail to reply to, you can use a validation script to make sure those form fields are completed before a form is submitted.

Creating a Validation Test

To apply a validation test to a form field, first click on that field in a form. Then, with the field selected, choose **Window, Behaviors** to open the Behaviors panel.

The Behaviors panel opens as an empty panel, with a "+" and a "-" sign in the upper left corner. The bulk of the panel has two columns: actions and events, as shown in Figure 14.4.

With your form field selected, and the Behaviors panel open, click on the "+" symbol at the top of the Behaviors panel and choose **Validate Form** from the list of behaviors. The Validate Form dialog box opens as shown in Figure 14.5, with the selected form field listed in the Named Fields area.

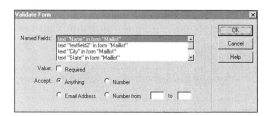

Figure 14.5

Defining validation options for a selected field.

To require that the selected field have some input, select the **Required** checkbox in the Validate Form dialog box.

To restrict the type of input, use the radio buttons in the Accept area of the Validate Form dialog box. Use the Number radio button to restrict input to numbers (for instance, to collect zip codes). Use the Number From areas to define a high and low value for numbers (for instance, if you are collecting a visitor's age, and only visitors over the age of 18 are allowed to submit the form, you can enter 18 in the first Number From field, and 150 (or some other high number) in the second Number From field.

Use the Email Address radio button to test input to make sure it is in a correct format for an e-mail address.

After you apply validation tests to all the appropriate fields in your form, you can save your page.

> **Inside Info**
>
> I emphasized in Chapter 13 that input forms cannot really be tested until they have been PUT (uploaded) to a server. However, you can test validation scripts in a browser using the Preview in Browser feature, since validation scripts are run right in the browser.

Changing Validation Tests

Once you generate a validation script, editing it is a little—uh, shall we say—"unintuitive?" You need to dig a bit into the Behaviors panel to tweak an existing validations script. Here's how:

1. Select the **Form** field to which the validation script was applied in the Document window.

2. Choose **Window, Behaviors** to view the Behaviors panel. The Behaviors panel will display an event in the Events column "onBlur," and an action in the Actions column "Validate Form."

3. Double-click on **Validate Form** in the Actions column of the Behaviors panel. The Validate Form dialog box opens.

4. The Validate Form dialog box is just like the dialog box you used to define the validation test originally. You can change or remove validation here.

5. After you edit the settings for your validation script, click **OK** to close the Validation Form dialog box.

You can test your revised validation test in a browser.

Creating a Jump Menu

Jump menus are an attractive navigation option. They don't take much space on a page, and allow you to provide many navigation options in a small space.

Jump menus are often effective in framesets, where one frame is used as a navigation frame.

Generating a Jump Menu

Dreamweaver generates the JavaScript necessary to create a drop-down list that serves as a navigation object.

There are, theoretically, a few options to trigger a jump in a jump menu. That is, supposedly you can decide if you want to make visitors click a "Go" button before they jump to the navigation target they select in the jump menu, or you want to just have the jump occur as soon as a visitor selects a link from the drop-down list.

Inside Info

Don't worry about the "onBlur" thing in the Events column. This is a reference to the act of leaving a form field. It means that the validation test will be applied when a visitor leaves the selected field—either by clicking in another field or by pressing the tab key.

Caution

When you rely on a jump menu in one frame to open a link in a second frame, you have to pay attention to defining a correct link target for your jump menu options. For a review of defining link targets in frames, jump back to Chapter 10. For a full discussion of links and link targets in general, flip back to Chapter 6.

I find that the *only* really reliable way to have your jump menu work in all browsers is to define the jump to occur when a visitor selects a target from the list (as opposed to having him or her click a "Go" button). So, in the following steps, I'll have you create the jump menu that way.

To create a jump menu, follow these steps:

1. On any page in your site (or a new page), choose **Insert, Form Objects, Jump Menu.**

2. In the Insert Jump Menu dialog box, Use the Browse button to navigate to the first link that will appear in the Jump menu list. Double-click on the link.

3. Dreamweaver will generate default text for your link in the Text area based on the page title of the link you defined. You can change this if you wish in the Text area of the dialog box.

4. Click the **+** symbol at the top of the Insert Jump Menu dialog box, and use the Browse button to navigate to your next navigation option. Choose a target frame or window for the link in the Open URLs drop-down list.

5. Continue to add more navigation options. You can reorder the options by using the Up and Down triangle/arrows at the top right of the Insert Jump Menu dialog box. The Move Item Up in List arrow (pointing up) moves a selected list menu item higher on the list. The Move Item Down in List arrow (pointing down) moves the selected item lower in the list.

6. Leave the two checkboxes at the bottom of the Insert Jump Menu dialog box unchecked. This will produce a more reliable jump menu that is triggered by a visitor selecting an option in the list you are creating. Your dialog box will look something like Figure 14.6.

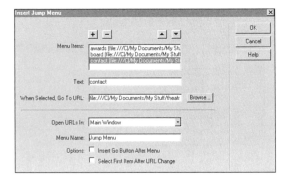

Figure 14.6

Defining a jump menu.

7. Click **OK** to finalize your jump menu options.

After you create your jump menu, test it. You can preview your page in a browser, and test your navigation jump menu.

Inside Info

One technique sometimes used by designers is to create a jump menu list option with text like "Navigate this site" and list that first, so it shows in the jump menu before a visitor clicks the down arrow to see all the available options. The "Navigate this site" option can either be linked to the site home page, or linked to no page at all (in which case it won't function as a link, it will just be display text).

Editing a Jump Menu

Editing a jump menu requires reopening the Jump Menu dialog box, and you can only do this through the Behaviors panel.

OK, I lied. You can *kind of* edit a selected jump menu in the Properties panel, but this has such frustratingly limited editing options that we're not even going to go there.

To change links or other settings in a jump menu, follow these steps:

1. Select the Jump Menu in the Document window.

2. Choose **Window, Behaviors** to view the Behaviors panel. The Behaviors panel will display an event in the Events column "onChange," and an action in the Actions column "Jump Menu."

3. Double-click on the Jump Menu text in the Actions column of the Behaviors panel. The Jump Menu dialog box opens, as shown in Figure 14.7.

Figure 14.7

Revising a jump menu.

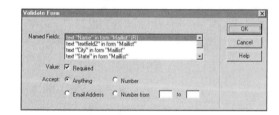

4. The Jump Menu dialog box is similar to the Insert Jump Menu dialog box. You can select a menu option, and use the "-" button to delete it. Or, you can use the Move Item Up in List or Move Item Down in List icons in the dialog box to change the order of list options. You can also edit the text or the Go to URL areas of the dialog box.

5. After you edit the settings for your jump menu, click **OK** to close the Jump Menu dialog box.

You can test your revised jump menu by previewing your page in a browser, and then return to the Jump Menu dialog box as often as needed to update or tweak your jump menu.

The Least You Need to Know

◆ Some form data is handled right in a visitor's web browser. It is not saved to a server.

◆ You can define validation scripts for input forms that test data in a browser before the form is submitted to a server.

◆ You can generate jump menus in Dreamweaver that are handy navigation tools. Dreamweaver creates the necessary JavaScript.

◆ You can edit an existing jump menu in the Behaviors panel.

Connecting to an Online Database

In This Chapter

◆ How Dreamweaver MX connects online data to your site

◆ Connecting your site to a server-based database

◆ Presenting live data in your Dreamweaver pages

◆ Sorting and filtering records

Dreamweaver MX is really two programs in one. Packed into MX is what used to be called UltraDev, a powerful program for creating online databases. Now, Dreamweaver MX allows you to display live (constantly updated) data in your web pages.

Mixing up live online database connections requires the assistance of folks who are experts at both databases and server management. If that's you, you're in business. For the rest of us, if you can find a database expert and a server administrator to hang with you while you set up your connections, you can display information from an online database right in Dreamweaver web pages. All it takes is a little help from your friends.

What's an Online Database, and How Does Dreamweaver Connect?

After hacking my way through enough Dreamweaver database hookups to give me a big headache, I'm reminded of the old Steve Martin joke about how to make a million dollars, and not pay any taxes.

Steve would start out by promising the audience the he had a surefire way to make a *million* dollars! And not pay any taxes. Well, the next line in the routine was, "OK, first get a million dollars, then I'll tell you how to not pay any taxes."

In somewhat the same way, I'll promise to show you how to display online data in Dreamweaver. Only thing is, I'm not going to show you how to create the database, or how to put it on a remote web server. That, I'm afraid, is the job of whoever writes books about online databases.

Inside Info
Okay, I'm exaggerating a little. I won't go into detail on how to set up an online database in this chapter. If you and/or your friendly database programmer have a basic idea of how to do that, you might be able to navigate your data onto your server based on what you find in this chapter. But for those readers who aren't comfortable with setting up an online database, I seriously advise you to have a database expert and a server honcho handy—at least for a few hours while you make your first connection. After that, you'll be able to manage the display of data yourself.

For those not familiar with the concept, a *database* is a collection of information. A database might be a directory of everyone in your organization, or it might be a list of products available. In essence, a database is a list of people, places, or things.

Databases are organized into fields and records. Fields are categories of information, like "Name," or "Product." Records are the individual items in the list. So, for instance, if your database stores a list of personnel at your company, each person is considered a record in the database. And if your database is keeping track of products, each product is a record.

When you embed a database in your website, visitors to your site can access the information in that database. Complex online databases are used to process orders through shopping cart programs. Other, highly complex databases are used to look up locations and provide directions, or present a list of movies in your neighborhood. That level of database programming goes way beyond what even an expert would do with Dreamweaver.

On the other hand, if you feel comfortable with the basics of managing a database, and you can get some help (which I'll walk through shortly), you can use Dreamweaver to incorporate database information in your web pages.

How Dreamweaver Makes the Hookup

Dreamweaver defines a live hookup between data saved in a database program (like Microsoft's Access), and your web page. That means that if you add a product to your database, or change an employee's e-mail in your database, that information is automatically updated online. And visitors see up-to-the-minute information at your site.

In order for Dreamweaver to display this kind of live data, the database file must not be stored on your local computer (where nobody will have access to it), but instead on a server that the web server has access to.

Posting a database to your web server is a lot more complicated than posting an HTML page, an image, or even a media file. In order to actually make a connection between your web pages and the information in the database, that database file needs to be defined on your web server as something called a *DSN*.

Making the Connection

You need several things to connect a database to a Dreamweaver website that you can't create in Dreamweaver. If you want to embed live data in a Dreamweaver site, you'll want to have all the elements in place before you start. I call them the *four needs*.

You need a *database* on your web server, preferably one created in Microsoft Access, with all the tables that you'll need to present information from that database.

> **Inside Info**
>
> The database only has to be on a server that the web server has access to. For security purposes, server administrators will not want to put database server software on the same web server that hosts your website.

> **Definition**
>
> **DSN** stands for data source name. This DSN tells your server how to connect to a database. DSNs use something called an open database connectivity driver (ODBC) to make this connection.

> **Definition**
>
> **Databases** can contain vast amounts of data. That information is broken down into tables. Each table holds some of the data in a larger database.

You need a DSN for your online database defined at your server. This is a job for your database guru and your server administrator. Make good friends with both of these folks, because you're very likely going to be spending some quality time on the phone with them as they help you get your database connection set up.

You need to know the path to the DSN file at your server. Once your database expert sends the database over to the web honcho, one or both of them need to provide you with a URL (web address) or a domain name and database name that leads to the file.

Finally, *you need* folders at your server that store your database configured so they support one of the scripting languages used by Dreamweaver to connect with a database. Those scripting languages are:

- ASP.
- ColdFusion.
- JSP.
- PHP MySQL.

As part of the preparation process of connecting Dreamweaver to an online database, you need to make sure your server administrator has set up a folder in your website that supports one of these scripting languages, and that allows you to access a database. Your server administrator will then need to let you know which scripting language is in place.

If your database has a DSN assigned, the database file is in a folder on your server, and that folder supports scripting, then you're ready to display content from that database in your website.

Inside Info

While defining a DSN is beyond the scope of this book, it might be within reach for those of you who are comfortable with some of the Windows operating systems. If you are using Windows 95, Windows 98, Windows 2000 Professional Edition, or Windows XP Professional, those operating systems come with built-in test servers, as well as features that allow you to define your own DSN, and you can find instructions for doing this using the help features of your operating system. You then need to activate the server software that comes with these operating systems, and copy your database into a folder in the server if you want to connect it with Dreamweaver on your own local computer.

Displaying Data in Dreamweaver

The first step in presenting data in Dreamweaver web pages is to define a connection between your site and the database DSN. When you create a new site, if you tell Dreamweaver that you are going to be using a live database connection, the setup wizard prompts you for information about that connection. I'm going to assume that you haven't already defined your connection to a database, and you've got an already existing site open.

Once you get your site connected to a database, the next step is to configure a page in your site to display that data. After that comes the fun part. After your site is hooked into a database, and your page is connected to that data, you can share information from that database with the world. The following sections will walk you through each step of this process.

Plug Your Database into Your Site

Even after you have your database file correctly copied to your server, defining the connection requires a lot of technical server assistance. Here again, I earnestly advise you to have your server administrator sitting next to you or on the phone with you while you go through this process so he or she can help guide you through the connectivity maze.

Does your administrator have a comfortable chair and a large cup of strong black designer-brand coffee? If so, you're ready to make the database connection.

With an existing site open, you can edit your site definition to include server connection information. To do this, choose **Site, Edit Sites.** Choose the site you want to change, and click, on **Edit.**

Select the Advanced Tab of the Site Definition dialog box, and follow these steps to define your database hookup.

1. In the Local Info category tab, you'll see the information you've entered that defines the connection info to your local folder (for more on setting up a local Dreamweaver site, see Chapter 1.

2. In the remote info category, you've already defined the connection to your remote server. If you need help with this part of the connection, check back to Chapter 2 and Chapter 3.

3. Select the Testing Server category. In the Server Model drop-down list, enter the server program used. This is part of the information you need to obtain from your server administrator.

> **Inside Info**
>
> If your server model is ASP, you can generally select ASP VBScript if your administrator has not specified a type of ASP to use.

4. From the Access drop-down list, choose **local network** or **FTP**. This is part of the information on connecting to your DSN file that you need to get from your server administrator.

5. In the Testing Server Folder box, enter the path to the folder with your site. You'll probably want to consult with your server administrator for this information.

6. You don't need to check the Refresh Remote File List Automatically, you can use the Refresh button in the Site window to update file lists as needed.

7. In the URL Prefix area, enter the http:// address (or IP address). Obviously, your settings will differ from mine, but your site definition should look something like the one in Figure 15.1.

Figure 15.1

Creating a connection between your site and a database.

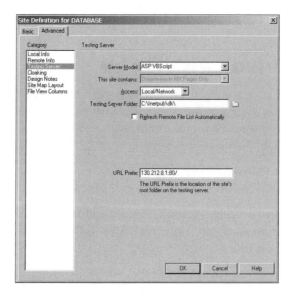

Connecting Your Database with a Web Page

If you've made it this far, give yourself a hug. You're half way home. The next part of the journey is to connect a page in your site with the database, and decide what information to present.

The web pages you use to present live data have a different filename extension than other pages. For instance, if your server is using ASP as the scripting language to maintain your database links, pages that contain live data will have an ASP extension. Pages might be named index.asp, data.asp, and so on.

When you create a new page in a folder that your server administrator has designated to support a server script, Dreamweaver will automatically assign an appropriate extension (like ASP) to those files.

The first step in presenting live data, then, is to create a new page with an appropriate filename extension. Do this by selecting the folder in your Site window with your database, and choosing **File, New File** in the Site Window menu.

If the new page does not have a script filename extension assigned by default (like ASP), contact your server administrator. Dreamweaver is not finding support for a script in the database folder.

With your database web page open, the next part of the process is defining a connection between that page and your database. To do that, follow the steps below.

1. Choose **Window, Databases** to display the Databases panel group.

2. Select the **Databases** panel within the panel group. Click on "**+**" and choose **Data Source Name (DSN)** to begin to define a database connection to the open page. The Data Source Name (DSN) dialog box opens.

3. In the Connection Name area of the Data Source Name (DSN) dialog box, make up a name that will help you remember which database you are connecting to. Stick to letters and numbers for this name, and don't use spaces.

4. Consult your server administrator as to whether your database is on a Local DSN or Using DSN On Testing Server, and click the appropriate radio button.

5. In the Data Source Name drop-down list, select a DSN. If you've correctly connected your site to a database in the previous section, you'll see a list of available databases (maybe just one). Your Data Source Name (DSN) dialog box should look something like Figure 15.2.

Figure 15.2

The DSN info comes from your database manager. The connection info comes from your database guru.

Inside Info

If there are no databases listed, you need to go back to the previous section and make sure the server settings connecting your site to your database were defined correctly. This is one of the hardest things to do in Dreamweaver, because it really does require a team of people who are proficient in Dreamweaver MX (that's you!) configuring your server and managing your database. That's why you spent all that money on designer coffee for your server administrator and database guru.

6. Generally, no user name or password is required. After you've entered a connection name and defined your data source, click **OK.**

You're close to home now. You've connected your database to your site, and you've connected the database to your web page. Before you can start displaying information, you need to choose what's called a *recordset.*

Definition

A **recordset** is a subset of all the records in your database. Here's where you'll choose from one of the database tables created by the database programmer. If you run into trouble in this next part, you might want to consult with your database guru on what information is in which table within the database. But you might well be able to figure that out as you go without help.

To define a recordset to display on a page, follow these steps:

1. Select the **Bindings** tab in Database panel group.

2. Click the "**+**" symbol, and choose **RecordSet** Query.

3. In the Name area, make up a name for your recordset. Don't use spaces or special characters.

4. In the Connection drop-down list, choose the connection you named and created in the previous set of steps in this section. If your connection is valid, a set of fields will display in the Columns area, as shown in Figure 15.3.

Figure 15.3

A peek at the fields that will be available with your selected recordset.

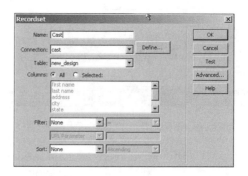

5. Use the Table drop-down list to choose one of the tables in your database. Since a list of fields will appear in the Columns area, you can get an idea of what information is included in each table if there are more than one.

6. Choose the **All Columns** radio button to access all data columns. You can exclude some data columns (fields) later if you wish, so select All now.

7. For now, leave the Filter and Sort drop-down lists set to None. Filtering and sorting data is cool, but we'll get to that later.

8. Click **OK** to close the Recordset dialog box.

Presenting Live Data in Tables

Whew! Connecting your database to your site, and then to a page took a lot of work! Now comes playtime. You get to display live data on your pages.

Data is almost always displayed on web pages in tables. Tables allow you to list information from a database in rows and columns for easy reading. So, the first step in displaying data is to create a table.

Data tables are generally two rows. The first row is used to display field names, like "Name," "Address," or "Product." That way, visitors know what it is that's being listed in the column on the table.

> ### Inside Info
>
> If the first row in a database table displays column headings, why is there *just one* additional row? The reason is that you'll use Dreamweaver to change that one row into an unlimited number of rows to display all the records you want to present on the page. I'll show you how to do that shortly.

You'll need one column in your database table for each field you want to display. So, if you're displaying name, department, and e-mail address for people in your organization, you'll need three columns in the table.

At the top of each column in your table, enter the field name you want to display that will describe the contents of that column. Figure 15.4 shows a table ready to display name, address, and phone information.

You're free to use all the wonderful table formatting tools covered in Chapter 7 to make your table look really spiffy. But since we're so focused on creating a database connection, I'm not going to worry about that right now.

To display data in a table, follow the steps below.

1. Select the **Bindings** panel in the Database panel group.

2. Click on the small "**+**" (not the big "**+**" at the top of the panel, but the small "**+**" next to your recordset) to expand the Query Table, and display all the fields in that table, as shown in Figure 15.5.

Figure 15.4

Preparing a table to display information from your database.

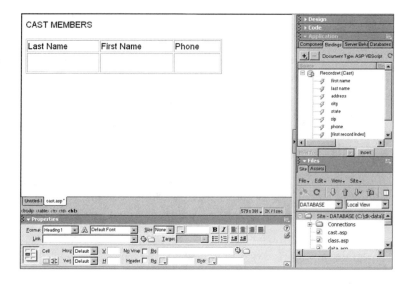

Figure 15.5

Changing the last row of the table to one that repeats until all data is displayed.

Inside Info

In addition to fields that display data, your database might well contain fields used for internal management of the database. These fields will be in parentheses, and you won't be displaying them on your page.

3. Place the cursor in the first column and second row of your table. You're ready to place live data here.

4. Click and drag the lightening rod icon next to one of the fields in the recordset (in the Bindings panel) into the table column, as shown in Figure 15.6.

5. Drag additional fields into other columns of your database.

Figure 15.6

Placing a field in a table.

So far, you've created an online database that will display the first record in the database, not bad start. Of course you'll want to display more than one record, and I'll show you how to do that next.

If you want to test your page at this point, don't try to use the Preview in Browser feature in Dreamweaver. To test your embedded data, you need to look at your site in a browser window with a real live connection to your server. So, open your site URL in a browser, and navigate to the page with your data. If you can see one record in your table at this point, you're there.

Repeating Records

Since you'll normally want to display many (maybe all) records in your database, not just one, you'll want to let Dreamweaver generate more rows in your table. To do that, follow the steps below.

1. Select the entire row in your table that displays data (the second row) by moving your cursor to the left edge of the table until it turns into an arrow, and then click to select the entire second row.

2. In the Server Behaviors panel in the Database panel group, click "**+**".

3. Choose **Repeat Region** as shown in Figure 15.7. The Repeat Region dialog box opens.

Figure 15.7

Transforming a table row into a repeating database region.

Caution

Remember, when testing pages with live data, you can't preview your work using the File, Preview in Browser command. That just generates a temporary HTML page that is not connected to your server. Since your data is not on your local computer, but instead on your server, you need to actually look at your site in a browser window to test it.

4. In the Repeat Region Dialog box, enter either a number of records to show at a time, or all records. In Figure 15.8, I've chosen to display all records.

5. Click **OK** to close the Repeat Region Dialog box.

Test your data display by looking at your page in a browser with a live connection to your site.

If you want to change your repeat region settings, double-click on **Repeat Region** in the Server Behaviors panel to reopen the Repeat Region dialog box. Here, you can change the number of records that display.

Figure 15.8

I'm going to include all records in my web page.

Sorting and Filtering

I warned you that complex online database management requires a whole other set of skills than web design. But hey, let's go there anyway!

I won't venture *too* far into database management, but at least I'll show you how to sort the records you display, and how to allow visitors to search for selected records using a filter.

Sorting Your Data

You can sort the way data is presented on your page. Any field, such as name, product name, and so on can be used as sort criteria. And you can sort the information in a field in ascending order (A on top, Z at the bottom, or 1 on top, 1,000 at the bottom), or descending order.

To sort the display of data, double-click on the Recordset name in the Server Behaviors panel. This opens the Recordset dialog box.

Choose a field from the Sort list at the bottom of the Recordset dialog box, and then choose either Ascending or Descending from the list next to the Sort drop-down list, as shown in Figure 15.9.

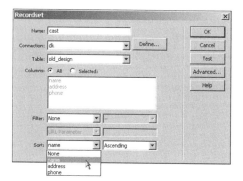

Figure 15.9

The Server Behaviors panel allows you to easily sort page data in ascending or descending order.

Filtering Records

If your database is very large, you'll want to allow visitors to search your database for information. For instance, if a visitor knows the name of someone in your organization, you can help them find out contact information for that person. Or, if a client is looking for information on a product, he or she can enter the product name and your database will display more information about that product.

Allowing visitors to search your database is done through filtering. Filters sift through all the information in your database and filter out everything except the record (or records) that a visitor is looking for.

To define a filter for your database, you'll need to create two additional pages in your site. One page will supply visitors with a search box that allows them to look for visitors. The second page will display results.

Before you embark on this process, think first about which field in your database you want to use as a filter field. Name? Product Name? Look at the Bindings panel for your database, and note the exact field name that you'll use as a search criteria.

Follow the steps below to set up your lookup and results pages.

1. Create two new pages, lookup and search. If your server script is ASP, your pages will be named lookup.asp and results.asp.

2. Open the lookup page, and create a form with one text field. In the Name area of the Properties Inspector for the form, type the field name you noted earlier for the field that will be your search criteria.

3. Add a submit button to your form.

4. Add some text to tell visitors what to enter in the text field, as shown in Figure 15.10.

> **Inside Info**
>
> For creating forms, see Chapter 13 and Chapter 14. In this section, I'm going to assume you're comfortable with the form and form field routines I explained in those chapters.

Figure 15.10

Visitors will use this search box to look up names in the database.

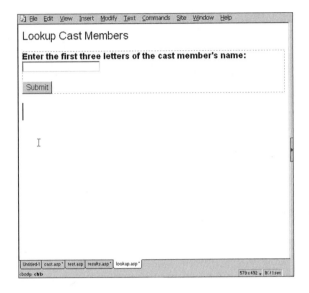

Inside Info

In Figure 15.10, I'm telling them to use the first three letters because I'm going to make it easier to look up names that way later.

5. Select the Form itself. You can do this by clicking on the red dashed line around the form, or by clicking on the <Form> tag in the Quick Tag list at the bottom of the Dreamweaver screen.

6. In the Form Properties panel, choose **POST** from the Method list, and use the **Browse for File** icon to navigate to the results page you created.

7. Save your page, and PUT (upload) it to your server. The query part of your search filter is done.

You've created a form that will take visitors' input, and search your database for matching records. And, you told Dreamweaver to send visitors to a results page to see what names came up. The next step is to configure and format the page that will display the results of the query. To do that, follow the steps below:

1. Open the results page.

2. In the Bindings panel, click "**+**" and choose **Recordset (Query).** The Recordset dialog box opens.

3. You can enter a name in the Name field of the Recordset dialog box (no spaces or special characters) or accept the default.

4. In the Connections drop-down list, choose your DSN connection.

5. Choose a table from the Table drop-down list.

6. In the Filter list, choose the field that you are using to let visitors search the database. In the drop-down list next to the Filter list, choose **Begins With.** This makes it easier for visitors to look up a name (all that is needed are the first few letters, or even the first letter of the name).

7. In the drop-down list under the Filter drop-down list, choose **Form Variable.**

8. In the box to the right, enter the field name you are using as a search criteria, as shown in Figure 15.11.

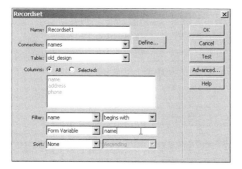

Figure 15.11

Connecting a search to a results page.

9. You can test your search criteria by clicking the **Test** button. You'll be prompted to enter search information. If you followed these steps, you can simply enter a single letter to search for all records that start with that letter. The test will display a list of matching records.

10. Click **OK** to close the Recordset dialog box.

11. With your connection defined, create a table to display matching records, as shown in Figure 15.12.

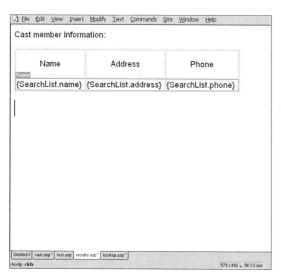

Figure 15.12

Creating a table with repeating rows to display results of a search.

If your lookup page and results pages are set up correctly, you can test your filter by entering information in the lookup form, and seeing the results on the results page.

The Wide World of Web Databases

If you've defined a database connection to your Dreamweaver MX site, you've just scratched the surface of the kind of information you can present at your website.

In large part, further development of your Dreamweaver-database connection is really database work. You can set up more complex searches, and you can present information in more organized ways. If you want to pursue online data management, you'll want to find an expert level book that specializes in the Dreamweaver features that used to be called UltraDev. And, you'll want to explore database theory.

The Least You Need to Know

- ◆ To place database content in a Dreamweaver page, you need a database on your server with a defined DSN (you need to know the name of that DSN and the URL path for that DSN).
- ◆ Your online database must be in a folder that supports one of the scripting languages that Dreamweaver uses to communicate with databases. You also need to know which language is being used.
- ◆ Once you have connected your Dreamweaver site and page to a database, you can display the contents of that database online, including up-to-the-minute changes in the information in that database.
- ◆ You can define what part of a database to show in your Dreamweaver web page by defining a Recordset, which is similar to a database table.
- ◆ You can display all or just part of a database on a page. You can sort the data, allow visitors to search your database for records, and then display only the records that match the search criteria.

Part 6

Putting On a Show (Multimedia)

Sound, video, interactivity, and animation add life to your website. In the next set of chapters, I'll show you how to make your page go "ding," your buttons go "bonk," and video rock your website.

I'll also show you how to use Dreamweaver Behaviors to make your pages react to visitors' activity, and how to add animation using Dreamweaver Timelines.

Chapter 16

Action in a Flash

In This Chapter

♦ Creating Flash animation in Dreamweaver

♦ Linking to Flash movies

♦ Embedding Flash movies in a Dreamweaver page

♦ Adding interactivity from Fireworks

I'm cynical of claims by one or another software manufacturer that their suite of products has some special synergy. I have no problem mixing up a drawing from Adobe Illustrator with a movie from Macromedia Flash.

But I will confess that Macromedia's Flash, Fireworks, and Dreamweaver form a pretty potent combination when it comes to creating an animated, interactive website.

Due to size constraints (both on the number of pages allowed in this book, and the size of my brain), I can't offer an introductory course in Flash and Fireworks in this chapter. But I can and will show you how to combine the web objects you create in those programs with Dreamweaver sites.

How Flash and Fireworks Connect with Dreamweaver

Animation and interactivity are increasingly integral elements of web design. *Animation* means that instead of your page content just sitting there on the page, it moves around. Movies are an example of animation.

Interactivity means that page content responds to actions of a visitor. An example of an interactive button would be one that changes color as a visitor rolls his cursor over it. An interactive navigation changes its appearance and displays more navigation options when a visitor rolls over it.

Inside Info

If you include Flash objects in your website, visitors must have the Flash Viewer program to see these elements. The Flash Viewer is included with recent browsers and is a free download for any Windows or Mac user who wants to use it. Some estimates claim up to 80 percent of all web browsers currently have the Flash Viewer already on their computers.

By the Way

For a quick and free introduction to Flash, check out the Flash tutorials at my website, www.ppinet.com. For a quick, cheap introduction to Flash, check out my *Complete Idiot's Guide to Flash 5*.

Both Flash and Fireworks can be used to generate interactive and animated objects for web pages. The underlying technical difference between the two is that Fireworks' interactive objects usually rely on JavaScript to power their activity, while Flash objects generally rely on a *plug-in* program, the Flash Viewer, which works with a visitor's browser.

Flash objects are used for many purposes on the web, including:

- Movies.
- Interactive games and presentations.
- Artwork that will print at a higher resolution than normal web graphics.
- Publications that would be enhanced by embedding fonts to preserve text formatting.

Figure 16.1 shows a Flash movie in a web page.

Fireworks is a multifaceted graphics editor that is used to edit images for both print and web output. But perhaps the most exciting feature for web development is Fireworks' ability to create interactive graphics that respond to being hovered over.

Figure 16.2 shows a Fireworks navigation icon in a web page.

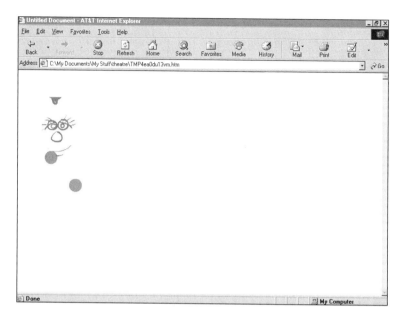

Figure 16.1

A Flash movie in a web page.

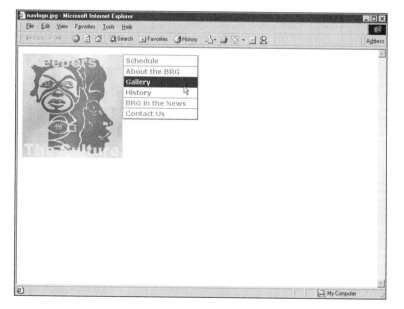

Figure 16.2

Adding a Fireworks navigation icon to a page.

Generating Flash Objects in Dreamweaver

While Dreamweaver does not create media files, it does include a little subset of Flash that allows you to create animated buttons right in Dreamweaver. Dreamweaver allows you to generate interactive Flash buttons and Flash text.

Caution _____

Remember, when you include Flash objects in your page, you are counting on visitors having the Flash Player installed. If you anticipate some of your visitors might need to download the Flash Player, you can include a link on your page to the Macromedia site (www. macromedia. com), with a warning that visitors need the Flash Player to see the page.

Caution _____

I'll emphasize the point: Don't move or rename the SWF files that are generated when you create a Flash object. With other embedded files—like images—you can move and rename files in the Site window and Dreamweaver will adjust links and HTML code so that the images remain embedded in your page. But don't try that with Flash objects.

These Flash buttons and text are almost always used as navigation icons. They are interactive in that they can change color, size, background, and other properties when rolled over.

You'll assign links to Flash buttons, including defining target frames for those links, so you might want to review Chapter 6 if you've blanked on how to do things like open a link in a new browser window.

Under the Hood—How Flash Objects Are Created in Dreamweaver

When you define Flash buttons and Flash text in Dreamweaver, Dreamweaver actually generates Flash *files* in the SWF (Flash Player) format. These Flash Player files are saved as part of your site. Dreamweaver saves these files in the same folder as your page so that browsers can find them. While you can select file names for your generated Flash objects, you *cannot* change the folder in which they are saved. Dreamweaver will pick an appropriate folder in which to save the file, and you just have to let it do that.

Dreamweaver then, also, generates HTML code to link these embedded Flash Player files in your page.

Dreamweaver does this all for you. But I figured you'd want to know what's going on behind the scenes when you create a Flash object in Dreamweaver.

While you don't need to worry about the details of how Flash objects are created, it's important that you do not rename or move these files once they have been generated by Dreamweaver. If you do move or rename these buttons, you'll break the links that embed them in your page.

Creating Flash Buttons

Flash buttons combine predefined graphic backgrounds, colored text, and interactive effects (like color changes) to make fun navigation links. In Figure 16.3, I'm rolling over a Flash button in a browser. You can see that its appearance has changed from the rest of the buttons in the set.

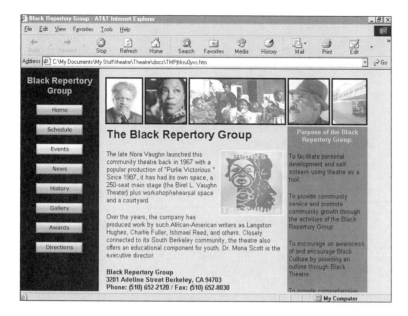

Figure 16.3

This Flash button changes color as it's rolled over.

To create Flash buttons, you choose a background (button) image, text to put on the image, and a link to associate with the button.

Follow the steps in this tutorial to generate Flash navigation buttons:

1. Open an existing page, or if you are working on a new page, save the page. You can only insert Flash buttons in a saved page.

2. Set your insertion point and choose **Insert, Interactive Images, Flash Button.** The Insert Flash Button dialog box opens.

3. Choose a Style from the Style list. As you do, the style will be previewed in the Sample area at the top of the Insert Flash Button dialog box.

4. Enter button text in the Button Text area. This can be any text, but keep it short so it fits on the button.

5. Select a Button font in the Font area, and a font size in the Size area.

6. Use the Browse button to navigate to and select a link target for the button. Or, type a URL (the *complete URL* including http://) in the Link Area.

> **Inside Info**
>
> In order to make sure that a browser can locate the Flash file that will be generated for your button, Dreamweaver needs to know the location of your page file.

7. In the Target area, choose the target browser window or frame for your link. If you leave this blank, links will open in the same browser window as the open page.

8. Use the Background Color swatch to change the background color for your button. Dreamweaver will select a compatible text color for the background you choose.

9. The safest way to handle naming your Flash button is to accept the default file name suggested by Dreamweaver. If you want to change the file name, enter a new name with a filename extension of SWF in the Save As area. But don't change the folder in which the file is stored. Your Insert Flash Button dialog box should look something like the one in Figure 16.4.

Figure 16.4

Generating a Flash button.

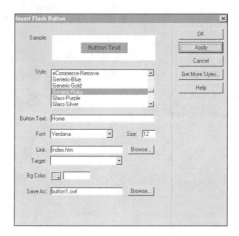

10. Click **OK** to generate the button.

You can resize Flash buttons in the Document window. Select the button, and click and drag on a side or corner handle to resize the button.

To edit a Flash button, double-click on it. This reopens the Insert Flash Button dialog box. After you change a button, and click OK, the Flash (SWF) file is resaved.

Normally Flash buttons are created in sets, and you usually keep the same color and style settings consistent for an entire set. I think I know what you're thinking "Can I just copy and paste to create a bunch of Flash buttons with the same style." Yes, you can, but remember to change the file name for each new button before you click OK. Otherwise, you'll replace your old Flash button as well as creating a new one.

After you generate your Flash buttons, you can test your buttons in a browser.

> **Inside Info**
>
> Flash "text" is not technically text. What looks like text is really a Flash format graphic file. In order for Dreamweaver to make sure the links between the generated Flash file and your page are protected, you need to first save your page.

Creating Flash Text

Flash text is a slightly less flashy (sorry) way to include interactive navigation links on your page. When buttons are a bit much, consider Flash text as a way to make your page more energetic.

You can define a font size, type, and color for Flash buttons, a background color, and also define a new color for text when it is rolled over.

Follow the steps in this tutorial to generate Flash navigation buttons:

1. Save your page. You can only insert Flash buttons in a saved page.

2. Set your insertion point and choose **Insert, Interactive Images, Flash Text.** The Insert Flash Text dialog box opens.

3. Choose a font, font size, and formatting attributes (like paragraph alignment, bold-face, or italics) from the Font area at the top of the Insert Flash Text dialog box. The Show Font checkbox displays selected font attributes in the Text area when you enter text.

4. Choose a text color from the Color swatch, and a rollover color from the Rollover Color swatch.

5. Enter text in the Text area. Even though Dreamweaver provides you with a large area to enter text, keep your text to one line if you want to use the Flash text as a navigation link.

6. Use the Browse button to navigate to and select a link target for the button. Or, type a URL (the *complete URL* including http://) in the Link Area.

7. In the Target area, choose the target browser window or frame for your link. If you leave this blank, links will open in the same browser window as the open page.

8. Use the Background Color swatch to change the background color for your text.

9. As I've cautioned earlier in this chapter, you must save your Flash text to the same folder to which the open page is saved. Again, the safest way to do this is to accept the default file name suggested by Dreamweaver. You can type a new name with a filename extension of SWF in the Save As area if you wish.

10. Click on **OK** to generate the Flash text.

Caution

Of course you want to avoid using a background color for your Flash text that is the same color as either the text or the rollover text. If you use the same color for text and background, the text won't be readable.

You can resize selected Flash text objects in the Document window by clicking and dragging on a side or corner handle.

To edit a Flash text object, double-click on it. This reopens the Insert Flash Text dialog box. After you change Flash text, click **OK.** The associated Flash (SWF) file is resaved.

Definition

Flash files are called Flash movies. A Flash movie, a Flash object, and a Flash Viewer file are all the same thing.

Presenting Flash Movies in a Dreamweaver Site

While I vowed not to tread too far into Flash territory in this chapter, Dreamweaver developers *do* have to be able to communicate with Flash developers (and if you're both the same person, than you need to talk coherently to yourself!).

There are two basic ways to include Flash movies in your website. You can *embed* Flash objects in a page. Or, you can include Flash movies as free-standing files in your website that open in a visitor's Flash viewer.

Embedded Flash objects are integrated into a Dreamweaver web page. It often isn't even obvious to a viewer that some of the content he or she is looking at or interacting with is Flash content. It all appears seamlessly as part of the web page. Only you (and others "in the know") can tell that the interactive or animated objects on the page are actually embedded Flash movies being presented because a visitor has the Flash Viewer plug-in.

Independent Flash files (in SWF) format can also be included in a site *without* being embedded in a page. For example, you might just have a link on your page that says "Watch a Flash movie demonstrating this product." Visitors who click the link will open an SWF file right in their Flash viewer, without seeing it in a web browser or HTML page.

Linking Flash Movies

Linked audio or video files are simply uploaded to your site (using Dreamweaver's Site window). By creating links to a media file, visitors download the file and view it in an independent browser window. A linked media file is illustrated in Figure 16.5.

Figure 16.5

The link to a Flash movie opened the movie in a separate browser window—here you see both the linked text and the small Flash movie.

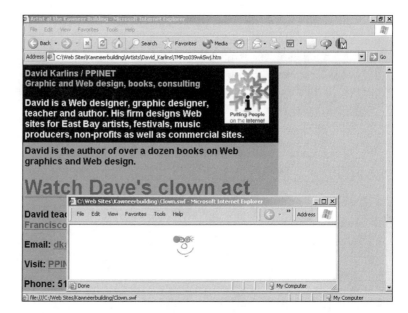

In the example above, the visitor clicks on the link, and opens the file (a Flash Movie) in the Flash Viewer he or she has on their computer.

At this point, any navigation links or other features to integrate the movie into your web-site are the responsibility of the Flash developer, who should provide some way for visitors to return to your site.

Combining Flash Movies with Dreamweaver Pages

There are two basic options for embedding Flash movies into Dreamweaver. You can save the Flash movie as an HTML page, or you can import a Flash movie directly into Dreamweaver.

If a Flash developer saves his or her object as an HTML page, Flash will create an HTML web page with the Flash object(s) embedded already. In short, Flash has done Dreamweaver's work, and all you have to do is copy the generated HTML page along with all associated Flash files into your site, and plug the whole thing into your site by including navigation links to the new page.

The limitations of this approach are that a) you can't edit the page as easily, and b) there's a danger of placing embedded Flash files in the wrong folder as you import the page, thus wrecking the Flash project.

These limitations aren't unsolvable—you can just be careful to put the HTML page and the embedded Flash files that come with it in the same folder. And, you can open the Flash-generated HTML file in Dreamweaver and touch it up.

The other basic approach is to have the Flash developer provide you with Flash Player (SWF) format files. Then you can embed those files yourself in an HTML page in Dreamweaver. The advantages to this approach are that you can control where the Flash file is saved and make sure it is in the same folder as the HTML page. *And,* you can do all the page formatting right in Dreamweaver.

In *both* of these scenarios, you'll end up with a Flash movie embedded in a web page. In the next sections of this chapter, I'll walk you through how to embed a Flash movie in a page, and how to format that embedded movie.

Embedding Flash Movies

Flash movies integrate smoothly with their Macromedia cousin Dreamweaver. Flash (or Shockwave) movies are embedded lists like pictures.

To embed a Flash (or Shockwave) movie:

1. With a page open in the Document window, choose **Insert, Media, Flash (or Shockwave).**

2. You can resize the movie just as you would an image, by clicking and dragging on sizing handles.

3. Use the Properties Inspector panel with the movie to define movie properties.

Your embedded Flash (or Shockwave) movie will look like the one in Figure 16.6.

Figure 16.6

The icon depicts an embedded Flash movie.

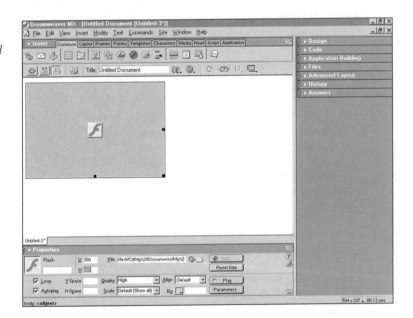

You can resize a selected embedded Flash movie by clicking and dragging on the side or corner handles. Click and drag on the middle of the movie to move its location on the page.

By the Way

You will often want to use tables to place a movie, just as you do with other page objects like text and images.

When you select a Flash movie, the Properties panel allows you to control many elements of how the movie plays, including:

- **Size** Determines the size of the display in a browser

- **Alignment** Allows you to flow text to the right or left of the movie

- **Background color** Determines the background color

- ◆ **Quality**   Determines the level of the movie quality
- ◆ **Looping**   Controls the repeat function
- ◆ **Autoplay**   Starts on page load

In Figure 16.7, I've set the Flash movie parameters to Autoplay and Loop (using the check-boxes), I've defined horizontal and vertical spacing of 4 pixels each, and I resized the movie to 100 pixels square.

Figure 16.7

The Properties panel allows you to format how a Flash movie will appear on the page.

Inserting Fireworks Objects

Fireworks is a full-featured graphic design and editing tool, and you can create web-compatible images with it and include them in your Dreamweaver sites.

Additionally, Fireworks is a good tool for creating simple animated graphics in Animated GIF format. These are GIF images that function as small movies.

If you create or edit an image in Fireworks, you can simply export it as a GIF (including an animated GIF), a JPEG, or just save the image in Fireworks' native PNG format. Then, insert that saved image into the Document window, as you would any web-compatible image.

Beyond that, Fireworks generates interactive objects, like navigation menus that expand, change, and contract as visitors roll over them. Transferring those objects into Dreamweaver is more complex than just importing an image, so I'll walk you through that process from the Fireworks and Dreamweaver perspectives in the following sections.

Preparing Fireworks Artwork for Dreamweaver

Importing a Fireworks-generated interactive object (like a pop-up navigation bar) involves importing a group of files that need to work together. These interactive objects typically include HTML code, images, and JavaScript coding that enable them to function interactively.

After you (or the folks creating the Fireworks object for you) create an interactive object in Fireworks, choose **File, Export** in Fireworks.

As much as I'd love to get diverted into launching into a Complete Idiot's Guide to Fireworks now, I'll have to restrain myself to offering a few words of advice on how to export your Fireworks object.

Following are some tips on how to best export a Fireworks object to files that will import smoothly into Dreamweaver:

◆ From the Save as Type list in the Fireworks Export dialog box, choose **HTML and Images**.

◆ Click the **Options** button in the Export dialog box, and choose **Dreamweaver HTML** from the HTML Style drop-down list in the HTML Setup dialog box. (There are many other options in the HTML Style dialog box, but if you select Dreamweaver HTML, you don't need to worry about them).

◆ In the Export dialog box, navigate to the folder in which your Dreamweaver site is saved. If you save the generated files to this folder, you won't need to import the files into your Dreamweaver site as a separate step.

◆ I advise using the **Put Images In Subfolder** checkbox. By default Fireworks will save all image files associated with your object in a subfolder called /images. If you want to change that, click the **Browse** button and locate a different folder.

> **By the Way**
>
> You might want to make a note of the folder in which your Fireworks object is saved—just to help yourself find the generated files when you import them into Dreamweaver.

With that advice to guide you or the team preparing your Fireworks objects, you can export files you'll use in Dreamweaver.

Bringing Fireworks Objects into a Page

The hard part of importing Fireworks objects into Dreamweaver sites is just making sure the files all match up. The images that are required for an interactive object like a pop-up menu all need to "find each other." In addition, the linked pages associated with a pop-up navigation bar, for instance, all need to be in the right folders.

> **Caution**
>
> While you can fix file relationships in Dreamweaver, the process is smoother if you followed my advice in the previous section for saving your Fireworks file.

The good part of all this is that if you (or your associates) weren't sure which files you wanted to include in links, you can edit and fix these file relationships in Dreamweaver.

To import a Fireworks-generated HTML file into Dreamweaver, choose **File, Open.** In Figure 16.8, I'm opening a Fireworks pop-up navigation menu in the right (navigation) frame of a frameset.

Figure 16.8

The HTML I'm inserting was generated in Fireworks to define a pop-up menu.

Once you've imported a Fireworks pop-up menu into a Dreamweaver page, you can test the links associated with that pop-up in a browser (choose **File, Preview in Browser** and choose one of your installed browsers).

Editing Pop-Up Menu Links in Dreamweaver

There's a good chance the links won't work. Not because you're a bad person, but because only a very obsessively detail-oriented person could keep track of the folder structure of their site and design a Fireworks object at the same time.

Thankfully, you can edit the links associated with your imported pop-up navigation menu right in Dreamweaver. To do this, select your imported pop-up, and view the Behaviors panel. You'll see a command line in the panel where "Show Pop-Up Menu" is listed in the Actions column. Double-click on that command to open the Show Pop-Up Menu dialog box in Dreamweaver.

The Show Pop-Up Menu in Dreamweaver duplicates many of the features in Fireworks. In the Contents tab, shown in Figure 16.9, you can select any of the links associated with the menu, and then edit the properties of that link in the Text, Link, and Target areas of the dialog box.

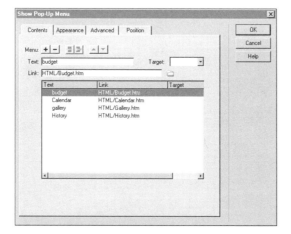

Figure 16.9

Editing the link properties of a pop-up created in Fireworks.

In the Contents tab, you can use the Browse for Folder icon to create or fix links that came with your Fireworks pop-up menu.

You can also define pop-up menus right in Dreamweaver from scratch. The disadvantage is that you can't edit images, as you can in Fireworks. The advantage is, you don't need to buy Fireworks (although if you're serious about creating attractive pop-up menus it might be a worthwhile investment).

I'll walk you through the process of defining pop-up menus in more detail in Chapter 19 when I explain how Behaviors work.

The Least You Need to Know

- Flash objects can add animation and interactivity (they respond to visitor actions) to a web page.

- Only browsers with the Flash Player plug-in can view Flash objects.

- Most Flash objects are made in Flash. But you can create Flash buttons and interactive Flash text right in Dreamweaver.

- Flash buttons must be saved in the same folder as the web page in which they are embedded.

- Fireworks is a web graphics editing tool that creates images in PNG, GIF, and JPEG format for websites. These images can be easily inserted into Dreamweaver pages.

- Fireworks also generates interactive objects like pop-up menus.

- You can import Fireworks pop-up menus into Dreamweaver and edit the links using the Dreamweaver Behaviors panel.

Chapter 17

Bap, Boom, Bang! Adding Sound

In This Chapter

- ◆ How sound files work on the web
- ◆ Where to get sound files
- ◆ Playing a sound file as a background to a web page
- ◆ Attaching sounds to action on your page

With the increasing availability of high bandwidth (fast) Internet connections, the last few years have seen an explosion of the exchange of sound files over the web. While the news focus has been on Napster and similar music-exchange operations, there are many good reasons to include sound files in your own site.

Sound files can include a personal vocal greeting to visitors, a sales presentation, a cut from your new CD, or appropriate background music that plays while visitors browse your site content.

I'll explain how to use all these options in this chapter.

Where Do Sounds Come From?

You can create your own sound files rather easily these days. Or, you can get them from somewhere else.

Both Windows and Macintosh operating systems include primitive sound recording software that allows you to record through the microphone jack in your computer. These files are often of sufficient quality for voice recording. They can be used to create sales presentations, educational content, or sounds that play when a button is pushed (like "Thanks for selecting this option, one moment please while we load your page.").

More complex and high quality audio files are created using more sophisticated software and recording equipment. You can find a wide variety of sound clips available by searching the web, ranging from snippets from movies, sound effects, and music that is sold over the web.

Once you download or create the sound files you want for your website, the first step is to copy them into your locate Site folder so they are easily available for implementation in Dreamweaver.

The Downsides of Sound

While sound files can bring your site to life, they can also provoke rather high levels of irritation.

One potential problem with sound files is that they are much larger than text or even images, and therefore take much longer to download into a site. Visitors with dial-up connections may have to wait mega-minutes to hear your voice or music.

It can also cause a lot of hostility when a sound file starts playing unexpectedly. Visualize a sound clip from a CD, or even a sales pitch for a product blasting in a crowded office and you get the picture.

These problems can be managed. You can include text content in your page alerting visitors that a sound file is going to play. You can warn visitors that a sound file is large and will take a long time to download over a dial-up connection. And, you can present sound in embedded plug-in players that allow visitors to control the volume or stop the sound if they wish. I'll explain how to do that in the section "Embedding Playable Sounds with Dreamweaver" later in this chapter.

Many Formats for Sound

Unlike image files, where there are three widely supported file formats (GIF, JPEG, and PNG), sound files are an anarchistic bunch. There *is no* "standard" sound file format for the web. So there is no single file format that you can use to present sound that is guaranteed to be heard by every visitor.

Sound files require additional *plug-in* software to be heard. Let's walk through how this works:

While browsing the web, a visitor opens a sound file in his browser. The visitor's computer (not the browser software) looks at this file and says, "Hey! I've got a program that's configured to play when I see one of these files." And then, the visitor's computer launches whatever program has been defined on that computer to play that sound file format.

You may have noticed that as you download sound files, or download media software, you're often prompted "Make ME your default player for WAV, MP3, AIFF sound files." If you click OK, you're redefining your system's file associations, and changing the player that will launch when a sound file is opened.

Most new computers have media player software included. So do new operating systems. And browsers often come with included media software.

In short, it's insane out there! As a web designer, you don't know what program will open the sound files you include in websites, and you don't even know if your visitors will have a media player that supports the sounds you include in your site.

Caution

Let me bang that point home more harshly: Students, readers of my books, and just folks I run into on the bus often accost me complaining that the sound file they put on a web page "looks funny" or "doesn't work" on a friend's computer.

Doesn't surprise me! That's the way it is in the scary world of computer sound. Chances are, if you use one of the sound file formats I list in this section, visitors will hear that sound file one way or another. But whether they hear it in the background, or it plays in a huge media player that takes over their screen depends on what kind of media software is installed on their computer, and how it is configured.

All this demands some flexibility in page design. You can include text in your page that warns visitors that a selected file requires a sound player, and takes some time to download. The text in Figure 17.1 is an example of how you can make this clear to visitors.

Figure 17.1

Warning! Sound files coming.

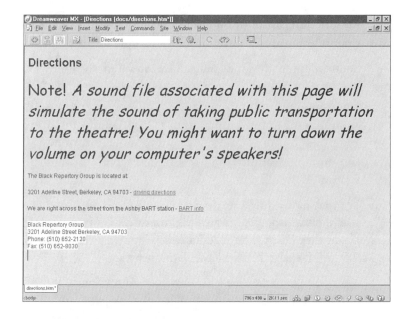

As I mentioned, there is no "standard" sound file format for the web. But frequently used, and widely supported sound file formats include:

◆ Real Media (RM, RA, or RAM) requires the proprietary Real Player, which visitors must download. Real Media files are *streaming* media files, which means they begin playing on a visitor's computer even before they are completely downloaded.

◆ WAV (pronounced *wave*) files are played by the windows media player, and require no additional plug-in software for Windows users. WAV files are larger than other sound file formats.

◆ MP3 files are relatively good quality, relatively small in size, and widely supported by media players including the QuickTime player and the Windows Media player.

◆ MIDI files are very widely supported by media players. They are small, relatively low quality sound files often used for sound effects.

Embedded vs. Linked Sound Files

Including a sound file in your website can be as simple as copying the sound file into your local site and using the PUT feature in Dreamweaver to upload that file to your site. Once it's there, you can simply link to that sound file. Visitors who follow the link will play the sound in whatever media player is installed on their computer.

Sometimes you want more control over how sound files are presented. You might want to embed a media player right into your page. When you embed a player (a plug-in) for a sound file in Dreamweaver, you have some control over how that player will display in a browser.

Once sound files have been added to your site, you can embed an associated player (plug-in) in the Dreamweaver Document window.

To embed a sound player and a sound file in your page, follow these steps:

1. Copy a media file (in a format like MP3 or WAV) to your site folder.

2. With a page open in your Document window, choose **Insert, Media, Plug-In.** The Select File dialog box appears, as shown in Figure 17.2.

By the Way

If you want a sound to play automatically when a page is opened, you do that by defining a Behavior. I'll show you how to do that later in this chapter.

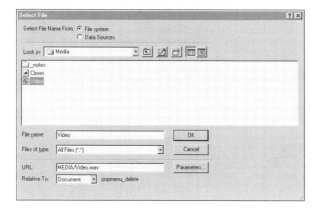

Figure 17.2

Choosing a sound file to play in a plug-in.

3. In the Select File dialog box, navigate to the sound file and click **Select.**

4. Select the plug-in icon that appears on your page, and view the associated Properties panel. Figure 17.3 shows both a plug-in icon, and the associated Properties panel.

5. Using the W and H areas of the Properties Inspector, define the size of your plug-in player.

6. In the Plg URL area of the Properties panel, enter the URL where visitors without a player can download an MP3 player. This is the URL that will display for visitors who do not have a player for this media file.

Inside Info

As I've emphasized earlier in this chapter, you're defining a space to display a media player without knowing which media player will display in that space. That's the crazy logic of defining media plug-ins. But I usually define a plug-in size of 200 pixels wide by 40 pixels high. This often results in a media player display that includes the media player controls in a visitor's browser.

Figure 17.3

The plug-in icon represents an embedded sound file.

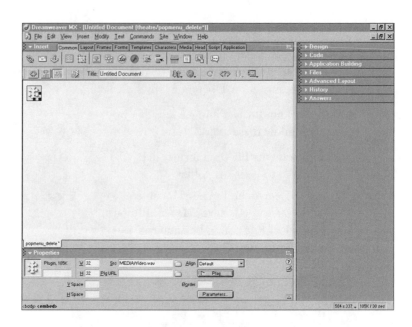

7. Test your media player in a browser. If necessary, tweak the size of the display.

Figure 17.4 shows a media file playing in a browser.

Figure 17.4

Playing music in a browser with an embedded player.

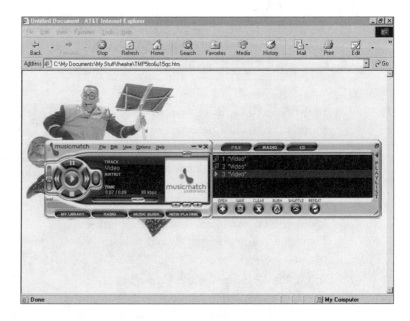

Attaching Sounds to Pages and Buttons

In addition to sounds triggered by embedded media players or links, you can define sounds to automatically play when a page is opened, or when a visitor interacts with an object on the page.

For example, you can assign a small sound file to repeat endlessly while visitors browse a page. Or, you can define a "click" sound to play when a visitor clicks on a button on a page.

Assigning sounds in this way can be rather invasive in that visitors won't necessarily have any conscious control over whether the sound file plays, or how loudly it plays. For those reasons, you should use page background sounds judiciously.

> **Inside Info**
>
> You can use http://www.microsoft.com/windows/windowsmedia/en/default.asp for WAV or MP3 files, www.real.com for the Real Media player, or research your own URL for an appropriate downloadable player.

Page Background Sound

When you assign a sound to a page, that sound file will play when, and only when, the file downloads. If you attach a large sound file to a page, it's likely that the sound file will not be synchronized with the page opening, and instead the sound will suddenly erupt seconds or minutes after the page has opened.

Therefore, sound files that play when a page is opened should be *very small*. A repeating MIDI file might be appropriate, while a large WAV file probably is not.

Once you've located an appropriate sound file to associate with a page opening, follow these steps to attach the file to the page.

> **Inside Info**
>
> Attaching a sound file to a page opening requires invoking Dreamweaver Behaviors. All Behaviors involve both an event and an action. In this case, the event will be a web page opening. In order to define this event as the triggering action for the sound, we'll have to associate this behavior with the Body tag in the page HTML. I'll walk you through how to do this in the steps below, and I'll explain how Behaviors work in more detail in Chapter 19.

1. Make sure, before you start, that the sound file you wish to attach is in your local site folder. This will make it easier to attach the sound to a page.

2. Open the page to which the sound will be attached in the Document window.

3. View the code for the page by choosing **View, Code** from the menu.

4. Look around in your HTML code for a tag called "Body." This tag might include other parameters (like Body bgcolor or something like that). That doesn't matter. Click in the Document window to select the Body tag as shown in Figure 17.5.

Figure 17.5

Selecting the Body tag makes it easier to associate a sound file with a page opening.

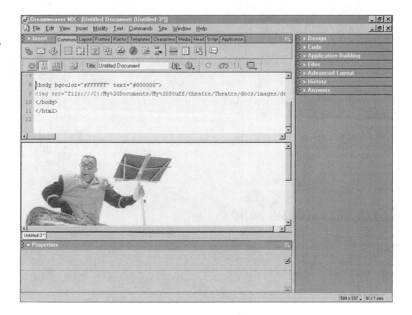

5. With the Body tag selected, open the Behaviors panel by choosing **Window, Behaviors.**

6. In the Behaviors panel, click the "**+**" sign and choose **Play Sound.**

7. Use the Browse button in the Play Sound dialog box to locate a sound file. Then click **OK** to close the Play Sound dialog box. The command onLoad appears in the Events column of the Behaviors panel, and Play Sound appears in the Actions column, as shown in Figure 17.6.

By the Way

You can return to Design view and make that scary code go away by choosing View, Design.

You have now associated the selected sound with the page loading, and the sound will play when the page is opened in a browser.

You can change the sound file by double-clicking on the **Play Sound** command in the Actions column of the Behaviors panel. This reopens the Play Sound dialog box, allowing you to change sound files.

You can remove the Behavior by selecting **onLoad** in the Behaviors panel, and clicking the "-" symbol at the top of the Behaviors panel.

Figure 17.6

Defining a sound to play when a page loads.

"Click Me" Sounds

In addition to triggering a sound by opening a page, you can define sounds that will play when a visitor *does something* at your site, like click on a text link or an image.

When you assign a sound to an object, you can define what kind of action will play the sound. For example, you can trigger a sound to play when a visitor *rolls over* a picture, *clicks on* a link, or *double-clicks* on a button.

Caution _____

When I say that a sound file will play, I mean it will begin to download. So, if you expect visitors to hear a long sound file play instantly when they click on a button, you and they are in for a disappointment. As I've redundantly overemphasized throughout the chapter, keep those sound files small if you want them to play quickly. A tiny "click" sound in MIDI format will download fast enough to associate with a button. A 10-second song clip will not.

Once you've located an appropriate sound file to play when an action takes place on your page, copy that file into your local site folder. Then follow these steps to attach the file to an object on your page.

1. With your page open in the Document window, select an object (it can be text, a button, or an image) that will act as a trigger for the sound. Figure 17.7 shows an example of a "click here" button that will trigger a sound.

Figure 17.7

Choosing a button to use as a sound trigger.

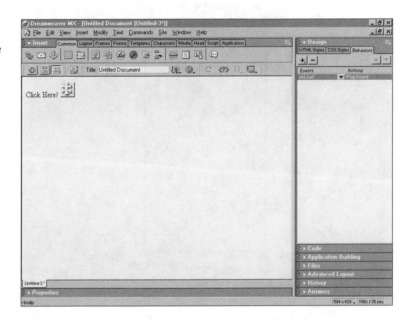

2. With the object tag selected, open the Behaviors panel by choosing **Window, Behaviors.**

3. In the Behaviors panel, click the "**+**" sign and choose Play Sound. The **Play Sound** dialog box appears.

4. Use the Browse button in the Play Sound dialog box to locate a sound file. Then click **OK** to close the Play Sound dialog box. The action "Play Sound" appears in the Actions column of the Behaviors panel. I'll show you how to define a triggering action in the next step.

5. With the Play Sound action line selected in the Behaviors column, click the down-triangle at the top of the Events column to view a list of available events to trigger your sound, as shown in Figure 17.8.

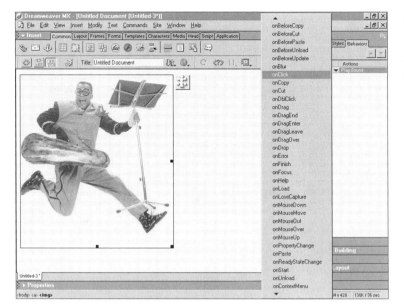

Figure 17.8

Choosing an event to trigger a sound—in this case, clicking.

6. Choose an action that will trigger a sound. OnClick triggers the sound when a visitor clicks on the selected object. onDblClick plays the sound when the object is double-clicked. onMouseOver plays the sound when a visitor rolls over the object.

You can test your action-triggered sounds in a browser. You can change the triggering event by selecting the event in the Behaviors panel, and then selecting a different event from the Events drop-down list. You can change the sound file for the action by double-clicking on the Play Sound action in the Behaviors panel. And you can delete the whole sound by selecting it in the Behaviors panel and clicking the "-" symbol at the top of the Behaviors panel.

Inside Info

The list of available events is constrained by the browser you chose to define events for. You can change this by selecting **Show Events For** from the Events drop-down list, and selecting another browser. Your list of events will likely be different than the one shown in Figure 17.8, since different events are available for different browsers.

The Least You Need to Know

- Unlike image files, which are supported by browsers, sound files require special plug-in programs to be heard by visitors.

- Sound files take a long time to download, and so they should be kept as small as possible and used judiciously.

- Sound files will play in whatever media player is configured with your visitor's system. You have very little control over how sound files are displayed.

- You can embed a media player in a page in Dreamweaver.

- You can use Dreamweaver to define a sound file that will play when a page is opened.

- Dreamweaver can attach a sound file to actions on a page, like clicking a button, double-clicking on text, or rolling over an image.

Chapter 18

Roll the Video

In This Chapter

- ◆ How to get online video
- ◆ The ups and downs of including video in your site
- ◆ Importing videos into Dreamweaver
- ◆ Embedding video plug-ins in Dreamweaver web pages

Dreamweaver makes it easy to include QuickTime movies, Windows Media movies, Real Media movies, and other animation formats in your web pages.

These movies "play" in a visitor's browser when, and only when, the visitor has the required media software to support these media files.

Adding Movies with Dreamweaver

Video has arrived on the Internet. With the widespread availability of high bandwidth (fast) connections, millions of people watch movie previews, news clips, instructional videos, and independent films online.

Videos obviously add tremendous communication and entertainment value to your site. The big challenge in including video in your site is that the files are *large*. How large? Well, by comparison, a seven minute video file can easily be as large as 1,000 large JPEG images. If you've ever sat and waited for a JPEG image to download over a dial-up connection, multiply that wait by one thousand and you get a sense of the challenge of sharing video over the web. Figure 18.1 provides a comparison between the file size of an HTML page, an image, a sound file, and a video file.

Figure 18.1

Video files are huge.

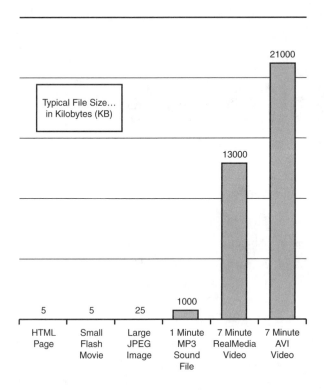

Before a visitor can see a video, the video file must download into his or her local computer. However, the *entire* video doesn't have to download before the show starts. Often, videos are downloaded using *streaming* techniques—so that part of the video starts before the end of the video has finished downloading. Streaming is programmed into the video itself, and not something you control when you place the video in your website.

Dreamweaver manages the process of adding movie files to your website and managing links that will open (play) those movies. You can also use Dreamweaver to embed movies right in your page.

Figure 18.2 shows a movie embedded in a web page in the Dreamweaver Document window.

Embedded movie

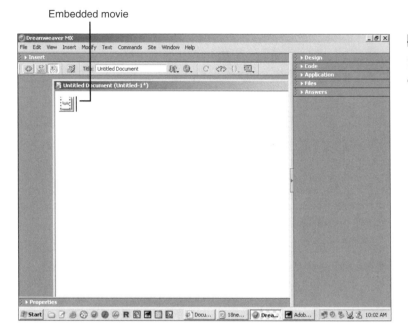

Figure 18.2

The icon represents an embedded movie.

Where Do Web Movies Come From?

Seems like every new PC advertises itself as the ultimate for do-it-yourself video editing. Having taken a crack at using the built-in software with my Sony Vaio, I can say that this software is fun, but hardly intuitive.

If you're serious about video editing, you'll want to check out a more sophisticated video editing package, like Adobe Premiere or Ulead MediaStudio Pro. These programs allow you to transfer video to your computer, cut and paste video clips, synchronize sound, add effects, and export your video to many video formats.

Inside Info
I produce digital instructional videos for my online classes that consist in large part of captured actions on my computer screen. For this, I use a program called Camtasia. Free trial versions are available at www.camtasia.com. This program allows you to capture anything on your computer screen (including animation) and save it to popular online video file formats.

Of course producing digital video is well beyond the scope of web design, per se, and most of the video you include in websites will probably be provided by a client, downloaded from a source on the web, purchased, or developed by an outside team.

Once a digital media file is delivered to you (or once you create it), you can place it in a website.

Movies Need Players

Before I walk you through the process of adding a movie to your website, it's important to break down exactly how that video will get played on a visitor's computer.

Browser software, like Internet Explorer or Netscape Navigator, is not capable by itself of playing a video. Additional *plug-in* software is required.

Don't let that alarm you! Most operating systems come with built-in video players that will handle many popular video formats. Macs come with QuickTime player, and PCs come with Windows Player. Both of those players can handle many popular video formats.

Other video formats, however, are not supported by the video players that come with operating systems. Flash movies (and their Shockwave cousins) are not playable in a QuickTime or Windows Media player. Neither are RealMedia (RM) video files.

By the Way

In Chapter 16, I explained how to include Flash movies in your website. Because Flash is made by the same folks who make Dreamweaver and because there is essentially only one player that plays Flash movies, you have more control over how Flash movies are placed in Dreamweaver web pages than you do when you embed other types of video.

RealMedia movie files have the advantage of using the most advanced downloading features—called *streaming*—which means visitors start watching a movie well before the entire movie file has downloaded to their system.

Flash movies have the advantage of being very compact in file size. Flash movies also support streaming, and provide a high-quality video experience for online viewers.

What this all means is that if you are going to include video in your site, you should let visitors know where they can get the software needed to play the video.

Table 18.1 identifies the most popular types of online video, as well as download sites for the required player.

Table 18.1   Popular Video Formats and Players

File Extension/Type	Player	Download Site
MOV/QuickTime	QuickTime and others	www.apple.com/quicktime/
AVI/Windows Audio Video	Windows Media Player and others	http://www.microsoft.com/ windows/windowsmedia/ download/
SWF/Flash	Flash Player	www.macromedia.com/ downloads/
MPEG/Windows Animation	Windows Media Player and others	www.microsoft.com/ windows/windowsmedia/ download/
RM/RealMedia	Real Player	www.real.com

Opening Movies in a New Browser Window

OK, now that you're clear on where movies come from and how they get played on the Internet, putting a movie in your web page is the easy part.

The simplest way to include a movie in your site is to add the video file to your site, and then provide a link to that file. To do that, follow these steps:

1. Copy a MOV, SWF, MPEG, RM, or other media file into your local Dreamweaver site folder.

2. View your site in the Site window. Your media file will be visible. If you wish, you can safely organize your media files in a separate folder, like the one in Figure 18.3.

3. In the Document window, create a text link to the media file, as shown in Figure 18.4.

4. It's a good idea to open a video in a new browser window, so when a visitor closes the video, he or she returns to your web page. Do this by choosing **_blank** in the Target area of the Properties panel for your link.

Inside Info

In Chapter 19, I'll show you how to use Behaviors to test visitors' browsers, and determine if they need a plug-in to view movies on your page.

Inside Info

Remember, it's helpful to include text explaining that visitors are about to open a video file, that it might take some time to download, and that they will also need a player for that file. I usually include a link to a site where visitors can download an appropriate player file, as shown in Figure 18.4.

Figure 18.3

Organizing videos in the Site window.

Figure 18.4

Linking to a movie.

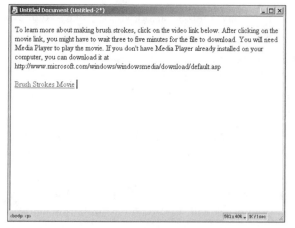

Plugging In Movies

Embedded movies are different than movies you simply link to in that they appear within your web page.

Embedded movies appear in a web page with player controls. The weird part of this is that you don't know which player controls will appear in a visitor's browser. Remember, as I explained in the beginning of this chapter, in general media players depend on which operating system a visitor is using. And, with each iteration of Windows or Mac OS (the media player gets "enhanced" with new buttons and stuff).

Figure 18.5 shows a movie viewed with the Mac QuickTime player. This same movie would be viewed in the Windows Media Player if the visitor was using a PC.

Figure 18.5

A Windows Media movie playing in the QuickTime player on a Mac.

Placing a Movie on a Page

You can embed QuickTime movies, Windows Media movies, and other animation formats by choosing **Insert, Media, Plug-In,** and navigating to a video file.

QuickTime (MOV) and Windows Media (AVI and MPEG) files fit quite nicely into Dreamweaver pages. You can define the size of the player and other parameters like border size and spacing.

RealMedia files don't plug in so well. It bugs me that the manufacturers of the Real player can't sit down with the folks at Macromedia, bury the hatchet, and find a way to make their products work together. You *should* be able to embed Real movies as easily as MOV and MPEG files, but in my experience, you can't reliably embed Real video files. Perhaps Real and Macromedia will learn to get along at some point, and if and when that happens, you'll be able to embed Real movies just as you can the other popular formats.

The routine for formatting video files is very similar to the routine for embedding audio files. The main difference is that you will want to define the plug-in size large enough to present the movie. You'll need to experiment with different plug-in sizes.

Inside Info

This unpredictability is not an issue with Flash movies, which require and play with the Flash player no matter which operating system they are viewed with.

To insert a movie plug in, follow these steps:

1. In the Document window, choose **Insert, Media, Plug-In**.

2. In the Select File dialog box that appears, navigate to the MPEG, AVI, MOV (or other) video file you wish to embed in your site.

3. If the movie is outside of your local site folder, you'll be prompted to copy the file to your local site folder. Click **Yes** in the dialog box prompting you to save the file to your site folder and navigate to a folder within your site. Then, click **Save in the Copy File** dialog box to save the file to your site.

4. The movie plug-in will appear as a small icon in the Document window. You can resize this icon by selecting it, and clicking and dragging on a side or corner handle, as shown in Figure 18.6.

Figure 18.6

Resizing a movie in Dreamweaver.

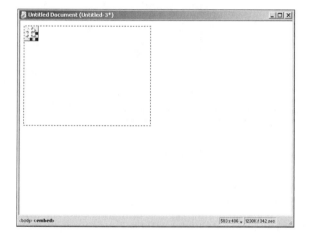

After you embed the video, save your page. You can preview the movie (choose **File, Preview in Browser**, and select a browser). Return to the Dreamweaver document window, and continue to resize the video for the optimum display.

Defining Movie Properties

Once you have successfully embedded a video into your page, you can define how that video displays in a browser. Sort of.

Remember, if you're embedding an MPEG, MOV, or AVI video, you don't really know what video player will

> **Inside Info**
>
> To maintain the height-to-width ratio of your video as you resize, hold down the Shift key and click and drag on the corner handle.

> **Inside Info**
>
> You can preview a selected movie right in Dreamweaver by viewing the Properties panel and clicking the Play button in that panel.

appear in your visitor's browser. But you can have *some* control over how the video is displayed, including the location of the video on the page, the size of the video player, the thickness of the border around the video, and other formatting.

To define how your movie will look, select your movie and choose the Properties panel. The Properties panel for a selected movie is shown in Figure 18.7.

Figure 18.7

Defining movie properties.

The Properties panel for a selected movie allows you to define how big the movie will be in your page, how it will align on the page, as well as other display options. The display choices in the panel are listed below.

- ◆ The W and H areas of the Properties panel define the width (W) and height (H) of the movie in pixels.
- ◆ The Src area defines the video file.
- ◆ The Plg URL defines a URL (web address) to display if a visitor needs a plug-in player to see the movie.
- ◆ The Align list allows you to align a video left or right, and to wrap text around the video just as you would an image.
- ◆ The V (vertical) and H (horizontal) space areas allow you to define buffer space between the video and surrounding text. Use these areas if you align the video, so that your video doesn't bump right up against the text flowing around it.
- ◆ The Border area defines border thickness in pixels. Border color is defined by the color of surrounding paragraph text.
- ◆ Use the Play button in the Properties panel to preview your video right in the Document window.

> **Inside Info**
>
> Sometimes the Play button works, sometimes it doesn't. To really preview how your running movie will look in a web page, preview the page in a browser.

Defining ActiveX Objects

Active X is Microsoft's version of plug-in software. It can be configured to present all kinds of interactive objects, but for our purposes here, it works pretty much like the Plug-In option. You can add a video file as an ActiveX object instead of a plug-in. It will look the same in most browsers.

To embed a movie as an ActiveX control, follow these steps:

1. In the Document window, choose **Insert, Media, ActiveX.**

2. With the new ActiveX control visible, view the Properties panel (as shown in Figure 18.8).

Figure 18.8

Defining Properties for an ActiveX object.

3. Select the **Embed** checkbox, and click on the **Browse for File** icon next to the Src area in the Properties panel. Use the dialog box that opens (it varies depending on which plug-in you selected recently) to navigate to and select a video file.

4. Most of the features in the ActiveX Properties panel are the same as those for plug-ins. Some additional areas are used for programming your own ActiveX objects, and are not relevant to embedding movies.

You can test your ActiveX control in a browser. In most cases, it will look just like a plug-in.

The Least You Need to Know

◆ Movie files are huge, they take a long time to download.

◆ Dreamweaver doesn't create or edit video, but it manages placing video in your website.

◆ You can either link a video from a page, or embed a video within a page.

◆ When you embed a video plug-in (or ActiveX object) in a page, you don't know which video player your visitors will use to view the movie. That depends on your visitors' operating system.

Making Dreamweaver Behave

In This Chapter

- ◆ Understanding how Behaviors work
- ◆ Creating rollover images
- ◆ Making objects fly around with timelines
- ◆ Automatically opening custom-sized browser windows
- ◆ Changing status bar text
- ◆ Detecting visitors' browsers and plug-ins

Dreamweaver Behaviors allow you to add *animation* and *interactivity* to your web pages. By animation, I mean you can make stuff move around on your pages. By interactivity, I mean you can create page objects that react to things a visitor does—for instance, a picture that changes when a visitor rolls over it with his or her mouse cursor.

In previous chapters, I've touched on the use of Dreamweaver Behaviors to create things like scripts that test form input before a form is submitted, or sounds that play when a page opens.

How Behaviors Work

Behaviors mainly work by generating *JavaScript*—a programming language that is interpreted and acted on by visitors' browsers.

JavaScript is very widely supported by browsers, so many Behaviors work in almost every browser, going back to Netscape Navigator version 2 and Internet Explorer version 3.

Definition

The technology used to generate complex Behaviors is sometimes referred to as **DOM**, or Document Object Model. DOM includes advanced, complex CSS (cascading style sheets) that allow for exact placement of objects on pages.

Complex Behaviors are built on JavaScript, but rely on more recent innovations in browser technology that are not supported by even the current version of Netscape Navigator.

Dreamweaver allows you to choose a set of available Behaviors depending on what browser you want to design for. If you want to ensure that all the Behaviors on your page work in all browsers, the choice of options is smaller than if you want to create pages that will work well in IE 6, but might not work in older or other browsers.

Behaviors and Browsers

Since not all Behaviors work in older browsers, Dreamweaver allows you to disable Behaviors that won't work in browsers that you select. So, for instance, you can decide that many of your visitors are still using Netscape Navigator 4.7, and you want to make sure that every Behavior on your page works for those visitors. Or, you can decide that most visitors will have IE 5.5 or higher, and those who don't can just miss out on some of the fun.

To define the browser and version for which you are designing Behaviors, follow these steps:

1. With a page open in the Document window, choose **Window, Behaviors** to display the Behaviors panel.

2. Click the "**+**" symbol at the top of the Behaviors panel, and choose **Show Events For** from the menu. A flyout menu displays browsers and versions, as shown in Figure 19.1.

3. Choose a browser and version. The list of available Behaviors will now match those that work in the browser you selected.

Figure 19.1

Defining which Behaviors you want to use.

Defining Events and Actions

Behaviors are generated using menus and dialog boxes. Most Behaviors are initiated by using the "+" symbol in the Behaviors panel. You can delete any selected Behavior by clicking the "-" symbol in the Behaviors panel.

After you create a Behavior, you will often want to change or edit it. You can do this if you understand that each Behavior is basically a set of events and actions.

Events are things that happen—like a page loading, or a visitor scrolling over a picture.

Actions are changes that are triggered by events. For instance, a picture changing, text formatting changing, or text appearing in a browser window status bar.

As we create Behaviors, we'll also explore the events and actions that make them do the things they do. And we'll edit events and actions in the Behaviors inspector.

Page and Object Behaviors

I find that it's helpful to think of them in two categories, page related and object related.

Some Behaviors react to *page* events—for instance, you can open a custom-defined browser window when a visitor opens or exits a web page.

Other Behaviors react to events that happen to text or pictures—for instance, a picture that changes when it is rolled over by a mouse cursor.

And, some Behaviors can react to either a page event or an object event. For instance, you can have a Behavior open a new window or a dialog box when a page opens, *or* when a visitors rolls over a button on a page.

The trick is to select the object to which you want to attach a Behavior *before* you start defining Behaviors in the Behaviors panel.

If you want to attach a Behavior to a page, switch to Code and Design view for a moment (choose **View, Code and Design**), and click on the **Body** tag. Don't worry if the Body tag has parameters, as long as you've selected it, as shown in Figure 19.2, you can go on to define Behaviors that are triggered by page events (like the page opening or closing).

Figure 19.2

Grabbing the <body> tag.

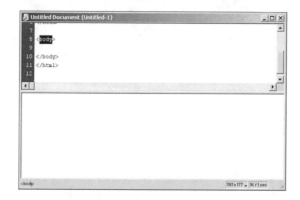

Pictures with Pizzazz

Dreamweaver can generate Behaviors that display more than one picture. The most commonly used is a rollover image, that changes when a visitor moves his or her cursor over it. Rollover images usually include links.

A more complex set of interactive images involves navigation bars. These bars are formatted automatically in tables, and display four different button images depending on whether a link is unused, used, hovered over, or active.

Create a Rollover

Rollovers are images that change when a visitor moves his or her mouse cursor over the image.

By the Way

You need to create the identically sized images for your rollover in a different program, like Fireworks.

In order for a rollover to work well, you need two images that are the same size. If the images are different sizes or shapes, the second image that is displayed will be warped or distorted, since it will get squished or expanded to fill a box the size of the original image.

Once you've created two identically sized images, you're ready to generate a rollover.

Follow these steps to generate a rollover image that serves as a link.

1. In a new or existing web page, choose **Insert, Interactive Images, Rollover Image.**

2. In the Insert Rollover Image dialog box, enter **Rollover1** in the Image Name area.

3. In the Original Image area, use the Browse button to navigate to and select the image file that will display before the image is rolled over.

4. In the Rollover Image area, use the Browse button to navigate to and select the image file that will display when the image is rolled over.

5. In the When Clicked Go to URL area, enter or browse to a URL.

6. **OK** the dialog box, and test the rollover in a browser.

Create a Timeline

Timelines create animation in Dreamweaver pages. They can be used to have a block of text or an image fly around on the page, either continuously, or just once.

Timelines have frames and layers. Frames work like frames in a movie. They display one-at-a-time at a rate (frames per second) that you define, and they create the illusion of animation for viewers.

Complex Timelines can involve multiple layers. But really, for that kind of complex animation you're better off just learning Flash. We'll confine ourselves to a one-layer Timeline here.

Figure 19.3 shows the Timeline panel, with the Frames row and Layers columns identified.

Follow these steps to create a Timeline that moves an image across the top of your page.

By the Way

Timelines work by combining JavaScript with Layer objects. In walking you through the process of creating a Timeline, I'll assume you're pretty comfortable with placing images and text in layers. If not, a quick review of Chapter 8 will be a good detour about now.

Inside Info

If you've worked with Flash, you're familiar with the Timeline interface.

1. Choose **Insert, Layer** to create a new layer.

2. Type text (like **"Welcome"**) in the layer. Format the text.

3. Choose **Window, Others, Timelines.**

Figure 19.3

The Timeline panel.

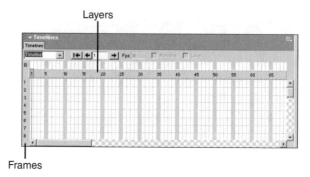

4. Drag the LAYER into the first layer, first frame of the Timelines inspector as shown in Figure 19.4.

Caution

You must drag the layer, not just the text, into the frame.

5. Click on the 15th frame in the first layer of the Timeline.

6. With the 15th frame selected, drag the layer (on the page) to the right side of the page, as shown in Figure 19.5.

Figure 19.4

Dragging a layer into a Timeline.

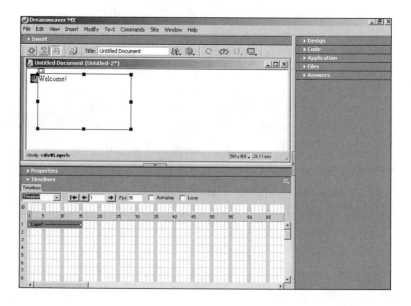

7. In the Timelines panel, select the **Autoplay** and **Loop** checkboxes. This will play the animation as soon as a page is opened, and continue the animation indefinitely.

8. Save your page and test your animation.

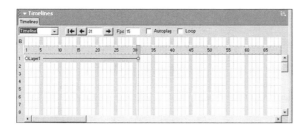

Figure 19.5

Defining an ending point for a Timeline animation.

Creating Page Associated Behaviors

Page-associated Behaviors include status bar text (messages like, "Special this week!—buy in the next 5 minutes!"), and having a browser window open with custom specifications.

The custom browser window Behavior is used frequently in websites. You can define a browser window with none, or just some of the usual browser elements (like a navigation bar). And you can custom size a browser window.

Defining Status Bar Text

Ever notice the text in your browser's status bar? It provides information, sometimes. When a page opens, the status bar displays information like "loading" or "done."

Since the browser window status bar doesn't include any particularly essential text, it works—from a design point of view—to stick your own text in the status bar.

Follow these steps to define status bar text:

1. With a page open in the Document window, view the Behaviors panel.

2. Click on the **+** sign in the Behaviors inspector, and choose **Set Text, Set Text of Status Bar** as shown in Figure 19.6.

3. In the Set Text of Status Bar dialog, enter some text to display.

4. **OK** the dialog box.

5. Use the Events drop-down list to change the triggering event to OnLoad. This will display the status bar text when a page *loads* (opens).

6. Test your page in a browser. Figure 19.7 shows a browser window with custom-defined status bar text.

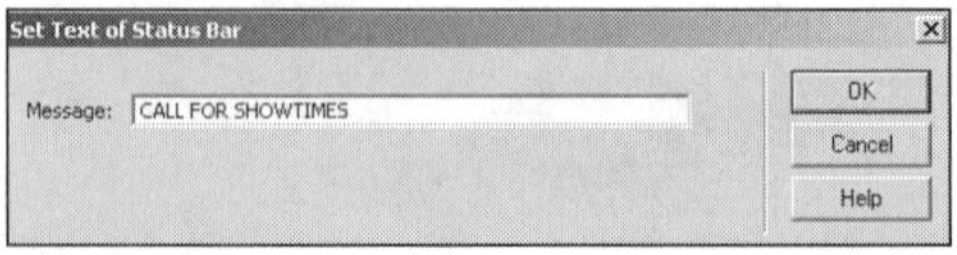

Figure 19.6

Defining new status bar text.

Figure 19.7

This text was defined with a Behavior.

Status bar text

Opening a New Browser Window

Among the most frequently invoked JavaScripts are those that open a new browser window.

Frequently the new browser window displays an advertising special (for instance, as I write this book both Netscape and AOL bombard visitors with an obnoxious ad in a new browser window, and unfortunately this practice is becoming quite widespread in web design).

New browser windows can be closed by a visitor, without closing the web page that launched them.

When you define a new browser window with a Behavior, you can enable or disable the following attributes for the new browser window:

♦ **Navigation toolbar**   Back, Refresh, Home and other icons.

♦ **Location toolbar**   The line where a visitor enters or views a page URL.

♦ **Status bar**   The text on the bottom of the browser window.

♦ **Menu bar**   The File, Edit, Favorites, Tools, and other menu options for the browser window.

♦ **Scrollbars as needed**   Horizontal and/or vertical scrollbars if the defined window is too small for the page content.

♦ **Resize handles**   The ability to change the size of the browser window.

In addition, you can define the exact size (in pixels) of the browser window that opens.

Follow the steps below to open a new browser window when a page opens:

1. With a page that will launch the new browser window open in the Document window, view the Behaviors panel.

2. Click on the **+** sign in the Behaviors panel, and choose **Open Browser Window.**

3. In the Open Browser Window dialog box, enter a page (or image file) link in the URL to display area.

4. Define the size of the browser window, and which Attributes to include. Your dialog box should look something like the one in Figure 19.8.

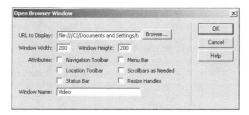

Figure 19.8

Defining a new browser window—this one will open 200 pixels square, with no browser toolbars or other attributes.

5. Make OnLoad the triggering Event.

6. Test your page in a browser.

Generating Pop-up Messages

Pop-up messages are a) cute and helpful, b) obnoxious and annoying, or c) depends. They are those little dialog boxes, like the one shown in Figure 19.9, that force a visitor to read and close them before the dialog box goes away.

Figure 19.9

Read this or else!

This dialog box is reminding visitors that the site has some new features.

You *can* trigger a pop-up message based on an event that happens to a selected object on a page. But more likely, you'll want to launch the pop-up message when a page itself is loaded (or exited).

By the Way

If you were looking for help on creating pop-up menus, you'll find that in Chapter 15, where I explain how to integrate pop-up menus created in Fireworks.

To create a pop-up window that opens when a page loads, follow the steps below.

1. With a page open in the Document window, view the Behaviors panel.

2. Click the "**+**" symbol in the Behaviors panel, and choose **Popup Message** from the list of Behaviors.

3. Enter some text in the Popup Message dialog box, as shown in Figure 19.10. This is the text that will display when the page is opened.

Figure 19.10

Defining a pop-up message.

4. Click **OK**. Note that the current setting in the Events column for this Behavior is OnClick. That's not the event you want if the pop-up window is going to launch when a page loads.

5. Choose **View, Show Code and Design View** to see some of your HTML code. Scroll up and down until you find the <Body> tag associated with your page.

6. With the <Body> tag selected, click on the **Events** column for your action, and choose **OnLoad,** as shown in Figure 19.11.

Figure 19.11

This Behavior will be triggered when a page is loaded.

7. Save your page and test the Behavior in your browser.

Making Browsers Behave

In the course of this book, and in this chapter, I've often noted things like "this doesn't work in Netscape Navigator 4.7." For instance, many Behaviors don't work in Netscape 4.7.

Aside from putting some text on your page that says something like "You need Internet Explorer 5 or newer to have much fun at this page," how can you detect and deal with visitors who don't have the right browser?

One option is to use a Behavior to automatically detect what browser a visitor is using, and send that visitor to a page that is created just for that visitor's browser. This approach obviously involved extra work, but for large volume sites, it's often a good way to maximize the experience of each visitor.

Inside Info

It doesn't matter what additional attributes are assigned with the Body tag, the important thing is to select the text "body" so Dreamweaver knows you are defining a Behavior that is linked to the page, not a specific object on the page.

Definition

The Behavior event OnLoad doesn't mean that an action will occur when a person viewing your site "gets loaded!" It means the Behavior will be triggered when the page is loaded.

You can also detect whether or not a visitor has the required plug-in software to experience all the content on a page. For instance, if you have a Flash movie embedded in a page, you can automatically detect whether a visitor coming to that page has the Flash viewer installed. And, if not, you can divert the visitor to another page.

Finally, you sometimes want to just automatically divert visitors who come to your site to a different page. In this world of quickly changing URLs and company and domain names, it's handy to just move someone who comes to cheappets.com to discountpets.com, without the visitor even being aware of a change in URL.

I'll show you how to do all that with Behaviors in this last section.

Checking Browsers

The Check Browser Behavior detects what version of a browser is being used by visitors to your page. Depending on which browser version they are using, you have three basic options:

- ◆ Have them stay on the page.
- ◆ Go to another page.
- ◆ Go to an alternate page set up for visitors who are using an older browser.

To define a check browser Behavior, follow these steps:

1. With the page open in the Document window, view the Behaviors panel.

2. Click "**+**"and choose **Check Browser** from the list of Behaviors. The Check Browser dialog box opens.

3. In the Netscape Navigator area, choose a version of Netscape Navigator to screen for.

4. In the Or Later drop-down list, define what to do if a visitor with the defined version of Netscape Navigator comes to your page.

5. In the Otherwise drop-down list, define what to do if a visitor *without* the defined version of Netscape Navigator (or newer) comes to your page.

6. In the Internet Explorer (IE) section of the Check Browser dialog box, define a version of IE to test for, and define actions (URLs to go to) if the visitor has, or does not have the version of IE (or newer) that you defined.

By the Way

The Check Browser Behavior is available for all browsers past version 3.

7. There are other browsers in the world besides IE and Navigator. Since many of those other browsers don't support Dreamweaver Behaviors, they won't detect or react to *this* Behavior anyway! Therefore, this section of the dialog box is kind of a waste, and there's not that much reason to mess with it.

8. After you define the Check Browser criteria, your dialog box should look something like the one in Figure 19.12. Click **OK.**

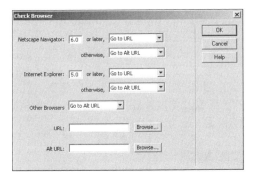

Figure 19.12

This Behavior will detect visitors with browsers older than Netscape Navigator 6, or IE 5, and send them to a special page that does not require modern browser features.

Are You Plugged In?

Plug-ins are required to play media files like Flash movies or sound files. You can define a Behavior that will automatically test the browser of a visitor to your page, and detect whether or not the visitor has the necessary plug-in software on his or her computer.

Normally, if a visitor *has* the required plug-in software, there's no need to do anything. The visitor can enjoy your web page and all the content on it.

If a visitor *does not* have plug-in software required by media on your page, you can send him or her to another page. That alternate page might be a different version of your page content without the Flash movie or QuickTime animation. Or, it might be a page that instructs the visitor on how to download the plug-in needed to view the media on the page.

By the Way

For more discussion of media plug-ins and including media on your site, jump back to Chapter 18.

Follow the steps below to create a Behavior that tests for a plug-in, and reroutes visitors without that plug-in to an alternate page.

1. With your page open in the Document window, click the "**+**" symbol at the top of the Behaviors panel.

2. Choose **Check Plugin** (I know, it's usually spelled with a dash, but the Macromedia programmers liked "plugin" better here) from the list of Behaviors. The Check Plugin dialog box opens.

By the Way

The options are Flash, Shockwave, LiveAudio, QuickTime, or Windows Media Player. For an explanation of what the heck these players do, see Chapter 16 or Chapter 18 for more info on the Flash player.

3. In the Plugin drop-down list, choose the media player plug-in required for your page.

4. In the Otherwise Go To URL area, enter (or browse to) a page to which you will redirect visitors who don't have the required software for your media files.

5. If a visitor's browser does not detect the necessary software, he or she will go to the URL you define in the Otherwise area. Sometimes, a browser will not detect a player on a system when it's actually there. For that reason it's a good idea to check the Always Go To First URL If Detection Is Not Possible checkbox, as shown in Figure 19.13. Then click **OK**.

Figure 19.13

If a browser can definitively detect that the Flash player is not installed, a different page will open.

Sending Browsers to a URL

There are many reasons why you might want to instantly redirect a visitor from one page to another. You or your client might have promoted a URL, only to change the company name. Or, you might want to redirect visitors from an old, out-of-date site to another site.

In any case, you can automatically reroute visitors to a new page using the **Go To URL** Behavior.

This Behavior is pretty simple to use. There aren't a lot of options. No matter what, visitors who come to your page will jump to another page.

By the Way

For an explanation of frames and links between them, see Chapter 10.

To define a Go to URL Behavior for an open page, click the "**+**" symbol in the Behaviors panel, and choose **Go To URL** from the list of Behaviors.

In the Go To URL dialog box, enter the new URL in the URL area. This is the page to which visitors will be redirected.

If you are defining this Behavior in a frameset, you can use the Open In area of the dialog box to define a target frame.

The Least You Need to Know

- ◆ Behaviors add all kinds of fun and excitement to your pages by making pages and objects move around and react to visitors.
- ◆ Behaviors use JavaScript, but you don't need to know JavaScript from the New York Knicks to use them. Dreamweaver handles all that.
- ◆ Older browsers don't support all Behaviors.

Part 7

Site Management and Maintenance

Once your site is finished, it's not really finished. You'll want to test your links, identify pages with problems, and keep track of the state of your site. In the following chapters, I'll show you how to use Dreamweaver's built-in reports to identify and fix site boo-boos.

I'll also turn you on to some tools you can use outside of Dreamweaver. Some of them are available through Dreamweaver Extensions, others add counters and search boxes to your site.

Chapter 20

Testing and Troubleshooting Sites and Links

In This Chapter

- ◆ Working with others on big projects
- ◆ Adding Design Notes to pages
- ◆ Generating site maps
- ◆ Testing your site for bugs and boo boos

Your car (or bike) needs regular maintenance. Your computer needs periodic (or perhaps constant) repair. Your filing cabinet needs to be weeded every once in a while. And your Dreamweaver website needs periodic testing, documenting, and cleaning up.

Dreamweaver provides many macro-tools to allow you to oversee and manage your site. These tools test your links, create a graphic map of your site (a site map), provide reports on the status of your site, and help groups of developers "talk to each other."

In this chapter, I'll introduce you to these tools, and show you how to keep your Dreamweaver site in nice working order.

Documenting Big Projects

A small site can be managed with some notes on the back of an envelope. But as your site grows, and as more developers join in the fun, you'll need more sophisticated methods for keeping track of your work, coordinating with others, and sharing an overview of your site.

By the Way

Design Notes are most often used to keep track of the status of HTML web pages. But they can also be attached to images, media files, or any file in your site.

Caution

Make sure you pull down the File menu in the Site window, not the File menu in the Document window.

Dreamweaver Notes allow you to add comments to every object in your site. Site maps are an important way to keep track of and share the link relationships in your site. And activating Dreamweaver's check in/check out features allow a team of designers to know who is working on what.

Takin' Notes

Design Notes can be used to assign a status level to a file (like draft, final, or something in between). They can also be used like digital "post-its," to keep track of any information you want to associate with a file.

To add notes to a file:

1. Select a file in the Site window.
2. From the Site Window File menu, choose **File, Design Notes,** as shown in Figure 20.1.

Figure 20.1

Defining a Design Note.

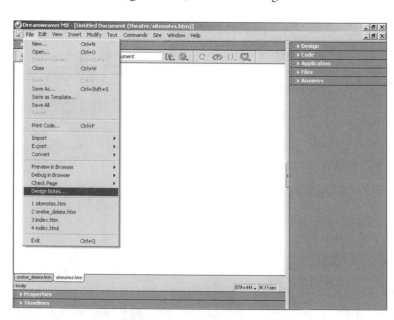

3. In the Design Notes dialog box, you can select one of the categories in the Status drop-down list. You can also enter free-form notes in the Notes area of the dialog box. Figure 20.2 shows a Status of Draft, and some notes.

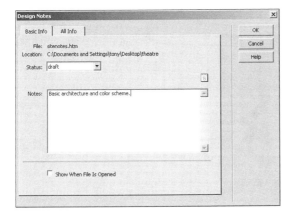

Figure 20.2

Defining draft status for an unfinished file.

4. After you define a note, click **OK** in the Design Notes dialog box.

By Default, a Notes column is displayed in the Site window. If you assign a status to all or most of your files, you can sort your project by work status. To do this, just click on the Notes column heading. Figure 20.3 shows a set of files organized by their task status.

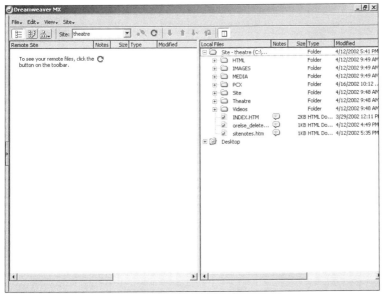

Figure 20.3

Organizing files by their state of completion.

Visualize This Site—Using a Site Map

A site map is like a blueprint for a building. Except that a site map can and often is generated not only at the beginning of a website, but also during, and at the end of a web design project.

Figure 20.4 shows a site map displaying the web pages in a site, and the links between them.

Figure 20.4

A site map.

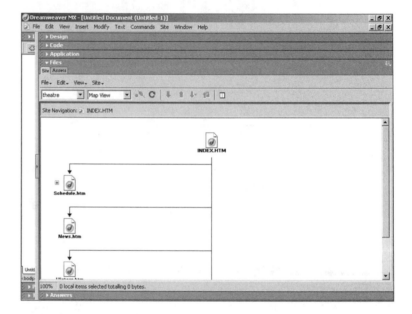

Inside Info

The Site Map icon drop-down menu also allows you to show just the site map (the Map Only menu option). Usually, you'll want to see both a site map and a list of your site files, so the Map and Files option is usually more helpful.

To generate a site map for your site, choose **Map and Files** from the Site Map icon drop-down menu, as shown in Figure 20.5.

The Site Map window can be changed to display page titles instead of page file names. This is often helpful since when you share an overview of a site with others, they are more likely to be interested in page titles (which tend to be more descriptive) than page file names. To change view, choose **View, Show Page Titles in Windows,** or **Site, Site Map View, Show Page Titles** on a Macintosh.

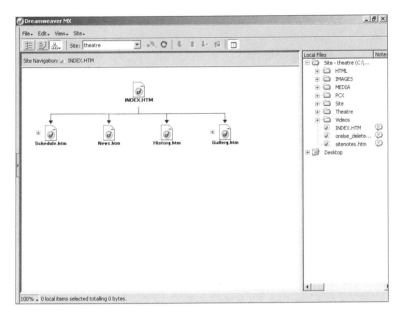

Figure 20.5

Viewing both the site map and site files.

Your site map displays existing links within your site. If you want to preserve this image, you can save it. To do that, choose **File, Save Site Map.** You can choose an image file format, a file name, and navigate to a folder in which you save the site map. You can then touch up and print the site map in your favorite graphics program.

The Site Map view can also be used to *define* links within a site. To define a link using the site map, click on a file in the site map, and then use the associated point to file icon to click and drag to a file—either in the site map itself, or in the regular Site window list of files. In Figure 20.6, I'm defining a link from a page in my site map to a file.

Links generated by clicking and dragging in the Site Map view are placed on pages as text links. These links can be edited or formatted when you open the page in the Document window.

Caution

Make sure you use the View menu on the Site window, not the Document window.

Checkin' In and Checkin' Out

David Byrne and the Talking Heads used to sing

> Checkin' in, checkin' out, woah-oh
> I got 'em wild, wild life

In the wild life of web design, it won't do to have two developers editing a page at the same time. I change the background color to blue. You change it to red. What a mess!

Figure 20.6

Generating links from the site map.

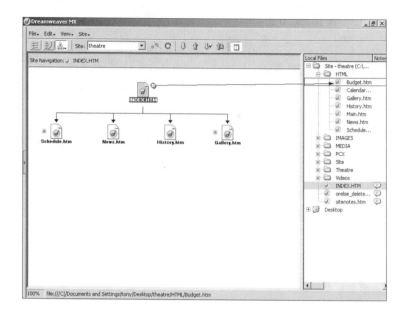

Dreamweaver's check in/check out feature allows multiple developers to check pages in or out the same way you check DVDs out (and back in) at your local video store.

To enable the check in/check out feature, follow these steps:

1. With your site open, choose **Site, Edit Sites, Edit** from the Site Window menu.
2. Click on the **Remote Info** category in the Category list.
3. Select the **Check In/Out** checkbox.
4. As soon as you select the checkbox, new options appear. By default, the Check Out Files When Opening checkbox is selected. This automatically informs others that you have a file checked out. The information associated with you checking out files is the name you enter in the Check Out Name, as shown in Figure 20.7.
5. Click **OK** to close the Site Definition dialog box.
6. Click **Done** to close the Edit Site dialog box.

Inside Info

Checking files in and out only works when you are connected to a remote site. If you're simply working on a local site, there is almost never a reason why two developers will have the same page open.

Once you've enabled check in/check out, you can select a file in the Remote side of the Site window (use Site Files view), and then click the **Check Out File**(s) icon in the Site window.

When you check out files, the Dependent Files dialog box will prompt you to check out additional files that are linked to or embedded in the file you are checking out. You can say Yes or No to that option.

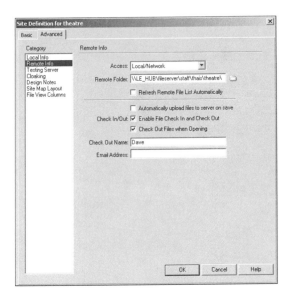

Figure 20.7

Files are checked out.

The Checked Out By column in the Remote Site window will tell your colleagues that you are working on the selected file(s). Figure 20.8 shows several files checked out to me. When I'm done, I'll check them back in.

After you're done, you can use the Check In icon in the Site window to remove your check out information from selected files.

> **Inside Info**
>
> You can select a single file to check out or many files at once. To choose a bunch of files listed together, use Shift+click and click on the first and last file to select all the files in between. To select a set of disconnected files, use Command/Ctrl+click.

Cloaking Files

Is "cloaking" a metaphor for checking in your coat in a cloakroom? Or for the "cloak and dagger" world of international espionage?

Whichever, it's a way of protecting selected files from all site operations, such as uploading (putting) files to the server, generating site reports, or link checking.

For example, you might want to put selected files in a folder with a PVT file extension (the folder can be called private.pvt). To turn that folder into a cloaked folder, file these steps:

1. In the Site window, choose **Site, Cloaking Settings**. The Cloaking tab of the Site Definition dialog box opens.

2. Select the **Enable Cloaking** checkbox.

Figure 20.8

Dave is working on these files now.

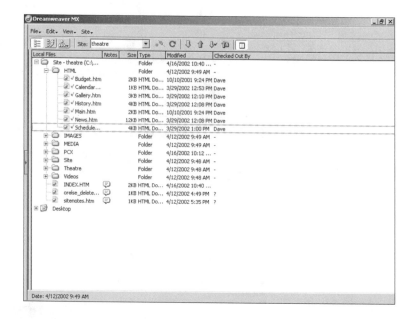

3. Select the **Cloak Files Ending With** checkbox, and enter a file name extension (like, for instance, pvt) as shown in Figure 20.9.

Figure 20.9

Cloak and daggering files.

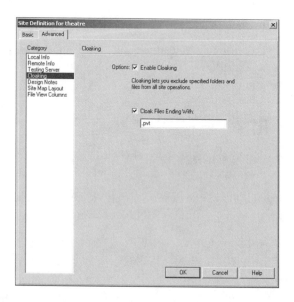

4. Click **OK** to close the dialog box.

Files you selected for cloaking will appear with a red diagonal line across their file icons in the Site window, as shown in Figure 20.10.

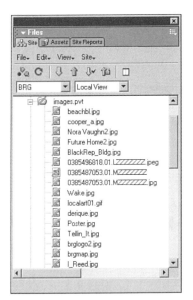

Figure 20.10

These files are cloaked.

Testing Links

In the fast-moving world of the web, links change all the time. The helpful link you provided to a resource yesterday might be outdated today.

Dreamweaver provides two useful site management tools to test and update links. You can use a special search-and-replace feature to update links. And, you can test all links in your site.

To test all the links in your site, choose **Site, Check Links Sitewide** from the Site window menu. This will test your links throughout your site.

After Dreamweaver checks your links, it displays a report that identifies broken links, all external links (links outside your site), or *orphaned files.*

Definition

Orphan files are files on your site that are not accessible from links on any page in your site. Often, orphan files are old files no longer used in your site, and you might want to clean them up (delete them). Other times, they are files you might want to keep on your site to store data at your server. Or, they could be files to which you have provided some people a direct URL for access. So you don't always want to delete orphan files, but often you do.

You can choose which set of files to view in your Link Checker report by selecting a report from the Show drop-down list. In Figure 20.11, I'm looking at the Broken Links list.

Figure 20.11

Identifying bad links.

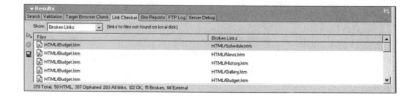

Inside Info

Files that are cloaked will be excluded from this process, as well as other site operations. I explained cloaking a bit earlier in this chapter.

To fix any identified broken or bad links, you can double-click on a file right in the Link Checker report. This opens the file in Document window for editing.

To globally change links within your site from one link to another, you can use the Change Link Sitewide feature. In the Site window, choose **Site, Change Link Sitewide.** The Change Link Sitewide dialog box appears.

Enter the old, out-of-date link you wish to change in the Change All Links to area of the Change Link Sitewide dialog box. Enter the *new* link, the one you want to replace the old link with, in the Into Links To area of the dialog box, as shown in Figure 20.12.

Figure 20.12

Changing an out-of-date link.

After you identify your old link, and specify a new link, click **OK.** Dreamweaver will search throughout your site and change all your links.

Site Reports

There are a million things that can cause a site to look tacky. Pages that don't have assigned page titles open with "Untitled Page" in the browser window title bar—a sure sign of an amateur (or overworked!) web designer. Visitors expect to see screentip text pop up when they roll over an image, and quality sites have such *Alt* text assigned to images.

Rather than raise your stress level by trying to examine each page in your site, you can let Dreamweaver search for bugs and boo boos like this, and provide you with a list of pages to fix.

Generating Reports

Dreamweaver provides two kinds of reports on the status of your site—workflow reports and HTML reports. The workflow reports generate lists of either files that have been checked out, or files that have notes.

The six HTML reports analyze the HTML in your pages, and do some fairly sophisticated summarizing of problems you might encounter. Some are useful to noncoders, some not. The available reports are:

- The **Combinable Nested Font Tags** report identifies badly done HTML code. If you rely on Dreamweaver to generate your HTML, this won't be a significant issue.
- The **Missing Alt Text** report identifies images that don't have associated ALT text. ALT text provides captions for visually impaired visitors, and shows as rollover text in most browsers.
- The **Redundant Nested Tags report** identifies even more arcane HTML errors than the Combinable Nested Font Tags report and is not a useful report if you rely on Dreamweaver to generate your HTML.
- The **Removable Empty Tags report** also identifies meaningless HTML coding sloppiness. So what!
- On the useful side, the **Untitled Documents report** lists HTML pages that do not have titles assigned. Titles show up in browser windows, and are essential for well-designed sites. You can add a title to a page in the Title area at the top of the Document window.

To generate any combination of the available reports, choose **Site, Reports** from *either* the Site or Document window. The Reports dialog box opens.

Use the Report On drop-down list to generate reports for an open document (current document), the Entire Current Local Site, Selected Files in a site (select them first in the Site window), or a Folder (this opens a dialog box where you can choose a folder).

By the Way

Normally, you'll want to test your Entire Current Local Site. That way, you'll check all files.

Select reports using the checkboxes in the Reports dialog box, as shown in Figure 20.13. Then, click **Run** to generate these reports.

Figure 20.13

I'm going to find all the missing page titles and missing Alt tags in my site.

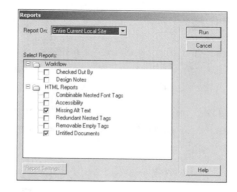

Fixing Site Boo Boos

Once you run a report, a list of files is generated in the Site Reports tab of the Site Reports window.

As you can see in Figure 20.14, when I generated a report for missing ALT tags and pages without titles, the generated report includes *both* problems.

Figure 20.14

All my bad pages are listed in the report.

If you want to sort the generated report by type of problem, you can click on the Description column heading in the Reports window to sort files by the problem.

You can fix errors on a listed page by double-clicking on the page. This opens the page in the Document window, where you can hunt down and fix mistakes.

Periodically checking for errors is an important part of maintaining a clean, attractive, usable site.

The Least You Need to Know

- ◆ You can add Design Notes to any file in Dreamweaver to help organize your work.
- ◆ You can generate a site map to present a graphical overview of your site and the links within it.
- ◆ If you work together with others on a large project, you can define check in/check out features that keep track of who is working on what.

◆ Links often go bad. Dreamweaver will test all your links for you and identify ones that need to be fixed.

◆ Dreamweaver will search your site and prepare reports on problems like missing ALT text for images or missing page titles.

Chapter 21

Extra! Extra!—Other Tools for Enhancing Your Site

In This Chapter

- ◆ Extending Dreamweaver with extensions
- ◆ Downloading and installing extensions
- ◆ More goodies for your site on the web
- ◆ Getting additional help with Dreamweaver

Throughout the course of this book, I've introduced you to a wide array of Dreamweaver tools, from page formatting to external style sheets, to Dreamweaver-generated animation. Whew! That was quite a ride.

Versatile as it is, Dreamweaver still won't solve *every* web design challenge you face. There are notable "missing links," like the ability to add counters to your pages, or search engines. Those two features are available online—often free—from other sources, and in this chapter I'll show you how to include them in your site.

Another important starting place for more web design features is the ever-expanding set of Dreamweaver *extensions*. Extensions add new features to your Dreamweaver program. They are developed in large part outside of

Macromedia and shared at the Macromedia extensions site. In this chapter, I'll show you how to download, install, and use extensions.

Using Dreamweaver Extensions

There are two steps to setting up a Dreamweaver extension—downloading it from the Macromedia site, and installing it in your local version of Dreamweaver.

Before I show you how to download an extension and install it, let's take a look at what's available.

Surveying Extensions

To check out the available Dreamweaver extensions, choose **Command, Get More Commands** from the Dreamweaver Document window menu. This launches your browser, and opens the Macromedia Exchange site.

The first time you visit the Macromedia Exchange site, you'll be prompted to register. Write down and save your login and password information for future visits.

There are a number of ways to survey available extensions at the Macromedia Exchange site. The site's home page usually lists new, featured, and popular extensions.

You can also search for an extension that serves your needs by using the search box at the page. For example, if you're looking for an extension that makes it easy to quickly generate a calendar on your page, try entering "calendar" in the Search Extensions search box. The search results will display all extensions that match your search criteria.

When you click a link to an extension, you'll see a set of information about that extension, including the author, the date the extension was posted, how many people have downloaded the extension, a rating (5 is best) based on feedback from users, and an approval logo from Macromedia if the extension was submitted to and tested by Macromedia.

When you follow a link to an extension, you'll also see information about what version of Dreamweaver is required to run that extension, as well as which browsers support the features created by the extension. Figure 21.1 shows information for a download.

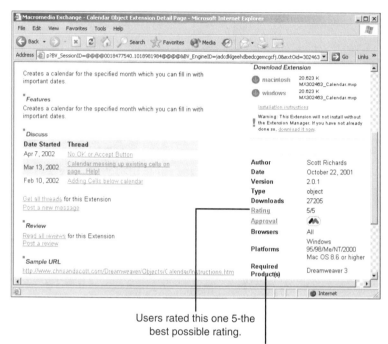

Figure 21.1

Checking out an extension before downloading.

Users rated this one 5-the
best possible rating.

This extension works with
Dreamweaver version 3 or newer.

Many extension descriptions include links to support pages, and even links to display sites, where you can see the extension in action before trying it yourself.

Finding and Downloading an Extension

Once you've determined that a desired extension will work, the next step is to download that extension onto your local computer. To do that, follow these steps:

1. Follow a link at the Macromedia Exchange to your extension.

2. Find the download icon for Dreamweaver Extensions, shown in Figure 21.2.

Caution

I'd avoid extensions that don't have the Macromedia logo, or that have an approval rating of less than 4.5. Extensions tend to be a bit buggy and tricky even when they work, and you'll avoid frustration by sticking with those that have been tried and tested.

Figure 21.2

Checking out an extension before downloading. Extensions have download links for Macintosh and Windows versions.

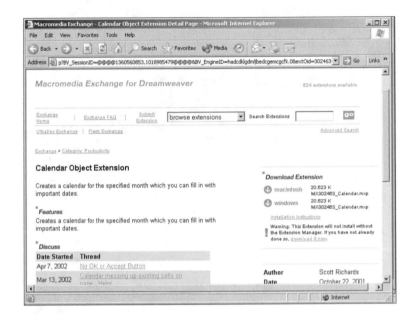

3. When you download the extension file, note the folder to which you save the file. You'll need to know how to find your extension file to install it.

After you've downloaded an extension, you're ready to install it to your version of Dreamweaver.

Installing an Extension

Once you've downloaded an extension to your local computer, you need to hook it up with Dreamweaver so it can become part of your (customized!) version of Dreamweaver. To do that, follow these steps.

Caution

The extensions you download from the Macromedia Exchange are not documented in Dreamweaver's help menu. Remember, you've customized your installation of Dreamweaver by adding extensions. You need to rely on the documentation for your extension, available at the Macromedia Exchange.

1. Choose **Commands, Manage Extensions.** The Macromedia Extension Manager window opens.

2. Choose **File, Install Extension.** The Select Extension to Install dialog box appears, as shown in Figure 21.3.

3. In the Select Extension to Install dialog box, navigate to your extension file (it will have an MXP filename extension) and select it. Then click **Install**.

4. After the extension is successfully installed, you'll be prompted to **OK** a dialog box telling you the extension has been added to your version of Dreamweaver.

After you install an extension, you'll see it listed in the list of extensions in the Macromedia Extension Manager, as shown in Figure 21.4.

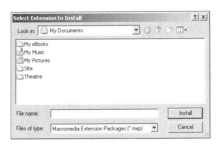

Figure 21.3

Choosing a downloaded extension to add to Dreamweaver.

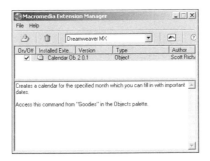

Figure 21.4

Listing installed extensions.

Running an Extension

Installed extensions actually become part of your Dreamweaver MX program. They are accessed via your Document window menu.

If an extension has been installed properly, just select it from the menu. Most extensions are added to the Insert menu.

Extra Stuff You Need for Your Site

There are some really useful website elements that you won't find in Dreamweaver, or in the Macromedia Exchange. For example, a counter is helpful at your site.

Another feature I add to almost all my commercial sites is a search box that allows visitors to easily search the site.

While these features are not available in Dreamweaver, they're available—often free (still!) as downloads.

Counting the Hits

Often we think of *counters* as a way to show visitors how many people have visited your site. Sometimes that is appropriate, sometimes not (ask yourself do visitors *really* care how many other people have visited your site).

Definition _____

Counters are sometimes referred to as hit counters, because they count hits—or visits—to a page.

Inside Info

Experts at JavaScript and HTML can create their own extensions for Dreamweaver, and use them at their own site and/or share them at the Macromedia Exchange. For those so inclined, you'll find all the info you need at the Macromedia Exchange page.

Inside Info

You get a report on who's searching for what, which I find extremely helpful in knowing who is going to my sites and what they're doing there. As a nice little touch for clients, I send them a weekly or monthly report on search inquiries placed at their site, which lets my clients know that the site I designed for them is generating quality visits.

The even more important thing about counters is that they can include reports for you to use in analyzing who is visiting your site, which pages are being visited, and what days and times are the most popular for visitors.

Check out the following sources for free counters:

♦ For nonprofit or free sites at http://counter. bloke.com.

♦ http://www.aaddzz.com/pages/counters.

♦ HC Hit Counters at http://butterpuff.com.

♦ CQ Counter's free version is at http://www. cqcounter.com/. The pay version provides reports without ads, and password protected access to your statistics.

Free Search Boxes

If there is a single, best free deal on the web for designers, my vote would go to the FreeFind search engine.

The Freefind search engine allows visitors to search either the web, your site, or both. As of this writing, it's still free, with no hassles and no registration. Download it from http://www.freefind.com.

After you choose a style and type of search box, FreeFind will display some HTML code. Copy that code, and paste it into the Dreamweaver Document window using the Edit, Paste HTML menu option.

After you install a FreeFind counter, you'll get weekly reports telling you what people searched for at your site.

More Help for Dreamweaver

If you've exhausted the information in this *Complete Idiot's Guide*, and you're ready to climb new mountains, there are a number of directions you can go.

As you've seen throughout this book, Dreamweaver generates all kinds of coding as you create pages in the Document window. Generated code includes:

- ◆ **HTML** (HyperText Markup Language)   The page formatting language.
- ◆ **CSS** (Cascading Style Sheets)   The coding used to define how style sheets are applied.
- ◆ **JavaScript**   Used for interactivity and animation in many Dreamweaver Behaviors.

Each of theses languages has a wealth of resources available, including books, websites, and instructional venues. I'll recommend a few here.

My favorite HTML book is Liz Castro's HTML for the World Wide Web, Visual Quickstart Guide (Peachpit). The World Wide Web Consortium (W3C), depository of web standards, has free and comprehensive HTML tutorials at http://www.w3schools.com/html/default.asp. The folks at W3C also have free CSS online tutorials at http://www.w3schools.com/css/.

Free, online JavaScript resources include tutorials, but also many sites that provide complete scripts for useful page objects. To learn JavaScript for free, online, again I'd start with the W3C resources, including their JavaScript tutorials at http://www.w3schools.com/js/default.asp.

Dreamweaver generates Flash objects, like Flash buttons and Flash text. If you want to learn more about Flash, you might want to start with my Complete Idiot's Guide to Flash 5.

Finally, if you would like the warm, caring, fuzzy environment of a classroom to learn Dreamweaver, let me invite you to join my online Dreamweaver classes. You'll find information, outlines, registration stuff, and free sample videos from the class at www.ppinet.com.

The Least You Need to Know

- ◆ You can add features to Dreamweaver by downloading and installing Dreamweaver extensions.
- ◆ Dreamweaver extensions become part of your local Dreamweaver interface.
- ◆ Other web development tools that aren't available in Dreamweaver can be found free on the web, including hit counters and search engine boxes.

♦ Dreamweaver generates HTML code for page formatting, CSS code for style sheets, JavaScript for animation and interactivity, and Flash code for Flash objects. You can learn any or all of these coding languages to develop more advanced web elements.

♦ Many online resources, including free resources, are available for learning more about Dreamweaver and HTML.

Dreamweaver Web Design Glossary

Adobe Photoshop   The industry standard program for creating bitmap graphics for the web.

Alt text   Text that is displayed in Internet Explorer when a visitor rolls over (moves his or her mouse over) an image.

applets   Small programs composed of a few dozen or less lines of programming code.

ASP   A server scripting language promoted by Microsoft and used by Dreamweaver to connect with a database.

Assets   Every color, image, and URL you add to a page is saved by Dreamweaver and displayed in the Assets panel.

AU   A sound file format.

bandwidth   Measures the capacity for transferring information to and from the server.

behaviors   Allow you to add animation and interactivity to your web pages. They rely mainly on generated JavaScript and are defined and controlled in the Behaviors panel.

browser-safe colors   The 216 colors that are reproduced faithfully on the overwhelming majority of operating systems and browsers. Many modern monitors support millions of colors. Other, older monitors support only the browser-safe set. Therefore, professional web designers restrict themselves to the browser-safe set.

CGI   Stands for Common Gateway Interface, and refers to scripts (usually written in languages like PERL) that manage form data. Many web-hosting services provide CGI scripts.

check boxes   Input form elements with two states—checked or not checked.

check in/check out   Feature that allows multiple developers to check pages in or out to keep track of who is working on what.

client-side processing   Used to manage input form data in a browser and used (for example) in validation and jump menus.

cloaking   A way of protecting selected files from all site operations, such as uploading (putting) files to the server, generating site reports, or link checking.

ColdFusion   A scripting language promoted by Macromedia used by Dreamweaver to connect with a database

CSS   (Cascading Style Sheets) These files store global formatting for a website—created in Dreamweaver or hand-coded using CSS code.

database   A collection of information. For example, a directory of everyone in an organization or a list of products.

database table   A table holds some of the data in a larger database.

description   A meta-tag used by search engines to summarize your page content when your page appears in a search results list.

design notes   Comments you can add to a file that don't appear when the file is viewed by a visitor in a website. Design notes can be used to assign a status level to a file (such as draft, or final, or something in between).

DOM   Stands for Document Object Model and refers to the technology used to generate complex behaviors. DOM includes advanced, complex CSS that allow for exact placement of objects on pages.

domain name   Since the IP addresses used to identify and locate websites are hard to remember, a domain name system associates easy-to-remember domain names (such as ppinet.com) with IP addresses and allows visitors to find a site by typing in a domain name instead of a number.

DSN   Stands for Data Source Name. A DSN tells your server how to connect to a database.

extensions   The ever-expanding set of new features you can add to your Dreamweaver program. They are developed in large part outside of Macromedia and shared at the Macromedia extensions site.

firewall   Software that protects a server from unauthorized access (hackers).

Fireworks   A full-featured graphic design and editing application from Macromedia used to create web-compatible images and animation.

Flash   A vector-based animation and interactivity application from Macromedia.

folder   The hierarchical structure in which files on your computer are organized.

form fields   The areas in a form where web pages collect information from visitors.

frames   An effective way to narrow page display and provide navigation sections of your website. Frames can be used as a navigation structure for a site and as a way of framing content inside other content.

GIF   Stands for Graphics Interchange Format. The GIF format is one of the universally supported web-compatible graphic file formats. GIF format supports transparency and animation and is reliably supported by every major operating system and browser. GIF images are limited to 256 colors, and therefore are not well suited for digital photographs, for instance.

hidden fields   Provide a way for you to embed information in a field that will be sent to the server without any input from the visitor.

home page   The page visitors see when they enter your URL into their browser's address bar. Alternate names for home pages include index.html, default.htm, or default.html. Each site generally has just one home page.

hotspots   Clickable areas inside any image—each with its own link target.

HTML   Stands for HyperText Markup Language and is the way web browsers (such as Internet Explorer or Netscape Navigator) look at and display text and images on your page.

HTML styles   The set of heading styles (Heading 1, Heading 2, and so on) and other styles (such as Paragraph) that are accessible from the Format drop-down list in the Properties panel.

images   Static (not animated) pictures on a web page. Dreamweaver keeps track of where these files are stored on your local site and maintains the integrity of the links between those images and your page—so long as you are working in a defined Dreamweaver site.

inline formatting   Formatting applied to selected text.

input forms   Areas of a web page that collect data. Forms are made up of three main elements: the Form, Form fields, and a Submit (and Reset) button.

Internet   The global network of servers that makes your website available to people around the world.

Internet Protocol (IP) Address   The way servers identify and locate websites. An IP address is a set of numbers.

intranet   A restricted network of connections that makes your site accessible to people in your company or organization. Servers that are accessible to a limited, authorized audience.

JavaScript   A programming language supported by all modern web browsers. It's a language that runs right in the browser.

JPEG   Stands for Joint Photographic Experts Group. As the name (Photographic) implies, this format was developed to present photos on the web.

JSP (Java Server Pages)   One of the server-scripting languages used by Dreamweaver to connect with a database.

jump menu   Drop-down menu used to navigate a site. Dreamweaver generates the JavaScript necessary to create a jump menu. You can edit an existing jump menu in the Behaviors panel.

keyword   A meta-tag is used by search engines to categorize your site.

layers   A page layout tool that provides more control over object placement than tables. Layers can be overlapped, providing some 3-D layout capability. Layers are less predictable than tables because they rely on browsers interpreting the latest version of Cascading Style Sheets (CSS-2) to support absolute placement of objects.

Library Assets   Objects that can be embedded many times in a website. If a Library Asset is changed, that change is automatically updated throughout the site.

link   The property assigned to an object (such as selected text or an image) that connects to a new address on the web. Links are (basically) displayed in four states: untouched (normal), hovered over, active (clicked), and visited. By default, browsers display links as underlined text in blue; visited sites are displayed in purple; and active links are displayed in red.

list menu   A form field that collects data from a drop-down list and sends it to a server.

meta-tags   Provide additional information about your page that does not display in a browser but is used by search engines to identify the content of your page.

MP3   A popular, compressed sound file format.

MPEG   A media file format promoted by Microsoft.

ODBC   Stands for open database connectivity driver. Used to define Data Source Names (DSN).

orphan files   Files on your site that are not accessible from links on any page in your site. Often, orphan files are old files no longer used in your site, and you might want to clean them up. Other times, they are files you might want to keep on your site to store data at your server.

page titles   *See titles.*

PHP MySQL   One of the server-scripting languages used by Dreamweaver to connect with a database.

plug-ins   Programs that allow web browsers to display text, graphics, and media that are not interpreted by the browser itself. Some of the most popular plug-ins are the Flash Player (which displays SWF files) and the Adobe Acrobat Reader (which displays PDF files).

PNG   Stands for Portable Network Graphics and provides more reliable cross-browser and cross-operating system color consistency than GIF images. However, PNG images are not supported by all older browsers.

Properties panel   The most useful panel in Dreamweaver. It changes to allow you to define properties for selected objects.

QT   QuickTime media format promoted by Apple.

radio buttons   A type of field used in forms. Radio buttons must be created in groups.

recorded commands   Recorded sets of steps that you can repeat.

recordset   A subset of all the records in your database.

RM   A media file format associated with RealMedia presentations.

root folder   The highest level folder in your site. Your home page file (index.html or something like that) must be in your root folder.

scripts   Little programs—composed of a few, or a few dozen, lines of programming code; scripts can add interactivity to your site.

server   A server is computer and software combination that stores files accessible to others—either over the Internet or via an in-house intranet.

site   Websites are made up of HTML, image, and media files, as well as scripts and other files used to define and maintain the pages.

site map   A graphical display of your website map with links displayed as lines between pages.

style sheets   *See CSS.*

SVG   Scalable Vector Graphics are vector-based images supported by the XML page description language.

SWF   The file format for presenting embedded animated or vector images in websites using the Flash viewer plug-in. SWF files are created in Macromedia Flash, Adobe Illustrator, CorelDRAW, Macromedia Freehand, and other vector-based graphics programs.

tables   The basic tool for controlling page layout in web page design. Tables are used to create a layout grid for a web page and allow you to closely define where objects sit on the page. Tables are a fundamental building block of web design.

templates   Refers both to model pages used to generate other web pages and to the set of prefab design pages provided by Dreamweaver.

text area   An element of input forms used to collect multiple lines of text, such as comments, complaints, and other freestyle submissions from visitors.

text field   An element of input forms used to collect lines of text (such as a name or email address).

tiled images   Images that repeat as necessary to fill a browser window, a table background, or a table cell background.

Timelines   A tool for animating objects on your page. Dreamweaver creates Timelines by generating JavaScript to control layers.

title   The name of a web page that displays in the title bar of a browser window, not to be confused with the page's filename.

tracing image   If you have an image, such as a photo or a sketch, that you want to use as a guide to laying out your page, you can embed that image as a page background and use it as a design template in Dreamweaver. The tracing image is not visible in a browser.

UltraDev   Bundled into Dreamweaver MX is what used to be called UltraDev, a powerful program for creating connections between Dreamweaver and online databases.

Uniform Resource Locator (URL)   Refers to the address or location of any file on the World Wide Web. A URL can point to a web page, an image, a media file, or any type of file accessible on the web.

uploading   The process of sending files from your local computer to the remote server.

validation scripts   Small programs that run in a browser and prevent visitors from submitting data that doesn't match set rules.

WAV   A common sound file format promoted by Microsoft.

web pages Pages that display in a browser window and are often composed of an HTML file along with many embedded files, such as images, plug-in sound files, embedded Flash movies, and the like.

Web Photo Album This new feature in Dreamweaver MX works with Macromedia Fireworks MX to generate a page with thumbnail images linked to larger photos.

WMF A media file format promoted by Microsoft.

WYSIWYG Stands for "What You See Is What You Get." Dreamweaver's page design tools allow you to format your page much as you would a word processing document.

Real World Dreamweaver

In this book, I've shown you how to harness the enormous power of Dreamweaver to create websites. Along the way, I've shared a few "tricks of the trade," for approaching real-world design products.

In the following three sections, I want to take you inside my web design studio and demonstrate how I apply these techniques to create real websites that make my clients happy while keeping my hours down to a reasonable amount.

I'll use three examples—websites I've designed for artists, for a literary agency, and for a music production studio. These sites use everything from forms to embedded media, from frames to Flash objects. They'll provide a good way to see how the skills you learned in this book are applied to solve web design challenges.

Project 1—Displaying Artwork

One of my recent projects involved designing a site for the Kawneer Building, a block-long structure that houses studios for potters, glassblowers, watercolorists, muralists, musicians, and performers. You can visit the site at www.kawneerbuilding.com.

My concept for this project was to feature and shape the site around the works of art submitted by the different artists in the building. That's a little trick of mine. People often say "Oh, that page looks great!" What they mean is that the *artwork* on the page looks great. That's fine with me, I'll claim my small share of the credit if they like the pages. I think of myself as something like a picture framer—I'm not trying to overshadow the artwork, I'm trying to present it in an attractive way.

This project also required a lot of file management. Most do. Each artist in the building provided me with clippings, text on disk, scanned images, hardcopy artwork, and even a CD to pull a track off of. So my first task was to organize the files. Then, I built a template page that I would use as a basic framework for each page. I created a CSS file style sheet to attach to each page. And then the fun began—designing creative pages for each artist.

If you're ready to follow along, I'll show you how it all came together.

Step 1: Create a Template Page

Because I'm going to display the artists' pages in a frameset, and I want to keep the entire page width under 800 pixels wide, I'm going to constrain all my artists pages into the 550 pixel wide table shown in Figure B.1.

You'll note that I'm "cheating" on my page template. I'm not really using a Dreamweaver *Template* page, I've just created a regular ol' Dreamweaver page that I'll use over and over.

One thing that I've done is create "placeholder" images—by defining every attribute of an image *except* the file that will be displayed. I can adjust the size and layout of these images, but they give me a basic framework to create somewhat consistent looking pages.

You'll also note that I've divided the page into a two-row table. I'll standardize this approach for each artist—so there is a separate background color for a similar sized top cell in each artists' page. You'll see how this comes together when I start customizing each page, but you can see my (pseudo) template in the following figure.

Figure B.1

I'll use this page, with a two-cell table and image markers, as my template for each artist.

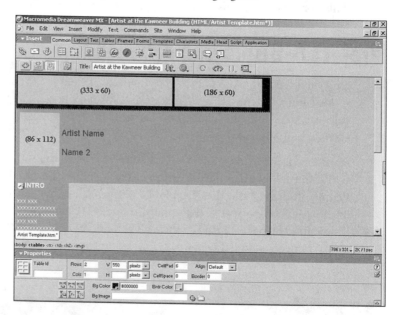

Step 2: Attach a CSS Style Sheet to the Template Page

Before I make a copy of the template page for each of my dozen or so artists, I'm going to assign a dummy CSS file to that page.

I haven't actually created the CSS file yet. So what. I will someday. And when I do, I'll want to be able to apply it to all the pages in the site to standardize font sizes and some other style attributes (like link displays).

In Figure B.2, I'm applying an (as yet undefined) CSS file to my template page. Eventually, I'll bring this style sheet to life by defining some tags, but for now, I'm just laying the foundation for doing that later. At this point, I'm not sure I'll need to apply site-wide styles because each page will be rather unique, but it doesn't hurt to assign a "dummy" style sheet now. A little bit of work now might make my job easier once the page content is done.

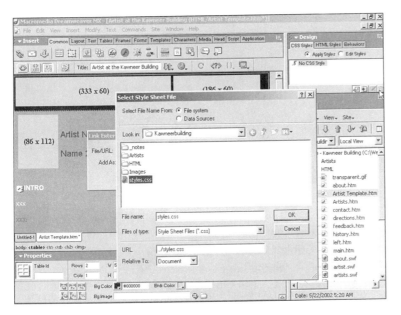

Figure B.2

Applying a style sheet to my "template" page will automatically attach that style sheet to each new page I generate from this page.

Step 3: Organize My Files

After I have a template page done, I'm going to create a separate folder for each artist and place a copy of the page in each artist's folder. I do that by just using File, Save As, and saving the "template" file with a new name in each folder.

There are different ways to organize folders. Sometimes it's best to organize similar file types in the same folder (like sound files, video, images, and so on—each with its own folder). In this case, I'm organizing the files by artist because most of the image and media files in this site will be used on the page for the artist they are associated with. And it will be easier for me to name and find them if I use this file management approach in this particular project. You'll see me take a different approach in the other projects in this book.

Figure B.3

I've organized my folders so each artist has his or her own folder, with the HTML, image, and media files I'll use on that artist's page.

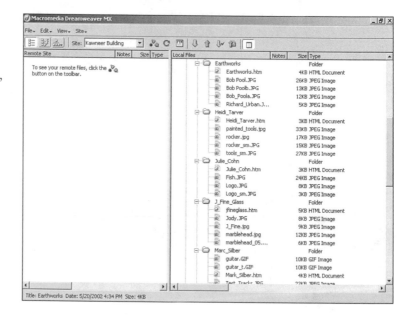

Step 4: Prepare Images

Because images are so central to this site, I'm going to standardize an approach to presenting them. Many of the artists have given me large images to scan or provided me with large digital images in nonweb-compatible formats. Others have provided me with JPEGs or (in a few cases) GIFs that are going to be too large for my 550 pixel wide pages.

My other consideration is download time. The large images I'm working with will create slow-downloading pages unless I do something with them.

After finding efficient ways to save or export images to JPEGs, I'm going to create a smaller image that is *about* 420 pixels wide. I'll also retain the original full size image. And, I'll create a link from the smaller image to the larger one, so if a visitor clicks on an image, they will see the original full size image. In short, for most of my large images, I'm going to save two versions—full size and smaller. I'll add ALT text to the smaller image on the page, so a visitor sees a message like the one in the following figure when he or she hovers over the picture.

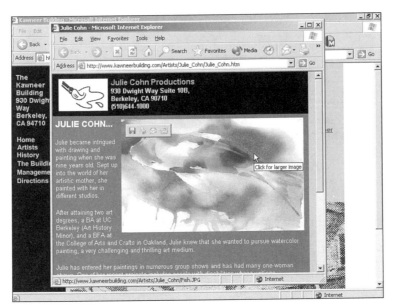

Figure B.4

A visitor can see the full 800 pixel wide version of this image, but I'll speed up page download by displaying one half that size with the page.

Step 5: Design Pages

Now comes the fun part. I'll design a distinctive page for each artist.

The first element in page design is to copy in the text content provided by the artists. Text is secondary to the message projected in this site, so I'm not going to trip much on text formatting. I'll keep it small and readable, and assign compatible font colors *after* I apply cell background colors.

Because I'm building around the artwork, I won't do much with formatting until I insert images into the page.

Once I have images to build around, I'll define a unique color scheme for each artist by drawing on the coloring of their artwork. An old friend of mine who did picture framing taught me to study the colors in a picture and select a frame color to draw out and emphasize a color within the picture. Dreamweaver's eyedropper makes that easy. In Figure B.5, I'm grabbing a section of the lamp that is "lit up" by the bulb and using it as a cell background to draw out the "light" from the page.

Step 6: Create a Directory Page

The individual artist pages will be accessed from an artist directory page. And that page will be part of a larger frameset that provides yet another level of navigation to the building management, history, and so on.

So my next step is to create the directory page to which the artist pages will be linked.

Figure B.5

I'm drawing on the color scheme of the artwork to define a color scheme for the page.

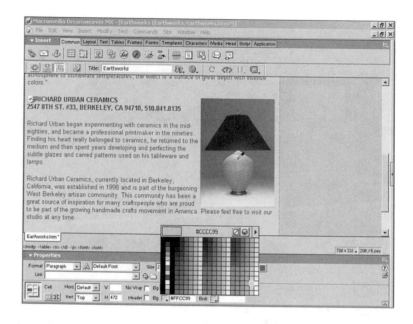

Because the Kawneer Building is famous for it's distinctive "sawtooth" profile, I'm going to use the building as a background for the artist directory page, as shown in Figure B.6.

I'll create this background by using a semi-transparent, enlarged, grainy black-and-white photo of the building as a table background, and enter text with links in that table.

Figure B.6

The profile of the building provides a distinctive page background for the artist directory.

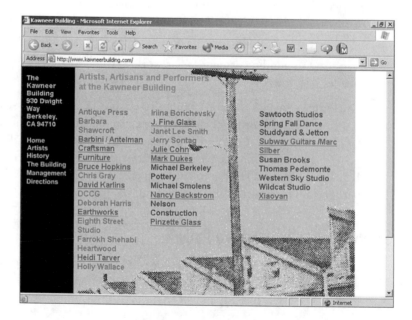

Step 7: Define the Frameset for the Site

As you've seen, in this particular project I worked from the particular to the general. I started by defining pages, and then created the directory page with links. Finally, I'll design a frameset to enclose the pages and allow links to other areas of the site.

My framed index page is shown in Figure B.7. As you can see, it's a simple two-frame frameset, with a navigation area on the left and a main display page on the right.

By restricting my left-side navigation frame to 200 pixels, my total page width comes to only 750 pixels. Even for visitors with 800 pixel wide monitor settings, the *entire* page width will fit nicely on the screen, with no need for tacky horizontal scroll bars.

For navigation, I've created Flash text in the navigation frame, with link targets in the main frame.

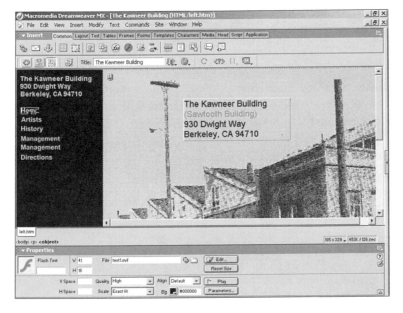

Figure B.7

This frameset will display the artist directory and artists' pages while providing constant navigation options to other areas of the site.

This page uses a layer with text placed on top of the page background.

To ensure that this layer doesn't get bounced around on the page in Netscape when the page is resized, I'm invoking the Add Netscape Resize Fix command. This generates JavaScript that will maintain the layer position in Netscape when viewers resize their browser window. Figure B.8 shows the command being invoked.

Figure B.8

This command will make my layer work more reliably in Netscape's browser.

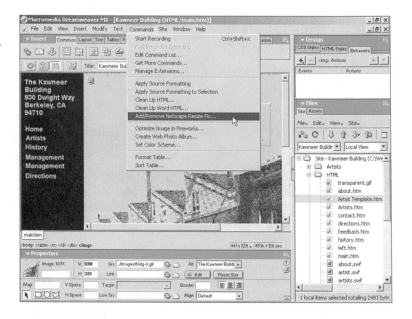

Now that my site is complete, all that's left is to test. And test. And test again. I'll view the site in Netscape 4.7, Netscape 6, IE 6, and I'll visit it on a Mac and a PC. I'll experiment with different screen resolutions, and I'll try resizing browser windows. I know that the site design will not be represented optimally in every environment, but I at least want to make sure it functions in every environment. Figure B.9 shows the site in Netscape 6.2, at an 800 pixel resolution.

Figure B.9

Test, test, test! I'm checking the page in Netscape 6.2 with Windows XP.

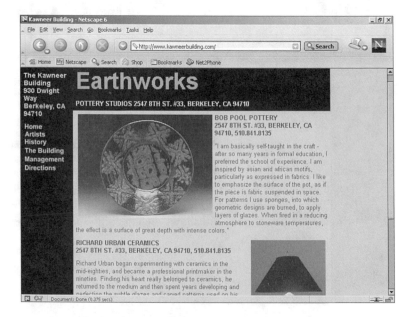

Project 2—Presenting Sound Files

Last year I designed a site for Marvin Productions to showcase a CD they produced. We wanted to include short clips of tracks from the CD. Here, I'll focus on how I included media files in the site.

I created the page layout shown in Figure B.10. I used artwork prepared by the producer to place a full-size image of the back of the CD on the page, and I placed a smaller image of the front of the CD on the page as well, along with a minimal amount of text.

As you can see in the following figure, this page is enclosed in a frameset that visitors can use to navigate to other parts of the site. I created the background of the left navigation frame as an image, and used that image as a table background.

One of my favorite tricks in presenting cuts from CDs is to create the illusion that visitors to a web page can click on a player that is attached to the CD cover. I do this by defining a plug-in that is the same width as the image, and placing it right below the image on the page. I'll show you exactly how I do this in the next set of steps.

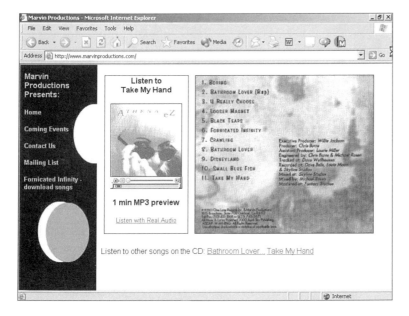

Figure B.10

The media plug-in is the same width as the CD cover image, making it appear that the image and media player are a single object.

Step 1: Prepare Audio Files

Preparing audio files for the web could be (and should be) the subject of a book in its own right. Here, I'll briefly walk you through the process of creating a page to share sample tracks for the web from the CD I was provided with.

I'll start by using one of the many free ripper programs available on the web to extract tracks from the CD and convert them to WAV files. Search for "free ripper software" to find the latest and greatest available versions.

Next, I'll use a program called CoolEdit (www.cooledit.com) to edit one minute samples from the CD tracks that I was going embed in the page. At this point, I have one minute long WAV files. I'll use CoolEdit to convert these WAV files to MP3 format for faster downloading. These MP3 files can be played by Windows Media or QuickTime players (or other players).

I also want to prepare alternative versions of my audio files in Real Media. This format is best for visitors with slow Internet connections. For this, I'll use the free RealProducer program available at www.real.com.

Step 2: Import Media Files into Dreamweaver

Now that I have my media files prepared, I'll import the files into Dreamweaver. I can do this using the file manager in my operating system, but I like to do all my file management in Dreamweaver's Site window just to keep things simple.

I'll use the Site, Import command (in the Site Window menu) to import my media files into a folder at my Dreamweaver site, as shown in Figure B.11.

Figure B.11

Media files are large! Here, I'm importing them into my Dreamweaver site.

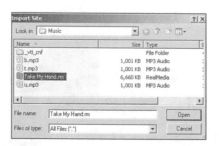

Step 3: Create Text Links to Media Files

The easiest way to share media files in a website is to simply create a text or image link to those files. When a visitor clicks on the link, the media file will play in his or her default media player.

In Figure B.12, I'm linking text to an MP3 file.

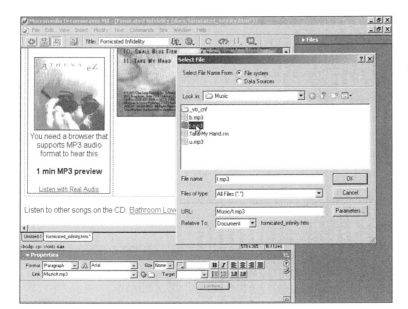

Figure B.12

This link will play the associated MP3 file.

Step 4: Create Image Map Hotspots to Play Media Files

Another trick I often use for pages like this is to create clickable hotspots on the CD cover. To do that, I'll just draw a hotspot on the back of the CD cover over the playable track. I'll make the hotspot link to the media file, as shown in Figure B.13.

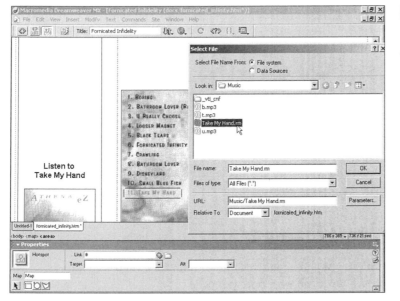

Figure B.13

This clickable hotspot is linked to a Real Media file.

Step 5: Insert a Plugin

So far, I've allowed visitors to play media files by simply clicking on text, or image hotspot links. These links open the visitor's default media player in a separate window.

I'm going to also allow visitors to play one sound file using a media player *embedded* in the page—so that the player controls show up in a small, rectangular area right in my web page.

To do this, I'll select Insert, Media, Plugin, and use the Src area in the Properties panel to embed a sound file.

Finally, I'll size my plugin display so it is the same width as the image—as shown in Figure B.14.

Figure B.14

This plugin display is the same width as the image of the CD cover—creating the illusion on the web page that visitors are looking at a playable CD.

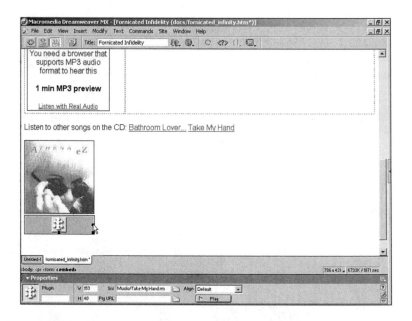

Since I can only guess what media players visitors will use when they open this page, I can't be sure the media plugin will fit nicely in everybody's display. I'll test the page in as many environments as I can, and with as many media players as I can to be as sure as possible that most visitors will see player controls on their page.

Project 3–Designing a Frameset

With the increasing prevalence of wide, high-resolution monitors, there's simply too much space on a typical monitor to fill with one web page.

This opens the potential for using frames as navigation and design tools. A left or top frame can serve as a conceptual site anchor as well as a navigation tool.

In Figure B.15, I've designed a frameset for the Black Repertory Group site (www. blackrepetorygroup.org) that appears to enclose the left, top, and right edges of the main frame.

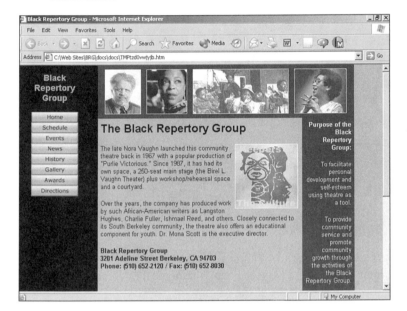

Figure B.15

This frameset appears to enclose the left, top, and right side of the main page. In reality, table cells form the top and right edge of the page layout.

Instead of defining multiple frames, I simply have one frame on the left for navigation, and a main frame. However, by including a top table cell, and a right edge table cell with matching background colors, I'll create the illusion that the frameset actually encloses three sides of the page.

Step 1: Create the Navigation Frame

To create the navigation frame, I'm designing a page with Flash buttons, as shown in Figure B.16. I can touch up the page after I incorporate it into a frameset.

I've centered all the page content. This will have the effect of centering the frame content when I squeeze this page into a 200-pixel-wide frame.

Figure B.16

This page will serve as my navigation frame.

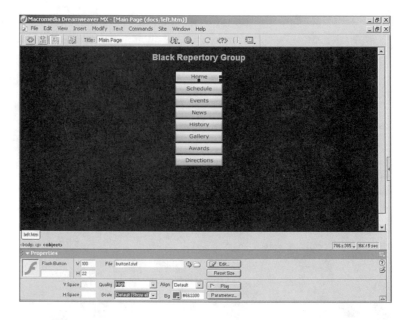

Step 2: Create the Main Frame

The main frame for this frameset is shown in Figure B.17. I've used cells with black backgrounds on the top and right edges of the page to create the illusion of a contiguous black frame enclosing the left, top, and right edges of the page.

Figure B.17

My main frame uses cell backgrounds to create a frame-like look.

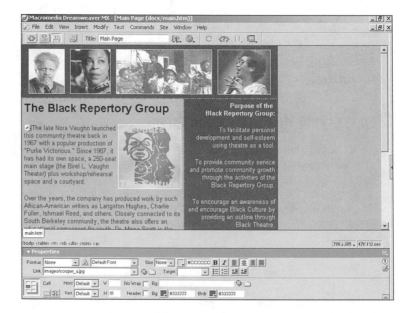

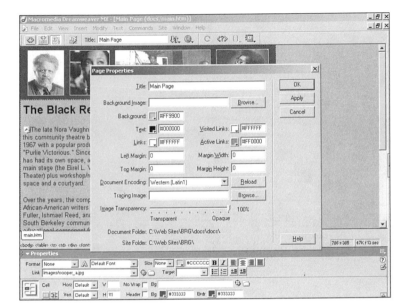

Figure B.18

By eliminating the default 10 pixel page margins, I'll get rid of any spacing between my framed pages.

Step 3: Define Zero Margins

To make the main page mesh cleanly with the left frame, I'll need to define zero margins for the top and left edge of the page. I'm doing this in the Page Properties dialog box (choose Modify, Page Properties).

Step 4: Package Pages in the Frameset

Now that the two framed pages are finished, I can package them in a frameset and touch up the pages to make sure they mesh well.

In Figure B.19, I'm creating a frameset named index.htm. I'm viewing the Frames panel (choose Window, Others, Frames). By clicking on the outline of the entire frameset in the Frames panel, I can access the Properties panel for the entire frameset.

I'm setting Border Width to zero, and choosing No from the Frames drop-down list to create a frameless looking frameset.

Figure B.19

I don't want my frame borders to be visible to visitors.

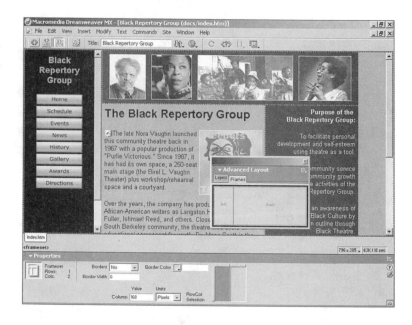

Figure B.19

I don't want my frame borders to be visible to visitors.

Step 5: Open Flash Button Links in the Main Frame

I held off on defining links for my Flash buttons so that I could make sure the links open in the Main frame.

By double-clicking on a Flash button, I can reopen the Insert Flash Button dialog box, and make sure my link opens in the appropriate target frame, as shown in Figure B.20.

Figure B.20

Make sure Flash button links open in the right frame.

If I want to make sure visitors have Flash-enabled browsers, I can use the Check Plugin behavior in the Behaviors panel, and divert non-Flash users to a different page.

In Figure B.21, I'm sending non-Flash folks to a special page that doesn't use Flash navigation buttons.

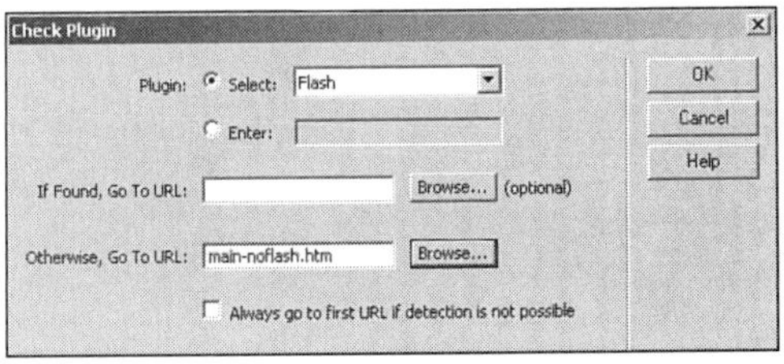

Figure B.21

If visitors don't have Flash-enabled browsers, they will jump to a page that doesn't use Flash objects.

As with every project, my next step is test, test, test. I'm assuming visitors will have browsers that support frames. If I wanted to be obsessively careful, I could send visitors with IE 2.0 to a different page, but I'm gambling that there aren't too many people browsing with that particular program any more.

I have defined an alternate page for Flash-less browsers, so I'll want to test my site in an environment where Flash is not installed.

Index

X-Y-Z